Feargus O'Connor

For

Catherine Barbara Pickering (1937–2003)

Feargus O'Connor

A Political Life

Paul A. Pickering

MERLIN PRESS

© Paul A. Pickering, 2008

First published 2008 by The Merlin Press Ltd.
96 Monnow Street
Monmouth
NP25 3EQ
Wales

www.merlinpress.co.uk

ISBN. paperback 9780850365610
ISBN. hardback 9780850365627

British Library Cataloguing in Publication Data
is available from the British Library

Printed in the UK by Imprint Digital, Exeter

CONTENTS

LIST OF ILLUSTRATIONS

Between pages 24 and 25

ACKNOWLEDGEMENTS

This book was conceived some time ago and the research for it was undertaken over several trips to Britain and in fits and starts in various Australian libraries. I am grateful for the assistance of staff at the following institutions: the British Library, St Pancras; the British Newspaper Library, Colindale; Chifley Library, the Australian National University; Manchester Central Library; National Library of Australia, Canberra; Staffordshire University Library (The Dorothy Thompson Special Collection); State Library of Victoria; The Working Class Movement Library (Salford); British Library of Political and Economic Science, London School of Economics.

Research for this book was funded by the Australian Research Council.

Not long into the project I came to the end of a lengthy period as a research fellow and took up the position of Director of Graduate Studies in the Humanities Research Centre (now the Research School of Humanities) at The Australian National University. Running a large and growing graduate program and supervising a number of graduate students has made significant demands on my time but it has also provided me with a wonderfully rich and vibrant intellectual environment. My thanks are due to all those who have participated in our thesis workshops and who have allowed me to share in their enthusiasm for their own research. I have learned more from my students than they have learned from me.

In addition I would like to place on record my appreciation to the following individuals: Glenn Airey, Glen Barclay; Malcolm Chase, Ian Donaldson; Vic Elliott; Jim Epstein; Tom and Lily French; Ann Jones; Nev Kirk; Iain McCalman; Tina Parolin; Moira Scollay; Barry Smith; Dorothy Thompson; Caroline Turner and Alex Tyrrell. Many thanks also to Anthony Zurbrugg and Adrian Howe at Merlin Press for their patience and professionalism.

I owe special thanks to Owen Ashton, Kate Bowan and Stephen Roberts for reading the manuscript and for making many valuable suggestions.

My children, Daniel, Jessica and Timothy, have had to put up with my preoccupation with the past and with extended periods when I monopolised the home computer. I thank them for their love, support and patience.

If there is one person who deserves to be singled out for thanks for their part in bringing this book to completion it is Suzanne Pickering. Often, over the past few years as I tried, at times falteringly, to balance teaching, administration, and other projects with this book she was the one to say four important words: 'But what about Feargus?' Feargus and I owe her no small debt of gratitude.

Paul Pickering, December 2007

1: A HORSE NAMED FEARGUS

In 1853 the road between the bustling port of Melbourne and Bendigo in the heart of the Victorian goldfields was a hazardous one. Travellers could easily be waylaid either by mud, as heavy traffic had ploughed the route into a quagmire, or by the bands of desperate 'robbers and cut-throats' who lay in wait in the damp and chilled shadows of the heavily-wooded Black Forest, the highest point of the journey across the Great Dividing Range. Heading to Bendigo to try their luck in central Victoria were William Craig and Joe Ogston. Ogston, according to Craig's memoir, had been active in the Chartist movement 'that disturbed the Old Country from 1838 to 1842', and was still 'keenly interested in politics'. Hauling provisions and equipment for the prospective miners on their journey was Ogston's horse, a 'brute' affectionately named Feargus, which he had purchased in a Melbourne sale yard. 'The horse Feargus I call after Feargus O'Connor', he told Craig, 'who was the mainstay of the Chartist party'.[1]

Travelling in the opposite direction to Ogston, Craig and 'Feargus' was another former Chartist, Charles Jardine Don, who had tried his hand at mining the hard ground of central Victoria and decided to return to Melbourne and to his trade of stonemasonry. Don had been born in Cupar, Fife, in 1820, and had been Secretary of the Glasgow Chartists before emigrating to Victoria. In Melbourne he became active in the flourishing masons' trade union, helped to found an organisation known as the Operative Reform Association, and, in 1859, he was elected to the Victorian Legislative Assembly becoming the first 'working man' in the colonial parliament. Working as a mason during the day and attending the Assembly in the evening, Don cut a formidable figure that reminded the hostile parliamentary correspondent of the Melbourne *Argus* of home. Don's first speech, lamented the reporter, 'was the fury and frenzy of Feargus O'Connorism of the most exaggerated kind revived'.[2]

These stories from the edge of the British world are a reminder of the capacious nature of Feargus O'Connor's impact on public life in the first sixty years of the nineteenth century. Like the eponymous nag hauling paraphernalia for prospective miners through the treacherous Black Forest, Feargus had carried the weight of the hopes for a better future of a generation of working men and women. Feargus might have smiled had he known of the equine namesake; he had welcomed the many 'Young Patriots' christened Feargus O'Connor during the 1840s. As the *Morning Chronicle* noted in 1849, 'a generation or so back' Feargus O'Connors 'were as common as blackberries'.[3] He would have recognized too the use of his name as a term of abuse by an antagonistic commentator frightened that he was trying to lead Britain towards a precipice of democracy and anarchy. As he vividly put it, his name 'actually stank' in the noses of the middle class.[4] His story touched the lives of many; it is worth telling.

In his prologue to his study of Alexander and Caesar, Plutarch begged his readers not to 'quibble' about his failure to 'report all of their famous deeds' and not even to 'report exhaustively on any of them, but do the majority in summary'. 'For it is not so much histories that we are writing', he continued, 'but lives, and there is not always in the most outstanding deeds a revelation of virtue or vice, but often a little matter like a saying or a joke hints at character more than battles where thousands die...'[5] This book is not intended to be a comprehensive biography: every day in O'Connor's life has not been considered, every file has not been opened. I offer the same explanation as Plutarch and humbly seek the same indulgence. Nor is it intended to supplant the two previous biographies – both now out of print.[6] My aim is to provide a sketch of O'Connor's career, to balance, more finely perhaps than previous studies, a consideration of his pre-Chartist and later-Chartist activities, and to better understand his ideas, both those which were quickly overtaken and those that were ahead of their time.

Musing on the nature of biographical enquiry and envisaging his own death, Roland Barthes argued for what he called 'biographemes', 'a few details, a few tastes, a few inflections'; fragments of a life (not unlike Plutarch's) rather than a fully shaped, unified account.[7] If nothing else the sources press for the study of O'Connor in this way. At his trial in 1843 he boasted that he 'never wrote a private political letter to any man...'[8] He was exaggerating, but not overly. There are few private letters (most of them frustratingly brief) and no private papers to allow us to do more than glimpse the private man behind the public performance. Students of O'Connor's life can take comfort from the words of a leading Australian biographer. Searching for the private man behind an Australian prime minister, Judy Brett decided that she had been looking in the wrong place: 'the public man *is* the real man and the task is to read his life and character where we find it – in the shape of the public life'.[9] This is also my task. Fortunately for the biographer the sources for the study of O'Connor's public life are rich, covering his pre-Chartist and later-Chartist exploits as extensively as the period for which he is best known. Fortunate too are we that O'Connor was his own favourite subject and there is a surfeit of material that allows us to record, if not interiority, what psychoanalysts would call his 'personal myth'.[10] If I can provide a few new tastes and inflections of a life lived in the full glare of public attention I will have achieved my objective.

Speaking in 1842 in the shadow of the new monument to the leader of the previous generation of radicals, Henry Hunt, O'Connor reflected that it 'was truly encouraging to those engaged in the cause of the people to know that their names and character would be respected after their departure'. In a moment of terrible irony he continued: '[H]ad he himself not contemplated that he should be respected not only when living, but after death he would have flagged long since'.[11] Feargus has not been treated kindly by history. By the time of his death in 1855 the *Nonconformist*, an unremittingly hostile journal with an extensive audience among the reforming middle classes, could dismiss his funeral, despite the 'immense crowd' it drew, as being of 'little or no political consequence'.[12] Three decades later in 1885, a monument to British reformers was erected in London's Kensal Green Cemetery within a stone's throw of Feargus's grave site.[13] The memorial features the names of eighty-five reformers: middle-class and working-class, socialist and liberal, male and female, English, Scottish, Welsh and Irish.[14] Despite his centrality in the story of nineteenth century radical politics, O'Connor's name was not carved into the stone. Finally then, this book is a plea for a place for Feargus O'Connor in British *and* Irish political history. He believed he had earned it. He had.

Notes

1   W. Craig, *My Adventures on the Australian Goldfields*, London, 1903, pp. 199-203.
2   *Argus*, 22 October 1859; *Hansard* [Legislative Assembly, Victoria], 20 October 1859, col. 62. See also P.A. Pickering, 'A Wider Field in a New Country: Chartism in Colonial Australia', in M. Sawer (ed), *Elections: Full, Free & Fair*, Sydney, 2001, pp. 28-44.
3   A.B. Reach's letter to the *Chronicle* reprinted in *Manchester and the Textile Districts in 1849*, Helmshore, 1972, p. 107.
4   'The Life and Adventures of Feargus O'Connor', *National Instructor*, 28 September 1850, p. 295.
5   Plutarch, *Life of Alexander*, 1.1-3. I am grateful to Timothy Duff for this reference.
6   D. Read and E. Glasgow, *Feargus O'Connor: Irishman and Chartist*, London, 1961; J. Epstein, *The Lion of Freedom: Feargus O'Connor and the Chartist Movement, 1832-1842*, London, 1982. Nor is it intended to preempt or preclude the publication of Glenn Airey's recent PhD thesis on O'Connor completed at Staffordshire University. I was pleased to read several of Glenn's thesis chapters in draft and encourage its early publication.
7   Cited in Ian Donaldson, 'Biographical Uncertainty', *Essays in Criticism*, vol. 54, no. 4, 2004, p. 308. I am grateful to Ian Donaldson for bringing this to my attention.
8   *The Trial of Feargus O'Connor and Fifty-Eight Others on a Charge of Sedition, Conspiracy Tumult and Riot* (1843), New York, 1970, p. 292. See also *Hansard* [Commons], 3 July 1849, col. 1275.

9   J. Brett, *Robert Menzies' Forgotten People*, Sydney, 1992, p. 198.

10   The term was coined in 1956 by noted psychoanalyst and art historian, Ernst Kris. See 'The Personal Myth—A Problem in Psychoanalytic Technique', *Journal of the American Psychoanalytic Association*, vol. 4, 1956, pp. 653-681.

11   *Northern Star*, 2 April 1842.

12   *Nonconformist*, 12 September 1855.

13   See P.A. Pickering, 'The Chartist Rites of Passage: Commemorating Feargus O'Connor', in *Contested Sites: Commemoration, Memorial and Popular Politics in Nineteenth-Century Britain*, Aldershot, 2004, pp. 101-126.

14   See P.A. Pickering and A. Tyrrell, 'The Public Memorial of Reform', in *Contested Sites*, pp. 1-23.

2: 'A MOST REMARKABLE FAMILY': THE O CONCHUIRS

Old Smithwick lately told me a characteristic story of Feargus O'Connor. Sir Edward Temple having named Frank O'Connor with praise in his book on South America, Feargus, in an ecstasy of inflation thereat, thus unburdened his delight. "Well, Standish, we are certainly a most remarkable family. My brother Roderic is the greatest man in Van Diemen's Land; my brother Frank is the greatest man in South America, and I, as I need scarcely tell you, am the greatest man in Ireland!"

William O'Neill Daunt (1861).[1]

Late in the afternoon of 4 August 1817 a sizeable crowd began to congregate along the High Street of Trim in County Meath at the front of the Court House where the district Assizes were shortly to commence. Built in 1810, a decade after the Act of Union that merged the Irish nation into a United Kingdom with England, Scotland and Wales, Trim Court House was an unequivocal symbol of domination, and never more so than on a day such as this. The crowd had gathered to witness the trial of one of the best-known men in the country, Roger O'Connor. In his mid-fifties, Roger O'Connor was probably at the height of his popularity in Ireland, as well as at the apex of his influence on Anglo-Irish politics. He was certainly at the peak of his notoriety. By 1817 O'Connor was no stranger to courts or gaols, having served periods of imprisonment for political activities during the 1790s, but the charge that he faced on this summer's day was ostensibly a criminal one: that some five years earlier, in October 1812, he had 'feloniously conspired, aided and abetted in the robbery of His Majesty's Mail from Dublin to Galway'.[2]

The daring robbery of the Galway Mail Coach, laden with cash for the Ballinsloe fair on the following day, had captured the headlines on both sides of St George 's Channel in 1812. In the days following the raid O'Connor drew attention to himself when he 'found' part of the stolen mail on his property at Dangan close to Dublin, but by this stage there were already persistent rumours about his criminal activities that would probably have made him one of the chief suspects in any case. Roger O'Connor's exploits were the stuff of popular legend. As early as 1809, for example, when part of Dangan Castle had been destroyed by fire, a handsome payout of £5,000 fuelled rumours of arson and insurance fraud.[3] Other tales – told and retold to countless wide-eyed children as part of a rich oral culture – held that O'Connor and his 'gang' (that, reputedly, included some of his sons) had committed a string of brazen mail coach raids and various other crimes against the British overlord.

According to witnesses for the prosecution in Trim, at approximately 5 pm on the evening of 2 October 1812 the gang – about a dozen men in total – had assembled at Dangan, where O'Connor distributed arms and issued final instructions, before riding some six miles to Cappagh Hill to lay in wait for the Galway coach. In the ensuing robbery a guard was killed and the coach's passengers handled roughly. A large amount of mail and other property was then allegedly taken back to O'Connor's castle where it was ransacked and the proceeds divided among the gang (each share was said to have been £530). The worthless mail was left for O'Connor to report, a gesture that was surely designed to taunt the Anglo-Irish establishment.[4]

Despite generous offers of reward, the increasingly frustrated authorities were unable to obtain the evidence needed to charge O'Connor and even when, in subsequent years, individuals were arrested for passing notes stolen in the robbery, none could be induced to betray their suspected leader. In March 1817, however, a highway robber under sentence of death offered to tell the whole story in order to avoid the gallows. Within a few days another former gang member was persuaded to corroborate the condemned man's account and in April O'Connor was arrested at a family property in Cork. Friend and foe agreed that, such was O'Connor's popularity among the local people of Cork, if he had decided to resist arrest, the authorities would have been powerless to take him into custody, notwithstanding the presence of a troop of dragoons.[5]

O'Connor's standing arose from more than his reputation as a generous and compassionate landlord. As a barrister, he had often represented local agricultural labourers and small farmers in cases involving their employer or landlord. As one commentator recalled, O'Connor 'generally attended the assizes at Cork as an advocate (to use his own expression) unhired, in favour of the poor, where in numerous instances he succeeded'.[6] Moreover, in the magical 1790s he had embraced the objectives of the French Revolution and become a leader of the United Irishmen in Cork. His activities ranged from drilling the local peasantry in anticipation of military assistance from a French expeditionary force to the production of a nationalist newspaper, the *Harp of Erin*.[7] In 1798 O'Connor was arrested; he refused to give evidence against his fellow conspirators and spent nearly three years in prison in Scotland. Released in 1801, O'Connor was banned from returning to the land of his birth for the duration of the French wars, and although this restriction was relaxed in 1803, he was still prevented from living in the south of Ireland, necessitating his relocation from Cork to Meath. According to a widely circulated rumour, O'Connor had purchased the 'magnificent' castle at Dangan in order to offer Napoleon Bonaparte suitable accommodation on state visits to a liberated Ireland,[8] but now it became his home. Exile and the subsequent removal to Meath dented O'Connor's financial security, but did little harm to his popularity. From the point of view of the British government the line between O'Connor's political and criminal activities was blurred: he was both a criminal thug and a dangerous revolutionary. To the people of Cork and Meath he was both a political hero and a martyr. 'In fine', he once boasted, 'many, very many, of the people of Ireland love me...'[9] (see plate 1)

Having spent over three months languishing in Newgate until his trial in 1817, O'Connor arrived at Trim Court House in poor health, but this was not immediately evident from his 'independent and dignified appearance'. As a contemporary report noted, O'Connor 'had a smile on his countenance' as he acknowledged the cheers of the crowd, no doubt because he recognised that here was an opportunity for vindication in the full glare of public attention.[10] As he strode into the Court he was linked arm in arm with his long time friend, Sir Francis Burdett, at one side, and at the other, one of his five sons, Francis (Frank) Burdett O'Connor. One of the most famous members of the House of Commons, Burdett, the Fifth Baronet of Foremark, was renowned for his political independence and for his support for radical causes. Burdett had met Roger O'Connor in the 1790s, and they became firm friends and close political allies. O'Connor had been on hand for most of the significant events in Burdett's career – for example, when he was committed to the Tower of London for libelling the House of Commons in 1810 – and the depth of the Irishman's affection was evident from the name he gave his son.

Understandably, the case for the defence was based on discrediting the Crown witnesses, a task that was accomplished with little difficulty given the circumstances under which they had testified. Burdett's appearance as a character witness however was undoubtedly the highlight of the unfolding drama. Had O'Connor needed financial assistance, Burdett testified, 'I can hardly mention the sum to which I would not go to accommodate him'.[11] He had 'felt ready to sink into the earth' when he had heard of the charges against O'Connor, he continued, a man of undoubted '*Worth* and *Honour*'.[12] Burdett's actions did little to endear him to the authorities. As Feargus O'Connor recalled later in life, when Burdett began to speak the Judge muttered audibly 'I WISH WE HAD BURDETT IN THE DOCK WITH HIM!'[13] Whether his testimony was decisive is doubtful given the inherent weakness of the prosecution case, but Burdett's performance subsequently embroiled him in the saga of the robbery in a way that he could have never anticipated. According to a popular version of events that was soon in circulation, O'Connor had robbed the Galway mail not for financial gain, but in order to retrieve compromising love letters that would imperil the reputation of his English friend and confidant.[14] With the introduction of a hint of sexual intrigue, the episode now had all the ingredients of a melodrama. For O'Connor's admirers, this new narrative added selflessness to his list of virtues; for his opponents it merely entrenched his reputation as an adventurer.

Shortly after Burdett stepped down the jury returned a verdict of not guilty (without bothering to retire) and O'Connor was freed to rapturous applause. The 'shouts from without re-echoed to those within', recorded one observer, 'a considerable time elapsed before the tumultuous joy subsided'.[15] O'Connor and Burdett battled their way from the court room into the hall against an 'immense' tide of well-wishers that pressed forward to share in the triumph, and repeated attempts to carry off the victor and his defender in an *ad hoc* procession through the town were only forestalled by the 'utmost entreaties' from the weary prisoner. 'The shouting and huzzaring continued in the town for near an hour after Mr O'Connor got into the street', noted one report, and the celebrations culminated in the lighting of numerous bonfires after nightfall.[16] Flush with victory, O'Connor issued an address to the 'People of Eri' that concluded in characteristically florid language: 'Whilst I live, I will be your servant', he assured them, 'my heart & soul are full of you'.[17] Acquittal, however, did not mean vindication. An ill-advised attempt to sue those who had given evidence against him failed, and his political influence sharply declined.

Frank O'Connor was not the only one of Roger's sons who had been present at Trim Court house to witness his father's ordeal: among the throng of supporters was Roger's twenty-one year old son, Feargus Edward O'Connor. Despite (and because of) his less prominent position, the trial is an ideal place to begin a portrait of Feargus O'Connor. On the one hand, it gives a clear indication of the size of the shadow that he had to emerge from. Roger's popularity condemned those of his sons who chose a public life to a crushing weight of expectation by virtue of his name. At the same time, the fact that Feargus did not march arm in arm with Roger, as Frank and Burdett had, provides an important clue to an ambivalent relationship between father and son. Feargus's early life was dominated – perhaps even blighted – by his relationship with his father; his political life was defined by his relationship to his family and by a quest to do 'justice to an injured father'.

Roger O'Connor had married Louisa Anna Strahan, the daughter of a local military officer, in 1784 and before she died in 1787 she bore him two children

(Roderic and Louisa). Roger remarried in 1788: his second wife was Wilhelmina Bowen, daughter of a well known Cork family, who was reputed to be 'a paragon worthy of imitation'. Roger and Wilhelmina had seven children: Arthur, Francis, Roger, Feargus, Mary, Harriet and Wilhelmina.[18] Feargus was born on 18 July 1796 at the family estate, Connorville, in County Cork.[19] He was still in his mother's arms, however, when the events of 1798 engulfed Ireland and led to the arrest of his father and his equally famous uncle, Arthur O'Connor, on charges of High Treason. Given his age he could have had little or no understanding of what was happening, but the disruption to his family life was severe. As Arthur O'Connor wrote in a furious public letter to the Chief Secretary, Lord Castlereagh, Roger's 'beloved wife and his eight infant innocents' had been 'scattered by marshalled blood-hounds, who have plundered his house, ravaged his demesne, and destroyed his property'.[20] The treatment that his father and uncle received at the hands of the British government also had a profound impact on Feargus's outlook. Decades later he was still consumed with righteous indignation when he recounted how Arthur and Roger had been 'immured in damp loathsome cells...My father was for several months, confined in an underground cell, nine feet square, until he lost the use of his limbs' so that he had 'to be brought to the air on a hand barrow'.[21]

'The people not only loved but adored both my father and my uncle Arthur', Feargus continued, they were 'two of the finest looking men, the most eloquent men, and the most highly educated men in the kingdom'.[22] Despite their prominence as wealthy members of the Protestant ascendancy (and their importance to understanding the life of Feargus O'Connor), Arthur and Roger O'Connor are little more than footnotes in Irish history. A lawyer by training, Arthur O'Connor was called to the Irish bar in 1788, but never practiced, setting his sights instead on a parliamentary career. Although it was later claimed that he had embraced republican principles following the American revolution, he entered the Irish House of Commons in 1790 in a conventional eighteenth-century manner – in a seat purchased for him by his uncle, Lord Longueville – and his early parliamentary record was undistinguished, voting invariably in support of the interests of his patron. By the mid-1790s, however, O'Connor had begun to assert his independence, a process that culminated in a celebrated speech in support of Catholic Emancipation in 1795. This speech earned him the plaudits of the crowd, and the wrath of Lord Longueville, who not only withdrew his support for O'Connor's seat but also disinherited him. Feargus O'Connor would later point to this as evidence of his family's incorruptibility.

Without his patron Arthur O'Connor resigned from Parliament, joined the United Irishmen, becoming a leading member of the Leinster Directory, and secretly negotiated the treaty with the French government that led to Hoche's ill-fated expedition. He was also involved in the clandestine military committee of the United Irishmen.[23] In another move that greatly influenced his nephew's later career, Arthur became the editor of a prominent nationalist newspaper, *The Press*, in 1796. Journalism, rather than conspiracy, led to his first brush with the law when he was imprisoned at Dublin Castle for six months during 1797 for seditious libel. In February 1798 O'Connor was arrested (with others) at Margate on his way to France. He was carrying a large sum of money that the authorities believed was intended to finance an army of liberation and he was charged with treason. Although he was not convicted, O'Connor was imprisoned (for some time with Roger) until June 1803 when he was exiled to France. Bonaparte welcomed O'Connor as an official representative of the Irish people and, in 1804, he commissioned him as a general in his army. In 1807 O'Connor married Eliza de Condorcet, the daughter of the famous *philosophe*, and, in 1808 they settled on an estate, formerly owned by Mirabeau, at Brignon.[24]

From Brignon Arthur O'Connor was an occasional commentator on Anglo-Irish affairs. In 1830, for example, he published a letter that mocked the efforts of British reformers, defying them to 'make a reform in their representation able to control prodigality and corruption'.[25] During the 1840s O'Connor (now calling himself Arthur Condorcet O'Connor) published his *magnum opus*: a rambling three-volume attack on 'Monopoly, the Cause of Evil'. Running to over 1600 pages *Monopoly* combines turgid prose with convoluted argument, but some sections are of great interest to the student of Feargus O'Connor. Feargus visited his uncle in France on several occasions and although he reportedly spent a lot of time playing billiards and eradicating rats,[26] he clearly imbibed many of Arthur's ideas. His influence can be seen in the following respects. First, Arthur made the case that was often put by Chartists (along with other advocates of the political reform) that all monopoly was evil, including a monopoly of political power. Monopoly, he wrote, 'is the cause of all existing misery – monopoly in land – monopoly in commerce – monopoly in throwing all the load on others, and throwing it off from themselves – in fine, monopoly of all the political power and with it, the subjecting of the people to all the abuses monopolists stand in need of to support their ascendancy'.[27] He also made out a historical case for political equality: the right of universal suffrage had, he argued, been sanctioned by Edward I five hundred years earlier.[28]

Secondly, by his example, Arthur O'Connor reinforced Feargus's appreciation of rural life. O'Connor referred to his estate at Brignon in the agricultural Department of Loiret in central France as 'my little commune', which he cultivated with his workforce of '450 souls'.[29] Finally, Arthur O'Connor offered a version of Irish history (recent and distant). On the one hand, O'Connor attacked the leading Irish politician of the day, Daniel O'Connell. O'Connell had 'destroyed' the unity of the Irish people that had been reflected in the composition of the United Irishmen by making himself leader of the 'popish population, or rather of the Jesuit priesthood who lead them'. O'Connor's *Press*, in particular, had promoted 'brotherly love' to 'every part of Ireland' in order to convince 'the Catholics their protestant countrymen had made their emancipation their own cause'. A purer nationalism, he claimed, was his family's legacy:

> Bred up in the traditions of my family, that I was descended from our ancient chiefs, from my infancy I have been a mere Irishman without any foreign mixture or alloy; my earliest passion was the history of my country, the more I studied it, the more strongly every energy of my soul was excited to rescue her from the oppression and misery which she has been suffering during six hundred years.[30]

It was Roger O'Connor, however, who was the chief custodian of this family tradition: when he addressed the 'people of Eri' he did so as the pretender to the ancient throne of Irish Kings. During Feargus's lifetime more than one version of his genealogy was published. One posited the family's move to Cork in the 1650s from Tralee as a flight from Cromwell's soldiers; another (emphasised by Feargus's opponents) traced the family to a Protestant English merchant (and Elizabethan settler) whose religion Cromwell had later arrived to protect. Both versions, however, agreed that Feargus was linked – however tenuously – to the 'royal' O'Connor clan of Kerry. Feargus never gave a detailed account of his lineage; his claim was both less specific and more ambitious, reaching back into the mists of the ancient Irish past. This story he learned from his father. According to his own account Roger O'Connor made four attempts to 'present the world' with what he called a 'faithful history' of Ireland: once during his imprisonment in 1797-8 (when his efforts were 'outrageously taken away' by British soldiers); in 1802-3 at Fort George; again in 1809 (when his labours and crucial documents were destroyed by the fire at Dangan Castle); and, finally, following his acquittal at Trim.

Published in two volumes in 1822 the result of this last attempt, *The Chronicles of Eri*, is a breath-taking epic tale that deserves to be regarded as Ireland's *Ossian*. Like James Macpherson, author of the famous collection of the poems of the third century Celtic bard, Ossian, O'Connor describes himself as translator, collector and interpreter. 'This history is a literal translation into the English tongue', he claimed, of ancient manuscripts in the 'Phoenician dialect of the Scythian language'.[31] Like Macpherson's *Ossian*, O'Connor's *Chronicles* were quickly denounced as a fraud. Unlike *Ossian*, which was tremendously influential in the century following its publication in 1765 (Napoleon was said to have carried a copy in his pocket), *The Chronicles of Eri*, left virtually no mark on the public imagination. Feargus O'Connor, however, never doubted their authenticity: they were his father's legacy and his inheritance.

Reaching back far beyond the time of Ossian (third century AD) and even the arrival of St Patrick in Ireland in 451 BC, the first section of the *Chronicles* records in meticulous detail the oral traditions of the Gaal-Sciot Ibeir who lived in the Gallice region of the north-western Spanish Peninsula from 5357 BC to 1335 BC. The second part records the history of the Gaal-Sciot people from approximately 1335 BC to 1006 BC when the 'flower of the race' emigrated to Ireland taking with them the sacred manuscripts on which O'Connor claimed to have based his discourse. The third part, written in Ullad (Ulster) continues the history from the 1006 BC to 7 BC. Even a brief summary of this grand narrative – including, as it did, the reign of a King Feargus from 143 to 131 BC – is beyond the scope of the present study, but because the nature of the community described by his father shaped Feargus's outlook in fundamental ways it is necessary to outline its most important features. Government of the Gaal-Sciot was by single chief, but this office, like all others in this social system, was elective: the *Cier-Rige*, the chief of the people, was an elected monarch. The business of the nation was conducted in public assemblies and in a *Teacmor on Tobrade*, a national assembly or convention, that was convened periodically. The 'commandments' of the Gaal-Sciot entreated them to mutual support; to 'Relieve the poor, the needy and distressed', to 'be kind, and minister unto the stranger', and to be 'merciful to every living creature'. Land was divided among the tribes, but 'the fair proportion of which no adult could be deprived' for Eri was 'the inheritance of all the children of the land, according to their due share of it'.[32]

Whether he knew it or not Roger O'Connor recognised the power of cultural nationalism, an impulse that would resonate with increasing volume as the century wore on. In a supposedly ancient commandment to 'Preserve the glory of thy race, die or live free', he could find an apposite message for Ireland after the Union: 'Sons and daughters of Eri', he wrote in the preface, 'shake off your stupor. And ah! If ye cannot feast each others ears with tales of joy, let not your sighs be articulated in language foreign to your lips'.[33]

O'Connor planned later volumes of the *Chronicles* to bring the story from 7 BC to his 'own birth' and beyond, but all he produced during the 1820s was a series of epistles to George IV that were published in 1828 using the pseudonym 'Captain Rock' (the name of the mythical leader of the 'Whiteboy' disturbances of the 1820s).[34] In 1824 the *London Magazine*, in a serialisation of Thomas Moore's *Memoirs of Captain Rock*, had suggested that the letters which comprised ROCK were merely initials, a thin disguise for an 'awful' prospect: 'Roger O'Connor, King!'[35] Addressing the actual king as 'My Cousin', O'Connor's

Letters are rambling and often disjointed, but they contain three elements that became cornerstones of his son's outlook. First, continuing the theme of the *Chronicles*, they plead for true Irish history. 'But though your Majesty be well versed in the history of *your* country', he wrote, 'I venture to assert, that your acquaintance with that of *mine* is very circumscribed'. Moreover, 'your knowledge thereof is not knowledge of the truth, but an accumulation of falsehoods, piled one upon the other by writers of your nation, hired by the ascendant faction, from time to time, to calumniate and vilify the Irish people'.[36] Secondly, the *Letters* outline the case for a true monarchy based on a direct relationship between the sovereign and the people. 'For all the miseries my country hath endured', he wrote, 'the Irish people lay not the lightest blame on your Majesty'. The problem was the 'oligarchy' that rules in the name of the crown. Thirdly, 'Captain Rock' made the case for reform: by urging George to invite Burdett to form a government as a prelude to the enactment of 'that chiefest of all blessings... a full, fair and equal representation of the people in *their House* of Parliament'.[37] Taken together these points are remarkably similar to Feargus's stated positions in later life.

The publication of the Roger and Arthur O'Connor's writings was in the future but the arguments on which they were based saturated the air that the young Feargus breathed. Roger O'Connor's inability to return to Ireland following his release in 1801 meant that his family removed to England and the five-year-old Feargus began his schooling at Mr Finlay's school at Streatham in Surrey, 'where the sons of all the first men were educated'.[38] By his own account the experience was traumatic. Although Mr Finlay was, according to Feargus' later estimation, a 'fine noble independent fellow and a great admirer of my father' he apparently took a disliking to his new pupil: 'scarcely a day passed', O'Connor recalled, 'that I was not flogged with a huge cane'.[39] Following his family's return to Ireland in 1803 Feargus was educated for a short time at a school in Clonmel before being enrolled with his brothers, Frank and Arthur, in Dr Leney's school near Dublin. The change of locality apparently did little to change the pattern established in Surrey. According to O'Connor the next eight years were an almost daily cycle of mischievous japes and misbehaviour interspersed with brutal beatings (at the hands of Dr Leney) that culminated in his expulsion for fighting in 1811.

Home offered the young Feargus no respite: as he later put it, 'My father had five sons...Roderic, Arthur and Roger were spoiled pets, while my brother Frank and I, being both rather wild, were awfully punished'.[40] In fact, Feargus appears to have been singled out for special cruelty by his domineering father. As he told it, gifts and money were lavished on the others, but he received nothing; they were taken on holidays, but he was often left in school. By his own estimation the detail of his brutalised childhood is an important part of his biography because of its impact on his psychological make-up, although in later life he sought to exculpate his tormentor, suggesting that the fault lay either with himself or the British: 'I can scarcely blame my father for the treatment I received as I was very wild, while probably it was the treatment that made me so'. 'The reader must understand', he continued, 'that this treatment was not a consequence of my father's natural cruelty, but consequent upon the change that his mind and disposition had experienced from persecution, tyranny and imprisonment'.[41]

Feargus's mother died in 1808 shortly before the fire at Dangan in 1809 (Frank later claimed that he had started it accidentally) although these events are not mentioned in Feargus's memoir. Indeed, apart from a couple of passing references, his mother is totally absent from O'Connor's account of his early life: she is never even mentioned by name. His sisters are not mentioned either. Even by the standards of the day, this gap in a memoir is extraordinary. Women do not enter into Feargus's account until shortly after his untimely expulsion from Dr Leney's school. Having enrolled at a school in Portarlington run by Mr Willis, O'Connor was deemed to be too old to sit in on classes with the other boys and was left to his own devices. Thus he 'amused' himself by 'walking and riding', dabbling in the study of medicine, and by pressing his amorous attentions on the headmaster's daughter. The proposal of marriage that quickly followed did not please his prospective father-in-law – precipitating his immediate expulsion – and it sent his father into a fit of rage ('he jumped and jumped like a madman', Feargus later recalled) at the prospect of marriage to a mere schoolmaster's daughter.[42] Signing himself 'Your tenderly affectionate father and true friend', Roger wrote to Feargus in January 1815, as soon as he had been informed of the affair, to berate him for pursuing 'the gratification of your own depraved, debased passion', and threatening him with dire consequences: 'never shall you see my face, nor ever during your existence shall you receive, nor any human being proceeding from you, the means of one hour's life from me'.[43] Despite his father's threats, Feargus continued to surreptitiously visit the girl – sometimes walking thirty miles a night to do so – but the passion did not survive long in the face of parental opposition from both sides.[44]

By this time, however, Feargus was no longer living with his father. Roger's letter of admonition also made clear that the family's fortunes were at an all time low; they were living, he told his son, 'with barely the necessities of life', waiting 'till such time as by our unwearied perseverance, we shall be able to live in some manner suitable to our pretensions'. Real or threatened loss of status was, as historians have shown, a common characteristic among political radicals, and undoubtedly Feargus O'Connor was affected by the sense of unease that had gripped his father.[45] Already the family had begun to split up: as one of O'Connor's cousins recalled, after the fire at Dangan and the loss of his wife, Roger O'Connor 'gave up housekeeping'[46] and Feargus and Frank were sent to live with their eldest brother, Roderic O'Connor. Apparently, the change of residence did little to improve the quality of Feargus's life; his elder sibling was, he later recalled, kind to his labourers but not to his brothers.[47] Before long the spirit of adventure and the rebellion that would later characterise the careers of both Frank and Feargus got the better of them and they ran away. In an act that lived up to their father's reputation for criminal conduct they stole two of Roderic's horses, rode them to Dublin, and sold them to pay passage to Holyhead. Their plan, according to Feargus's later account, was to seek 'independence' – a fundamental Chartist aspiration – in England (or even America) through honest endeavour: Feargus as a farmer, Frank as a fencing instructor (a skill he had learned from Burdett).

After they arrived in England, the boys walked to London via Bath, doing odd jobs on the way (they spent six days baling hay on Lord Aylesbury's estate), but by the time they reached the metropolis they were hungry and footsore. Avoiding any relatives, they decided to approach Burdett in the hope that he would finance their American adventure. Their wily father had, however, anticipated this move and written to his friend asking him to ensure that his delinquent sons returned to Ireland without delay. Instead of passage to the New World, the O'Connor boys left London with £50 from Burdett, having promised to return home. Every step they took on the long walk to Bristol, where they were to catch a steamer to Cork, must have redoubled their sense of foreboding. Not even a violent storm that came close to ending their passage at the bottom of St George's Channel was more terrifying than the reception they expected from their father. He did not disappoint them: according to Feargus, Roger's fury knew no bounds and their punishment was severe.[48] Feargus apparently learned little from the experience as he soon ran away again – this time with his brother Arthur – but on this occasion he hid in a cottage belonging to a tenant farmer on the property.

At about this time his father was arrested in relation to the Galway mail coach robbery. Feargus had not returned to school, but instead he had begun to manage a hundred acre farm (apparently a surviving part of his father's estate) and to indulge an interest in horse breeding. Following Roger O'Connor's acquittal, this interest was given a financial boost by Burdett who accompanied Feargus on a visit to his property, where he gave him £150 to purchase stock.[49] This was also the time Feargus decided to pursue a career in the law. What he later described as the 'one of the most important features' of his life began innocently enough. According to his version of events, he had been sitting in Trim Court House, in keeping with a habit he had developed, when a humorous answer by a witness had caused him to laugh uncontrollably earning him a rebuke from the bench and a whack on the head from the clerk. 'I got as red as fury', Feargus recalled, 'I jumped up, left the Court, and vowed that I would have privilege not only to laugh, but to speak in a court of justice'.[50] This decision led to yet another fight with his father. When Roger O'Connor discovered that Feargus had gone to Dublin to enter his name at the King's Inn – a prelude to training for a legal career in Ireland – he had 'fumed like a mad man', 'tore at his hair', and 'jumped about' because to appear before the Bar Feargus would have to take an 'OATH OF ALLEGIANCE to a foreign king'.[51] This dispute led to Feargus's disinheritance, he later claimed, although this could no longer have amounted to much. By this time the heavy debts stemming from the purchase of Dangan had all but bankrupted Roger O'Connor. Shortly after his liberation he finally returned to Cork and began writing furiously. Although he still dreamed of wielding a sword to recapture the throne of Ireland, Roger's active political career was at an end, but he added further weight to the tradition carried by his offspring in the series of extraordinary (if little studied) writings discussed above.

This was also the time when two of Feargus's brothers left Ireland. In 1824 his half brother, Roderic, removed to Van Diemen's Land where he quickly became an extensive landowner and laid the foundation of an enduring colonial dynasty.[52] O'Connor, as one historian has colourfully put it, 'sailed to Hobart on his own ship with his two bastard sons'.[53] Shortly after his arrival Roderic received a substantial land grant on Lake River south of Cressy in the island's central north where he established an antipodean version of the family seat of 'Connorville'. Armed with a letter of recommendation from the Under-Secretary of State in Whitehall, O'Connor soon came to enjoy the friendship and patronage of the Lieutenant Governor, George Arthur, which led to a succession of government posts and the consolidation of his empire. Known for his litigiousness, Roderic shared with his younger brother an obstreperous manner and an innate ability to excite strong reactions from those with whom he came into contact. According to one commentator Roderic was a 'man of blasted reputation, of exceedingly immoral conduct and of viperous tongue and pen'.[54] In political terms, however, he was a world away from his younger brother (and his father and uncle). Roderic O'Connor was an extensive employer of convict labour and a vehement supporter of convict transportation, a cause his half brother would have bitterly opposed. Feargus regarded emigration from Britain and Ireland as unnecessary – a symptom of bad government – and he condemned the transportation of radicals to New South Wales as barbaric. Similarly, he would have repudiated the actions of his elder brother in helping to organise bands of armed convicts charged with 'dispersing' – often a euphemism for murdering

– the local indigenous population. Roderic, a man familiar with convicts both as an employer and a magistrate, once quipped that the 'worst characters would be best to send after' the hapless Aborigines.[55] Roderic's enthusiastic support of the colonial authorities led to his nomination to the Legislative Council for two terms (1844-8, 1852-3), a route to public office diametrically opposed to that championed by his younger brother. It is unlikely that Feargus had direct contact with his brother (Frank and Roderic barely communicated in twenty years[56]) and therefore his estimation of Roderic's wealth and standing in colonial society was undoubtedly based on second-hand information. In many respects Roderic stood for everything Feargus despised; had he known that the soil of the Tasmanian Connorville was soaked with the blood and tears of others he would surely have been ashamed.

Feargus later attributed Roderic's decision to emigrate to the 'persecution' that had been visited on his family,[57] but the same cannot be said about the departure of closest sibling, Frank. In July 1819 Frank left Dublin as part of a regiment in the Irish legion bound for Venezuela to fight in the wars of liberation in Spanish South America. There, wielding the sword given to him by Burdett inscribed 'LIBERTY ABOVE ALL THINGS', he fought alongside Simon Bolívar, becoming a general in the Bolivian Republic that was formed in 1825. Francesco Burdett O'Connor (as he became known in South America) would, in his own words, weather many 'revolutionary storms' during a 'life of toil, trouble and uncertainty'. Before his death in 1871 he would found a dynasty based on his extensive land-holdings and attain high political office, serving as prime minister, in his adopted country.[58] Frank's departure in 1819 never to return must have been keenly felt. Despite their closeness Feargus and Frank kept in touch only infrequently in subsequent years.[59]

In the face of change Feargus threw himself into his equine business ('horse jobber', he described himself) and, according to his own account, he prospered during his first year of operation. He attributed this to the fact he was a good judge of horses, as well as to an aptitude for horse training by which he could improve the value of stock that he had purchased. At this point fate intervened to his benefit; as Feargus put it perfunctorily in his memoir: 'when one of my uncles died…I fell into a good fortune'.[60] During an earlier bout of legal and financial difficulty Roger's three youngest sons had been sent to Fort Robert at Ballyneen in County Cork to live with their uncle, Robert Connor. Robert Connor was a Tory in politics who, unlike Arthur and Roger, did not attach the nationalist 'O' to his surname. Many years before taking in his nephews he had even attempted to have his revolutionary brothers arrested for treason.[61] Robert Connor had three daughters – co-heiresses – who soon became romantically involved with their cousins. Roger and Arthur were married; Feargus was not, but his eldest cousin, Anne Connor, transferred her share of the property to him in any case. When Robert Connor died in 1820 Feargus 'inherited' a share of Fort Robert including the house and demesne.

Situated amidst the heavily wooded hills on the northern bank of the river Bandon near Ballyneen in the south of County Cork, Feargus's new home had been built by his uncle in 1788. According to one account the house was 'slightly ostentatious', jutting out of the top of a slope from which the bay windows of its large rooms afforded magnificent views of the river and woods below.[62] Ballyneen itself was a village that contained approximately 700 inhabitants when Feargus inherited Fort Robert. The town comprised about 120 homes clustered around two streets close to the 'spacious' ten-arch bridge across the Bandon. A court house, police station and medical dispensary made Ballyneen the administrative hub for a population of approximately 5,000 that lived in this part of the Bandon valley. According to a topographical guide published in 1837, a small number of the town's inhabitants were weavers – manufacturing coarse linen and cotton cord – but the vast bulk, like the surrounding district in general, were engaged in agriculture.[63]

O'Connor embraced his new life with characteristic verve. According to his cousin, William O'Neill Daunt, who lived close by, Feargus 'lived a jolly life, enjoying the society afforded by the neighbourhood, to which his entertaining conversation rendered him a welcome acquisition; playing whist, riding to foxhounds, outrivaling all his competitors in desperate horsemanship'.[64] Feargus also revelled in the role of farmer, reputedly spending many happy hours in the fields working alongside his tenants (later estimated to be between 100 and 130 in number).[65] His later speeches and writings are full of references to the virtues of rural life. He had made the transition from idle to industrious, he told readers of the *Labourer* in 1847, when he put his wig and gown away and got mud on his boots at Fort Robert.[66] The youth who had run away with the hope of becoming an independent farmer in America had apparently satisfied all of his aspirations in the land of his birth, but politics was like a stone in his shoe. Duty called. In 1836 O'Connor published articles advocating rural resettlement in the London radical journal, the *True Sun*, using the pseudonym 'Quintus Cincinnatus'.[67] He did not bother to explain his choice of *nom-de-plume* but anyone familiar with Roman history could not fail to grasp its significance. Lucius Quinctius Cincinnatus was an early Roman hero regarded as a paragon of virtue. Renowned for living a humble life on his small farm, Cincinnatus left his fields with his crops unsown to lead the Roman army against an invader. Having saved Rome he returned to the simple life of citizen-farmer on the land that he loved.[68] It would not be the last time that O'Connor imagined his own life according to a famous template. Like Cincinnatus he would forego the life he loved to save his people and, having done so, retire to his fields.

It was in the role of farmer that the first signs of political discord began to emerge. Disturbed by the practice of other local farmers who held back their crop in order to maximize the price, O'Connor decided to put his potatoes on the market as soon as they were ready, earning him the ire of fellow landlords in equal measure to the adulation of the local populace. Soon, however, he put down the shovel and picked up the pen, writing a furious denunciation of landlords, magistrates, parsons, middlemen and policemen. Although he was only a relatively young man when he wrote it, this pamphlet contains important pointers to the political ideology that he articulated in later life.

Addressing himself to the governing elite O'Connor presented a swingeing critique of the state of Ireland on behalf of those he called his 'co-slaves'. The tone was strident and ominous: 'you have added OPPRESSION to OPPRESSION; BRUTALITY to BRUTALITY; and have heaped IMPOSITION, UPON IMPOSITION, 'till you have at length driven the people of this country to desperation'.[69] The different elements of Church and State are accused in turn: absent landlords, 'enamoured with English *pomp* and English *splendour*', leave their estates in the hand of 'harsh agents'; Bishops ' know their parish only on the map', the clergy are the 'GREATEST OPPRESSORS'; magistrates and grand jurors are corrupt. The solution to the myriad problems of Ireland, however, appears relatively simple. Describing himself as a 'student of law' he suggested that the way to avert 'impending ruin' was 'an impartial distribution of justice': 'the Irish are a brave, thoughtful and generous people, who only require to be fairly dealt with, and have the laws properly administered, and impartially dispensed'. In 'one fortnight', he promised, Ireland could 'enjoy perfect tranquillity' if only landlords and the clergy 'made such conciliation as the present times and scarcity of money demand'.[70]

Whether he believed such an outcome would be possible without repeal of the Union is not made clear. What is clear is that O'Connor saw the need to communicate Ireland's claims to a wider British and European audience. In part this was a calculated attempt to combat what he believed was a profound ignorance in England about conditions in Ireland. 'You gentlemen, living on the other side of the water', he wrote, 'have no more conception of what is going on here than the merest African slave'.[71] At the same time, it is clear that even at this early stage, his strategy was to find allies for Ireland across the Irish Sea. Although Roger O'Connor had moved freely in London radical circles, it was his son who would make a combined struggle against oppression the cornerstone of his campaign. As we will see in later chapters, O'Connor never entirely reconciled the tension between Irish nationalism and trans-national solidarity. If 'the people of England' would not listen Ireland's cause must be taken up in

Europe: he would 'proclaim to all EUROPE WITH STENTORIAN LUNGS, that Irishmen shall at least enjoy an EQUAL participation of justice'.[72]

The pamphlet is important not only for what it tells us about O'Connor's formative ideas but also for the light it sheds on his motivation. It is clear that for O'Connor politics was an intensely personal almost visceral matter. The central importance of his family is evident in the title – *The State of Ireland* had been the title of a tract issued by Arthur O'Connor is 1798 – and, in many respects, the state of Ireland that Feargus outlined in the early 1820s was little more than a metaphor for the tribulations experienced by his family, and especially his father. At several points the pamphlet is addressed directly to Roger O'Connor: 'But oh! thou venerable and incorruptible sire, with what delight do I view you (having baffled their machinations)…As Hannibal to his father swore, I here pledge myself to seek justice for thy oppression from every earthly tribunal'. These wounds were raw: 'Here I must lay down my pen', he confessed at one point, 'and try to forget I ever had a father, otherwise I should pass all bounds'.[73] Roger, who had endured 'dungeons, tortures and perjurers', was still 'shining like a grand luminary' determined to 'rescue' Ireland 'from the hands of hireling historians', but vindication (and now recognition) had been denied to him. Trusting that 'no liberal person' would 'censure' him for 'trying to do an injured father justice', here was Feargus's mission. Insisting that he would deal with Ireland's oppressors 'more fairly… than they have dealt with my FA-THER!!!',[74] O'Connor made Ireland's liberation and Roger's vindication one and the same thing.

Whether Feargus remained in contact with his father as his political star began to rise is unclear. Given their tempestuous relationship it is unlikely, although Feargus later recounted a moment of rapprochement when Roger cast himself as a rueful Shakespearian figure: 'I am Lear; the only child that I have been cruel to is the only child who is kind to me in my old age'.[75] Roger lived his remaining years before his death in January 1834 in a humble cottage near Ballincollig west of Cork, with a 'peasant girl' whom he had re-named 'Finana', and was visited, according to one account, only by his daughter Harriet.[76] In his fragmentary memoirs, Feargus referred to his father being 'prematurely consigned to the cold grave', the ruination of his health evidence of British misrule.[77] If he shed tears it was not in public. Alive or dead Roger O'Connor's shadow was prodigious; restoration of his father's reputation remained at the heart of Feargus's political motivation.

The intensely personal nature of O'Connor's politics was also evident in the claim to personal and political independence that would become a constant refrain of his public life. In part this was again a family story: 'I belong to a family many of whom have lost their all from devotion to your cause, and some of whom are at this moment exiled from their country, from incorruptible attachment to you'. He was 'no cold-blooded politician', he wrote, 'whose very fortune depends upon your disaffection'.[78] There was also a distaste for party politics: 'I have sided with no party, being well convinced that those who are out, are trying to get in – and those who are in are determined not to gratify them'.[79] Corruption had rendered political ideas suspect – 'I am no wild theorist', he insisted – what mattered was personal integrity. O'Connor never wavered from his claim to be above party politics, carrying it through to the House of Commons where it earned him isolation and almost universal enmity from the political class. O'Connor concluded his pamphlet with a plea to the Irish people to 'avoid insurrection and civil war', but he was soon embroiled in a rebellion that would shatter his idyllic life as a rural squireen and take him to England and to a life of politics.

Notes

1   W.J. O'Neill Daunt, *A Life Spent for Ireland*, London, 1896, p. 182.
2   *Full and Accurate Report of the Arraignment and Subsequent Extraordinary and Highly Interesting Trial of Roger O'Connor Esq. of Dangan Castle, County Meath*, Dublin, 1817; *Cobbett's Weekly Political Register*, 12 May 1810.
3   See M.W. Patterson, *Sir Francis Burdett and his Times (1770-1844)*, London, 1931, vol. 1, p. 433.
4   See *Trial of Roger O'Connor*, Patterson, *Sir Francis Burdett*, pp. 436-455.
5   See Patterson, *Sir Francis Burdett*, pp. 438-9.
6   Sir B. Burke, *Vicissitudes of Families*, Second Series, London, 1861, p. 33.
7   See R.R. Madden, *The United Irishmen, Their Lives and Times*, Second Series, London, 1843, vol. 2, p. 294; W. O'Neill Daunt, *Eighty-five Years of Irish History*, London, 1888, pp. 131-4; *Dictionary of National Biography*, vol. XIV, pp. 839-40.
8   Daunt, *A Life Spent for Ireland*, p. 322-3; Burke, *Vicissitudes of Families*, p. 37. According to Daunt, there is a letter to that effect in the Napoleonic correspondence.
9   *Cobbett's Weekly Political Register*, 12 May 1810.
10   *Trial of Roger O'Connor*, p. 2.
11   Patterson, *Sir Francis Burdett*, p. 441.
12   Patterson, *Sir Francis Burdett*, p. 441; *Trial of Roger O'Connor*, p. 46.
13   'Life and Adventures of Feargus O'Connor', *National Instructor*, 8 June 1850, p. 57.
14   Patterson, *Sir Francis Burdett*, p. 444-5.
15   *Trial of Roger O'Connor*, p. 46-7.
16   *Trial of Roger O'Connor*, p. 47.
17   Patterson, *Sir Francis Burdett*, p. 442.
18   See Burke, *Vicissitudes of Families*, pp. 34-5; D. Read and E. Glasgow, *Feargus O'Connor: Irishman and Chartist*, London, 1961, p. 14.
19   There is a dispute about the year of his birth, 1794 or 1796, that can not be resolved

as the records were destroyed in 1922. The later date seems to accord more closely to his account of his education. There was also a dispute about the place of his birth. In 1843 the *English Chartist Circular* carried a description of a visit to O'Connor's 'birth place' in Dangan Castle, but this was incorrect. See *English Chartist Circular*, no. 138 , pp. 343-4.

20   *Arthur O'Connor's Letter to Lord Castlereagh*, Dublin, 1799, p. 44.

21   'Life and Adventures of Feargus O'Connor', *National Instructor*, 25 May 1850, p. 7.

22   'Life and Adventures of Feargus O'Connor', *National Instructor*, 25 May 1850, p. 8.

23   See R. O'Donnell, *Robert Emmett and the Rebellion of 1798*, Dublin, 2003, pp. 37-9.

24   'Life and Adventures of Feargus O'Connor', *National Instructor*, 25 May 1850, pp. 7-8; Madden, *The United Irishmen*, pp. 289-297; *Notes and Queries*, 19 June 1852; E.M. Johnston-Liik, *History of the Irish Parliament 1692-1800*, Belfast 2002, vol. 5, pp. 382-4; J.H. Hames, *Arthur O'Connor, United Irishman*, Cork, 2001.

25   A. O'Connor, *A Letter from Gen. Arthur Condorcet O'Connor to General Lafayette on the Causes which have deprived France of the advantages of the Revolution of 1830*, London, 1831, p. 22.

26   Hames, *Arthur O'Connor*, p. 257.

27   A. O'Connor, *Monopoly the Cause of All Evil*, Paris and London, 1848, vol. 1, pp. 109.

28   O'Connor, *Monopoly*, vol. 1, p. 230.

29   O'Connor, *Monopoly*, vol. 1, p. 300.

30   O'Connor, *Monopoly*, vol. 3, pp. 541, 549.

31   R. O'Connor, *Chronicles of Eri; Being the History of the Gaal Sciot Iber: or, the Irish People; translated from the original manuscripts in the Phoenician dialect of the Sythian Language*, London, 1822, vol. 1, p. xi.

32   O'Connor, *Chronicles of Eri*, vol. 1, pp. ccclviiif, ccclix, ccclix-x, 44; vol. 2, frontispiece, part 3, p. 431f.

33   O'Connor, *Chronicles of Eri*, vol. 1, p. ccclviii. See also J. Hutchinson, *The Dynamics of Cultural Nationalism: the Gaelic Revival and the creation of the Irish nation state*, London, 1987.

34   See C.G. Duffy, *My Life in Two Hemispheres*, New York, 1898, vol. 1, p. 9. According to Duffy, the 'Captain's name in those days was equivalent to a dynamiter or an Irish invincible...'

35   See *London Magazine*, June 1824, p. 585; T. Moore, *Memoirs of Captain Rock, The Celebrated Irish Chieftain, With Some Account Of His Ancestors. Written By Himself*, London, 1824.

36   Captain Rock [Roger O'Connor], *Letters to His Majesty, King George the Fourth*, London, 1828, pp. 11-12. The volume in the British Library identifies O'Connor as the author in the hand of its former owner, and O'Connor's friend, Thomas Hardy. There were numerous other individuals who were believed to be Captain Rock.

37   *Letters to His Majesty*, pp. 14, 363.

38   'Life and Adventures of Feargus O'Connor', *National Instructor*, 1 June 1850, p.

23.

39   'Life and Adventures of Feargus O'Connor', *National Instructor*, 1 June 1850, p. 23.

40   'Life and Adventures of Feargus O'Connor', *National Instructor*, 1 June 1850, p. 23.

41   'Life and Adventures of Feargus O'Connor', *National Instructor*, 1 June 1850, pp. 23-4.

42   'Life and Adventures of Feargus O'Connor', *National Instructor*, 1 June 1850, p. 24-6.

43   Cited in Read and Glasgow, *Feargus O'Connor*, p. 18.

44   'Life and Adventures of Feargus O'Connor', *National Instructor*, 1 June 1850, pp. 25-6.

45   See P.A. Pickering and O. Ashton, *Friends of the People*, London, 2002, pp. 153-4.

46   Burke, *Vicissitudes of Families*, p. 38.

47   'Life and Adventures of Feargus O'Connor', *National Instructor*, 8 June 1850, p. 40.

48   'Life and Adventures of Feargus O'Connor', *National Instructor*, 8 June 1850, pp. 40-2.

49   'Life and Adventures of Feargus O'Connor', *National Instructor*, 15 June 1850, p. 57.

50   'Life and Adventures of Feargus O'Connor', *National Instructor*, 15 June 1850, p. 57.

51   'Life and Adventures of Feargus O'Connor', *National Instructor*, 15 June 1850, pp. 47-8.

52   The dynasty has endured over seven generations down to the current Roderic O'Connor. See J. Dunn, 'Superfine Heritage', *Outback*, no. 40, April-May 2005, pp. 81-3. Andrew Gregg at the University of Tasmania is writing a history of the O'Connors in Tasmania.

53   R. Hughes, *This Fatal Shore: the epic of Australia's founding*, New York, 1987, p. 394. See also M. Clark, *A History of Australia*, Melbourne, 1968, vol. 2, p. 127.

54   Cited in P.R. Eldershaw, 'O'Connor, Roderic', *Australian Dictionary of Biography*, Melbourne, 1967, vol. 2, p. 296.

55   Cited in Hughes, *This Fatal Shore*, p. 418.

56   See National Library of Australia, Manuscript Department, MS 2630, F.B. O'Connor to R. O'Connor, 5 March 1836. See also L.M. Geary, 'Fraternally Yours: Roderic and Francis Burdett O'Connor', *Journal of the Cork Historical and Archaeological Society*, vol. XCV, no. 254, 1990, pp. 120-3.

57   'Life and Adventures of Feargus O'Connor', *National Instructor*, 25 May 1850, p. 9.

58   See 'Life and Adventures of Feargus O'Connor', *National Instructor*, 25 May 1850, p. 9; J. Dunkerley, 'The Third Man: Francisco Burdett O'Connor and the Emancipation of the Americas', *Warriors and Scribes*, London, 2000, pp. 145-167; A. Hasbrouck, *Foreign Legionaires in the Liberation of Spanish South America*, New York, 1928.

59   Dunkerley refers to one letter from Feargus to Frank, dated September 1843, in private possession. See 'The Third Man', p. 206n. I am grateful to Malcolm Chase

who has allowed me to consult a copy of the full letter which he intends to publish at an early opportunity subject to the permission of its owner. I strongly support his intention. The letter makes it clear that the brothers had not been in regular contact. A letter from Frank to Roger (c. June 1820), detailing some of the exploits of the Irish legion and his wounds in battle, was recently offered for sale from a private collection by Michael Brown, a Bookseller in Philadelphia, USA.

60 'Life and Adventures of Feargus O'Connor', *National Instructor*, 15 June 1850, p. 58.

61 Burke, *Vicissitudes of Families*, pp. 31-3; 'Life and Adventures of Feargus O'Connor', *National Instructor*, 22 June 1850, p. 71.

62 M. Bence-Jones, *A Guide to Irish Country Houses*, London, 1988, p. 126; Read and Glasgow, *Feargus O'Connor*, p. 20.

63 S. Lewis, *A topographical dictionary of Ireland: comprising the several counties, cities, boroughs, corporate, market, and post towns, parishes, and villages, with historical and statistical descriptions*, London, 1837, vol. 1, p. 159; P. O'Flanagan, 'Three Hundred Years of Urban Life: Villages and Towns in County Cork, c.1600 to 1901', in P. O'Flanagan and N. Buttimer (eds), *Cork, History and Society*, Cork, 1993, pp. 391-468.

64 O'Neill Daunt, *Eighty-five Years*, p. 134.

65 *The Trial of Feargus O'Connor and Fifty-Eight Others on a Charge of Sedition, Conspiracy Tumult and Riot* (1843), New York, 1970, p. 320.

66 *Labourer*, vol. 1, 1847, p. 147.

67 *English Chartist Circular*, no. 117, p. 257. The spelling was incorrect in the *Circular*.

68 For Lucius Quinctius Cincinnatus see Livy, *Book III*, xxvi, 1-8, xxix, 2-7, Leob edition, London, 1967, pp. 89-99. Cincinnatus was a hero of George Washington who served as inaugural president of the Cincinnati Society for officers of the continental army from 1783-1799.

69 F. O'Connor, *A State of Ireland, shewing the Rise and Progress of the Present Disaffection, with an Address to the Irish People*, 2nd edition, Cork, [1822?], p. 13. The British Library catalogue lists the year of publication as 1820(?). In his memoir O'Connor indicates that it was published in 1822. See 'Life and Adventures of Feargus O'Connor', *National Instructor*, 29 June 1850, p. 90.

70 O'Connor, *A State of Ireland*, p. 18.

71 O'Connor, *A State of Ireland*, p. 3.

72 O'Connor, *A State of Ireland*, p. 22.

73 O'Connor, *A State of Ireland*, p. 6.

74 O'Connor, *A State of Ireland*, pp. 6, 25, 29.

75 Life and Adventures of Feargus O'Connor', *National Instructor*, 1 June 1850, p. 26.

76 O'Neill Daunt, *A Life Spent for Ireland*, pp. 251-2; *Dictionary of National Biography*, vol. XIV, p. 853.

77 'Life and Adventures of Feargus O'Connor', *National Instructor*, 3 August 1850, p. 167.

78 O'Connor, *A State of Ireland*, p. 9.

79 O'Connor, *A State of Ireland*, pp. 3-4; see also p. 31.

1. 'Roger O'Connor "NO UNION, Erin Go Brach!"', *The works of James Gillray from the original plates, with the addition of many subjects not before collected*, London, H.G. Bohn, [1830?]. Reproduced with permission from the Rare Books collection of the University Library, The Australian National University.

2. O'Connor Liberation Medal, 1841. 'FEARGUS O'CONNOR. UNIVERSAL
SUFFRAGE AND NO SURRENDER'.
Original in the possession of the author.

3. O'Connor Liberation Medal, 1841 (reverse). 'FEARGUS O'CONNOR
WAS CONFINED IN THE CASTLE OF YOURK BY THE WHIGS FOR
LIBEL. LIBERATED 27 AUGUST 1841'. He was released on 26 August.
Original in possession of the author.

THE MODERN MILO.

Vide—"The Life and Times of Feargus O'Connor."

4. 'The Modern Milo', *Punch*, vol. 2, 1842.
Reproduced with permission from the collection of the University Library, The
Australian National University.

Feargus O'Connor. Esq.re
M.P. for Nottingham.

5. 'Feargus O'Connor Esq. MP for Nottingham', 1847.
Original in possession of the author.

6. O'Connor Monument, erected 1857, Kensal Green Cemetery, London.
Photograph by Alex Tyrrell.

7. 'Mr Feargus O'Connor, MP', engraving by Henry Vizetelly,
Illustrated London News, 15 April 1848.
Original in possession of the author.

8. Statue of Feargus O'Connor by J.B. Robinson, erected 1859, Nottingham
Arboretum.
Photograph by the author.

3: REBELLION AND REFORM

Rumours of the contents of O'Connor's pamphlet *A State of Ireland* were sufficient to cause one local magistrate to order its confiscation, and virtually all of the first edition – 3,000 copies – were seized shortly after publication. In part, the severity of the response was prompted by the troubled waters onto which the pamphlet was launched. During the early 1820s what O'Connor would later call the 'Whiteboy revolution' engulfed several Irish counties, with rural Cork among the most disturbed areas.[1] By April 1823 the Cork Grand Jury estimated that the local Whiteboys (or Rockites – followers of Captain Rock – as the Cork protesters were also known) had inflicted as much as £10,000 worth of damage 'by fire, destruction of cattle, breaking of machinery, etc'.[2] So called because of the white disguises they often wore on their nocturnal raids, the Whiteboys had first been seen in Ireland in the middle of the eighteenth century, and their subsequent appearance – in response to a range of grievances from the enclosure of common land and high rents to the burden of tithes – was a sure indicator of popular discontent.

O'Connor was moved to action by the misery that he saw around him. 'Although I was very young', he later wrote, 'I was capable of understanding the atrocious and tyrannical cause of the people's suffering'.[3] Ostensibly, his response to the events in Cork was constitutional. Following discussions with a group of local Catholic priests, O'Connor called a public meeting in the chapel at Enniskeane where he gave his first public speech. Looking back on the occasion in 1850 O'Connor recalled that his remarks contained 'a little spice of treason' (he was, he claimed, not as 'cautious' as in later years). His words earned him the plaudits of the crowd and 'literally flabbergasted their reverences, as they were aware of the influence my name would have with the people'.[4] In his own mind at least, it seems that O'Connor's family would be half a pace behind him whenever he stepped onto the platform. It is clear that the young man courted wider publicity for his actions: after the meeting concluded with the passage of resolutions 'condemnatory of the tyranny of landlords and parsons' it was O'Connor who sent copies, together with a report of the proceedings, to the leading Cork newspaper, the *Southern Reporter*.[5]

As the man who might have claimed to be a son of a pseudonymous 'Cap-

tain Rock', however, O'Connor may well have also taken a more clandestine
role in Cork's 'Whiteboy revolution'. Faced with the threat of draconian punishment, the Whiteboys carefully guarded their anonymity and the stories of
their periodic activities are thus invariably shrouded in mystery. Not surprisingly O'Connor's role is impossible to clarify with any certainty. In his memoir
O'Connor recalled that around the time of his public meeting he had received
a tip-off that he was going to be charged for involvement in Whiteboy violence,
in particular for his part in commanding the insurgents in what subsequently
became known as the battle of Deshure. What is clear about this clash with a
contingent of Scots Grays that had taken place at the end of January 1822 is that
one rebel was killed and twenty-nine others were arrested; it was also alleged
that a Whiteboy leader had been wounded in the leg during the melee and had
been lucky to evade capture.[6] Thirty years later, O'Connor openly implied that
he was this person. 'Well, curious enough to relate', he wrote smugly, 'there was
a burnt hole about the size of a bullet, in the skirt of my coat…and still more
curious to relate, I also had a sore leg at the time'. What is clear is that in 1822
O'Connor suddenly fled to England 'until the breeze had blown over'.[7]

O'Connor spent the next thirteen months in London. Living in a 'small garret' at 4 Northumberland Street near the Thames Embankment in Westminster
(Wolfe Tone's son also lived there), he began to mingle in the metropolitan
radical circles that had welcomed his father. Feargus was a 'young man of very
fine talents' who visited regularly reported Thomas Hardy, the veteran leader
of the London Constitutional Society, to Roger O'Connor.[8] But Feargus did
not pursue an active political career at this stage. Facing poverty O'Connor 'resolved upon training [his] mind to literary pursuits' in order to see if he could
earn a living by his pen. The battle of Deshure had, he claimed, convinced him
of the futility of armed rebellion, but in a cold London garret it became the
subject of his first work of fiction. O'Connor's novel in two volumes entitled
White Boy offered, according to his own evaluation, 'a fair, a critical, and not
an overdrawn character of English law, the English Parliament, Irish landlords,
Magistrates, middlemen, judges, barristers, juries, and the Catholic peasants'.
He followed this with four plays – two tragedies of five acts each, a comedy and
a farce – written in quick succession.[9]

The tragedies, he later stated, were 'Constantia and Cardenio', adapted 'from
a beautiful pastoral tale in Don Quixote', and 'The Princess of Spain' (about
which he says nothing); the comedy was 'an illustration of Irish manners and
customs, entitled Bull or O'Bull'.[10] For the subject of his farce O'Connor chose
George IV's visit to Ireland in 1821. The king's visit, the first by a reigning
monarch since 1399, was, as O'Connor noted, widely seen as a crucial step towards Catholic emancipation later in the decade, but it was also marked by

overt declarations of fealty by the leading Catholic politicians of the day, including Daniel O'Connell. As O'Connor recalled, the Earl of Fingall, a member of one of the oldest Catholic families in Ireland, had accepted 'some regal badge', while O'Connell had greeted the king on bended knee with an olive branch. In his memoir O'Connor gives few details of the text of this play, entitled 'Mock Emancipation', but he relates with considerable delight two 'caricatures' that 'adorned' it. In the first the king is depicted as administering an emetic ('a dose of physic') to Lord Fingall to prepare him for high office. After some straining the hapless Lord vomits a 'little black Pope' to rapturous applause from the court who declare him 'fit for the honours conferred upon him'. In the next scene O'Connell was also purged of Catholicism, but without any chemical assistance: as he bent to his knees to hand George the olive branch 'his breeches burst, and out flew the Pope to the astonishment and consternation of the Catholic beholders'.[11] During his short exile O'Connor had apparently imbibed the prurient humour that had characterised Regency politics, but he was not the only critic of Irish obsequiousness, particularly that of O'Connell. According to Oliver MacDonagh, O'Connell's foremost biographer, his 'fawning, courtier-like' performance 'aroused disgust and contempt among liberals in England'.[12]

O'Connor's literary efforts were neither published nor performed and none have survived in manuscript form.[13] According to Thomas Frost, a radical *litterateur* in his own right, the reason was easy to locate: O'Connor was 'as destitute of literary ability as any man of ordinary intelligence and education can be, his style being discursive, and his poverty of language, to say nothing of his imagination, extreme'.[14] There is no evidence about O'Connor's other activities at this time, and after little over a year, he returned to Ireland where he quickly settled back to the life of a rural farmer. If the authorities had unanswered questions about his earlier conduct, including the reason for his flight, they apparently did not pursue them. Despite his return to the land it is unlikely that politics was ever far from his mind, and before long O'Connor resolved to return to his study of the law which his father's example had shown him could be wielded as a political weapon. O'Connor had undergone the first part of his legal training at King's Inns in Dublin in the early 1820s, and late in 1826 he returned to London to complete his training by enrolling in the law society at Gray's Inn in Holborn, one of the four ancient Inns of Court that controlled admission to the bar. Over the next three years O'Connor accumulated the mandatory two years residence at Gray's Inn, and in 1830 he successfully applied for admission to the Bar.[15]

We have no information about O'Connor's activities during his time at this venerable institution, but we know what it was like to undergo the experience from other contemporary accounts. Whether or not his earlier sojourn in the capital had exposed him to the harsh reality of metropolitan life, O'Connor would have undoubtedly encountered it in Holborn. Gray's Inn lane was, according to one account, 'dismal and dirty at all times', its 'muddy pavement' lined with a vast range of shops – pawn brokers, old book stalls 'smelling like literary mausoleums', small public houses, and butchers' shops 'where pieces of unwholesome-looking meat lie in heaps'. The inhabitants of this district comprised 'groups of dirty, ruffianly-looking men' – Irish as well as English – who stood 'quarrelling about the doors of the dram-shops', 'still more dirty looking women, with loose drapery and scattered hair', and children, 'half-naked, shaggy-headed little savages'.[16] Later O'Connor's popularity would owe much to his easy manner in working-class company despite his relatively privileged background. Cleary his time in Holborn did much to prepare him for this.

The several buildings that comprised Gray's Inn were nestled in this district. According to one description the principal chambers were 'spacious and well adapted for permanent habitation'. The main hall of Veralum-buildings, smaller than those of the other Inns, was, 'nevertheless, imposing': 'The roof is of carved oak, divided into six compartments. The screen another magnificent specimen of carving, supported by six pillars of the Tuscan order, with caryatides supporting the cornice.' Portraits of Charles I, Charles II, James II, Bishop Gardiner, Lord Coke, and Lord Bacon, the society's most famous old boy, glared down at students such as O'Connor sitting in this hall; in the 'cosy' library another portrait of Bacon dominated the wall.[17] At least some former visitors did not recall the experience with pleasure. A junior law clerk during the 1820s, Charles Dickens, for example, remembered Gray's Inn as 'one of the most depressing institutions in brick and mortar, known to the children of men', and, writing in 1860, longed for the day when its 'staircases shall have quite tumbled down… when the last clerk shall have engrossed the last parchment behind the last splash on the last of the mud-stained windows' and when 'the last prolix old bencher…shall have been got out of an upper window by means of a Fire Ladder'.[18]

Of all the Inns of Court, Gray's was tinged with disrepute, a characteristic captured in a well-known quatrain that might have appealed to O'Connor's rebelliousness:

Inner Temple rich
Middle Temple poor
Lincoln's Inn for gentleman
And Gray's Inn for a whore.[19]

Nevertheless, attendance at any Inn of Court required considerable means. Students at Gray's Inn like O'Connor (there were less than 80 at any one time), paid about £35 per year in admission fees, £10-£12 a year in living expenses, as well as a 'stamp' of £50 required for admission to the Bar. By the 1850s the government could no longer ignore calls for reform of legal education (the 'Sahara Desert of the law', Dickens called Gray's Inn), but before then admission to the bar had little to do with gaining a comprehensive knowledge of the law; it was a rite of passage that was the preserve of a social elite (in 1833 there were only 1,130 Barristers in Britain).[20]

Having passed through this rite of passage O'Connor returned to Cork where he threw himself into building a career as an advocate. Whether he 'quickly acquired a very high standing' in his chosen profession, as later claimed, is difficult to say, but he undoubtedly earned popular approval by emulating his father's practice of defending the poor and the vulnerable without cost. In his memoir O'Connor provides details of numerous cases that he argued at this time, but he makes it clear that he quickly became angry and frustrated by the law. He singled out the case of a poor man facing transportation for stealing a goose as an illustration of how the court left his 'heart palpitating with indignation'. What angered him so was not that an innocent man had been falsely accused – in fact he makes it clear that the man had stolen the goose – but that a good man needed to steal a goose in order to feed his family. The symbiotic relationship between poverty and crime is a familiar trope to any student of Irish political discourse.

O'Connor claimed that the man with the goose was his 'last' legal case: so iniquitous was the application of the law in Ireland that he vowed that he would 'never again enter a court of law as an advocate'.[21] Although Parliamentary records show that this vow was apocryphal (O'Connor continued to argue legal cases on behalf of humble citizens in Cork well into the 1830s, a fact that helps to explain his enduring popularity), it is fair to say that by 1830 he had turned decisively away from the law to more direct political action. The change might have been expected sooner. For much of the later 1820s Ireland was in the grip of the nationwide struggle that culminated in Catholic Emancipation in 1829 and entrenched Daniel O'Connell as the pre-eminent Irish politician of his day. Surely emancipation – a cause that Arthur O'Connor had famously championed in the Irish Parliament in the 1790s – was the ideal issue for Feargus O'Connor to re-launch a political career? O'Connor, however, played no role in this campaign. The fact that he was at Gray's Inn for extended periods at this time only partly explains his lack of involvement. Most importantly, O'Connor believed that emancipation was of limited efficacy and had come at too high a price. The 'poor Irish Catholics' had been taught to regard emancipation as a panacea – 'exemption from tithes, and the release from bondage of every description' – but in practice it had merely led to the disenfranchisement of tens of thousands of voters. In fact, O'Connor continued, the only Irishman to have benefited from emancipation was Daniel O'Connell.[22]

O'Connor made his return to the political platform at the end of 1831 by intervening in a large public meeting in the County Court-House at Cork. The meeting had been called by the city's Whig grandees in support of the Reform Bill that was then under consideration by the parliament in Westminster. According to one observer, for most of the day speaker after speaker 'rehearsed the usual commonplaces of Reform' and 'talked in a tone of aristocratic condescension of the claims of the democracy'.[23] It was apparently all too much for O'Connor; towards the end of the proceedings he jumped up in front of one of the galleries and gave a 'rattling speech' that was 'beyond comparison the best speech of the day'.[24] The fact that O'Connor was not part of the platform party was not a disadvantage; far from it. Offering a rousing speech from the floor – a tactic he would use to good effect on many subsequent occasions – would have undoubtedly enhanced his distinctive message by imposing a physical distance between himself and every other speaker. His message was simple: whereas the Whigs and other reformers spoke of Reform, O'Connor told the crowd 'that Repeal alone could save Ireland from ruin'.[25]

This was the first time that O'Connor demonstrated his considerable skill as a public speaker before a large crowd and he left a lasting impression on friend and foe alike. 'You were charmed with the melodious voice, the musical intonations, the astonishing volubility, the imposing self-confidence of the man, and the gallant air of bold defiance with which he assailed all oppression and tyranny', recalled Daunt. 'It is true he dealt largely in bombast, broken metaphor, and inflated language', he continued, 'but while you listened, these blemishes were altogether lost in the infectious vehemence of his spirited manner.' Daunt also attested to O'Connor's ability to produce an 'extraordinary popular effect' through humour; his 'talents as a mimic were considerable'; he 'excelled in repartee'; he 'had strong satirical powers' and 'could pounce with merciless sarcasm'.[26] For Justin McCarthy, O'Connor was a 'splendid mob speaker, who could fight his way by sheer strength of muscle and fist through a hostile crowd'; for Georg Weerth (describing a much later speech) O'Connor's 'impression on the audience was indescribable':

> more than once the women who surrounded the speaker on the rostrum wiped the scalding tears from their cheeks, more than once they broke out into prolonged shouts of joy. On the faces of the men you could read what was going on in their hearts; the speaker's mood was mirrored there.[27]

For another admirer O'Connor was better at addressing a crowd than even the most celebrated Irish orator of the day: 'There was', he suggested, 'a wild, Ossianic spirit about O'Connor's spirit-stirring effusions that was altogether different from O'Connell's wearisome blarney and incessant cajolery'.[28] No doubt O'Connor would have been delighted by this comparison for a number of reasons. After all, he was the son of the man who saw himself as Ireland's Ossian and he would, before long, become O'Connell's foremost rival for popular support.

O'Connor's speech at the Cork Court House certainly caused the 'Aristocracy and Squirearchy of the County' to take notice. 'His principles astounded them by their violence', recalled one witness, and although they did not regard him 'as exalted enough to constitute an important opponent', the local 'great ones… stared at him for his confidence before them'.[29] This commentator emphasised O'Connor's 'comparative obscurity' at the time, but this did not last long. Following the meeting O'Connor embarked on a punishing program of meetings (another practice that would characterise his later career as a Chartist leader). 'His powers of locomotive agitation are wonderful', enthused one observer, 'his energies are sleepless; wherever popular passion was to be fed, or popular grievances to be consoled, there he was'.[30] 'O'Connor tried to crowd half a dozen lives into one', recalled another commentator.[31] It was a propitious time to establish a political career. As Daunt remembered, during the summer of 1831 a 'great movement against tithes and the Union became general through Ireland; the whole kingdom was astir', a situation that provided O'Connor with 'numberless opportunities for the display of his declamatory powers'.[32] Whilst repeal was his constant refrain, O'Connor's speeches were usually cleverly targeted to suit their audience – 'he has local abuses on the tip of his tongue', recalled one observer.

In particular, O'Connor established a reputation as a strident critic of tithes, the deeply resented levy imposed on the Irish people for the upkeep of an alien clergy. A report of a meeting at Dunmanway in western Cork shows him at work. Before a crowd estimated at approximately 50,000 people O'Connor moved the first resolution in a speech of stunning simplicity. Part of his address, as reported in the leading Cork newspaper, was devoted to O'Connor's favourite subject: himself. He began by confronting the accusation that he had been receiving money for speaking at meetings – a familiar charge that was levelled against popular agitators on both sides of St George's Channel. 'The only notice which I shall take of this aspersion', he stated indignantly, 'is, that I would rather starve than receive one farthing wrung from the hard-earned industry of my country'. Here was his cue to establish his record of public service: 'Did I require a bribe ten years since, in the awful year of 1822, when treason stalked abroad?

Did I not then come forward to advocate your rights, when a bare association with you was considered as little short of treason?'[33] Having spoken about himself at some length O'Connor then personalised the issue of tithes for his audience in compellingly uncomplicated language: 'Do the poor receive comfort or consolation from those who relentlessly extract from them the tenth of their poverty, their industry and their labour?' he asked. When the clergy visited the 'miserable hut of the peasant' did they come to offer 'comfort or consolation'? No: they came to 'snatch the last blanket from the bed of sickness and misery, and wrest the last morsel from the lips of the widow and the orphan'. After this peroration O'Connor returned by way of conclusion to speaking about himself. 'I shall ever, as I have done, devote myself to your cause, unpurchaseably and unflinchingly', he promised them, 'I am ready to spill the last drop of my blood in defence of the liberties of my Countrymen (cheers). No taunt, no threat, no scoff, shall make me desert your cause...'[34]

O'Connor's ability to involve his audience in his visceral political world was a powerful weapon. In fact, O'Connor's appeal seemed to draw on contradictory attributes: at times his manner was almost obsequious and subservient – 'homely and excessively good humoured' – and the common 'country folk' felt encouraged to talk with affectionate familiarity of 'Fargus' as if they were on first name terms with him. He was comfortable with ordinary people and yet, for some observers, he was separated from them by an 'indescribable swagger'. His demeanour was that of a 'far descended gentleman', a 'Celtic prince', a natural leader, and he appealed to what some commentators regarded as a deeply ingrained sense of deference among the Irish people. He was a 'whimsical genius', self-deprecating, but also 'vituperative', vain and arrogant.[35] During his Chartist career O'Connor retained this potent mix of fame and familiarity, although among the 'class' conscious British radicals his aristocratic status became less of an asset than a liability. Friend and critic agreed that O'Connor was an imposing physical presence: 'huge, boisterous, fearless', with 'red curly tresses overhanging the collar of his coat', piercing blue eyes 'flashing with fire', and 'a cajoling smirk' that denoted great personal charm and disarmingly good humour. 'He was full of frolic and threw himself *con amore* into whatever sort of merriment was going', recalled Daunt, 'Feargus was uncommonly amusing'.[36] 'O'Connor is a magnificent figure of a man', reported Weerth,

From his shapely, graceful legs and thighs rises a broad-shouldered, deep-chested torso, which carries an interesting rather than beautiful head with a broad protruding brow. O'Connor's hair is red, his eyes deep-set, his nose cocked-up.[37]

Another commentator recalled his 'herculean form, majestic head, sandy hair and splendid voice...'[38] O'Connor remained 'a picturesque agitator' until the end of his public life and in important respects he outshone the principles he stood for. An understanding of his public life is inextricably linked to an appreciation of his performative gifts and imposing physical presence.

Within a few months O'Connor's activities had taken him from 'comparative obscurity' to the centre of the political stage in Cork. Ironically, his rapid rise had been helped by the sustained attacks that he had attracted: from aspersions directed against his family and his financial motivation, to allegations that he was an enemy of the King and the Protestant church. As we have seen, O'Connor relished the opportunity that such attacks afforded him to speak about himself. When anti-tithe meetings were proscribed in Cork in July 1832 O'Connor defied the ban (an action for which he was later arrested although not brought to trial).[39] By mid-August his standing was such that a large public dinner was held in his honour in Enniskeane, the scene of his first public speech a decade earlier. It is clear from subsequent evidence that O'Connor played a central role in organising this dinner, even agreeing to underwrite the cost of the food and drink in the event that ticket sales should prove too slow. He need not have worried: despite inclement weather the 'little village was thronged from end to end with country people, assembled to hail and welcome the gifted, the patriotic, and public-spirited guest'.[40] Even at this early stage in his public life O'Connor had an acute sense of political dramaturgy and no detail was left to chance. The dinner guests – just over five hundred in number – were seated in a large white tent (240 ft x 80 ft), supported by 'rustic pillars, beautifully enwreathed with flowering shrubs' down the middle. A solid white wall behind the speaker's platform was also 'half covered' with green foliage giving one reporter the impression of the 'scenic illusion of a theatre, or some fanciful description in fairy tale'. It was both. The use of white was undoubtedly designed to convey O'Connor's freshness, his innocence, and his independence from the corrupt political class; the traditional green of Catholic Ireland (and the natural world) was intended to evoke old Ireland, a theme which was reinforced by the use of Irish as well as English during the proceedings. Not surprisingly, after O'Connor's speech the crowd sang a traditional air, 'The dear Irish boy', a tale of intimate lovers that also seemed to capture the developing relationship between Feargus and his audience:

My Connor, his cheeks are as ruddy as morning,
The brightest pearls do but mimic his teeth;
While nature with ringlets his mild brows adorning,
His hair Cupid's bow strings, roses his breath.

Smiling, beguiling,
Cheering, endearing,
Together how oft o'er the mountains we stray'd;
By each other delighted,
And fondly united,
I have listened all day to my dear Irish boy.[41]

So much care was taken to stage manage what became known as the 'Great Dinner' at Enniskeane because it was to be the platform from which O'Connor confirmed his candidacy for County Cork.[42] Some commentators believed that he had this end in mind from the moment he intervened in the reform meeting the previous December. Although this is probably true, O'Connor himself identified the passage of the Irish Reform Bill on 7 August 1832 as the crucial precondition. Reform, he told the crowd, had 'opened a wider sphere of exertion'. Before he made his announcement O'Connor had been shrewd enough to secure the support of Daniel O'Connell. His approach to 'the Liberator' had been suitably deferential – no hint of the mocking tone of his unpublished farce – and he subsequently used O'Connell's support to great effect: the letter of endorsement was read from countless platforms and published in the press. O'Connor was also 'profoundly deferential' towards the Catholic Clergy – he boasted that he was 'personally acquainted with a greater number of Catholic priests than any other layman in Ireland'.[43] His claim to the seat, however, was based on more than either Catholic support or O'Connell's imprimatur. In 'infancy', he told the dinner guests at Enniskeane, 'his spirit drank in the love of liberty' and he was now standing on a principle embraced as a child: repeal. The importance of this commitment should not be under-estimated. As one commentator explained, to 'understand fully the sources of O'Connor's popularity, the reader should bear in mind that at the period of his agitation there existed in Ireland a widely-spread hostility to the legislative union'.[44] But it was not only the message, it was also the tone of its delivery that set him apart. 'Feargus's daring defiance of all conceivable opponents, and his vehement denunciations of English misrule', remembered one observer, 'contrasted laughably with the quiet, mouse-like demeanour' of the other candidates, including his running mate, Garrett Barry.[45] As he would do in the twilight of his career, O'Connor offered a seductive combination of radicalism and nationalism. 'Irishmen! awake, awake!', ran his first election address, 'hold the ground for a Radical Candidate – a Lover of Liberty, and of the rights of man', a man who stood for 'REPEAL', for 'TOTAL ABOLITION' of Tithes, for the 'removal of the sinful wrongs heaped upon' Ireland.[46] The language was, perhaps, deliberately provocative – especially the reference to Tom Paine's rights of man – but tremendously appealing to a section of the populace.

This is not to underestimate the difficulty that confronted him. Winning the plaudits of the crowd – many of whom could not vote – was a far cry from winning the election. Few observers – certainly not O'Connell – gave O'Connor any chance of victory in what was regarded as the 'most aristocratic County in the Kingdom'. There were both general and particular reasons for this assessment. On the one hand, the representation of County Cork had been, over a long period, the exclusive preserve of a handful of aristocratic families (it had not been contested since 1812) and the Reform Bill was not expected to loosen their stranglehold on the seat. Certainly the political elite did not feel threatened by O'Connor; as one individual recorded in his diary, O'Connor was a 'man of no character, no property, and even no consequence'.[47] Others felt that O'Connor carried particular personal baggage. According to his own account, O'Connor was resented by some large farmers whose profits he had affected by putting his potatoes on the market early in the season (a practice he had begun shortly after arriving at Fort Robert).[48] For another commentator the problem was Roger O'Connor: the 'penumbral shadow of some of his father's irregular exploits created a large amount of prejudice against the son' among middle-class electors.[49] Indeed for some, father and son merged into one. One incident during the campaign so caught the public imagination that it reverberated in the halls of Westminster. O'Connor had reputedly addressed a crowd in familiar terms as 'My lads', adding 'you all know me', to which a well-placed heckler responded: 'Yes, you robbed the mail!'[50]

O'Connor recognised that victory would not be easy but he was convinced that the reformed system was 'as unwrought gold, and required to be worked out into utility'.[51] He set to work. 'I travelled the county by night and day', he recalled, 'frequently attending two, three, or four meetings a day, at a great distance from each other'.[52] He was not always present as the result of an invitation. As he told a meeting at Middleton, he had learned of their gathering four hours earlier from a newspaper 'and he hesitated not a moment to attend, nor did he exaggerate when he assured his friends that he rode during those four hours close upon fifty English miles (cheers)'.[53] Not only did he address meetings and canvass individual electors, but he also devoted considerable energy to establishing an organisational structure to enrol voters (for which he received considerable assistance from the Catholic clergy). Everywhere he went he reported progress and exuded confidence. 'It was said of him', recalled one commentator, 'that if the papal throne were vacant, he would offer himself with the utmost composure as a candidate for the popedom, if the notion caught his fancy.'[54]

The only interruption to the campaign came early in September when

O'Connor was arrested for allegedly breaching the ban on anti-tithe meetings. The summer of 1832 had seen a rapid escalation of what later became known as the Tithe War (by 1833 there were 22 counties in which more than half the tithes had not been paid) and O'Connor had done much to fuel popular unrest in Cork. The government soon had second thoughts and the charges against O'Connor and other anti-tithe agitators were dropped. Apart from adding the aura of political martyrdom to O'Connor's *résumé*, the brief interval also afforded him the opportunity to publish a short pamphlet addressed to the Lord Lieutenant, the Marquis of Anglesey, which essentially repeated the grim assessment of *A State of Ireland* that he published ten years previously.[55] O'Connor soon returned to the campaign trail, not only in Cork but also, such had his reputation grown, in several other contests. 'It would be absolutely ridiculous on my part', O'Connor wrote in his memoir, to describe the 'slavery and drudgery I had to endure, all parties and factions being opposed to me.'[56]

On election day, 22 December, a crowd estimated at up to 6,000 gathered before the County Court House for the nomination. O'Connor was nominated by Daniel O'Mahoney, a Cork freeholder, who admitted that he had never before exercised his vote, and who used his speech to reiterate O'Connor's commitment to repeal, as well as to the election of Magistrates, Triennial Parliaments and the vote by Ballot. O'Connor's seconder, Daniel Geran of Rushmount, described himself as 'one of the People' and gave a rousing speech that the candidate himself would have been proud of. 'We are termed by some individuals insane, because we seek Repeal', he stated, 'and others call us revolutionists and radicals. If to seek the independence of our country by every honourable and peaceful mode be insanity then we plead guilty to the appellation (cheers). If to endeavour the recovery of our rights by legal, and legal measures alone, be revolutionary – then we are Revolutionists – and as to Radicals, we glory in the name.'[57]

When accepting the nomination O'Connor declared himself to be a Reformer in England and a Repealer in Ireland. England was calling for a remodelling of her institutions (he supported the campaign for universal suffrage, annual parliaments and the ballot) 'but unhappy Ireland had unfortunately no institutions to remodel' (in later years he would argue that repeal without reform would be of little use). O'Connor also read sections of his 1822 pamphlet – 'to show the truth of his predictions respecting the Union and the Church' – and he aimed a withering assault at the aristocracy – the 'Conservative phalanx' – that provides an important benchmark for the development of his thinking in relation to social structure and the popular struggle. 'What means the people', he asked? 'It means the community save the Princes and the nobles'. In Cork, he continued, there were no Princes and their nobles were men 'who are decorated with exterior tinsel, armed with assumed powers, and distinguished by inferiority of intellect, and a firm and tenacious adherence to corruption, fraud and injustice'.[58] The impulse at the root of this attack on the aristocracy was not egalitarian; as Daunt recalled, O'Connor 'contemptuously' dismissed 'the peers of the county' as 'new families' – unlike his 'ancient blood' of real nobility. This was an organic view of society – a harmonious combination of democracy and hierarchy – similar to that evoked by Roger O'Connor in the *Chronicles of Eri* wherein a popular monarchy was sustained by community support and tradition. Standing behind O'Connor on the platform was not only Roger O'Connor but also the ancient kings of Ireland. Some electors undoubtedly took this seriously. As Daunt recalled, when O'Connor announced his intention to stand one farmer took the stage and proclaimed 'O, Fargus, Fargus ! is it not the murdher [sic] of the world to see you looking after the representation of a county in their English Parliament, instead of enjoying (as by right you ought) the royal crown of Ireland upon that honest red head'.[59]

Not surprisingly, O'Connor and Barry emphatically won the show of hands and a poll was demanded by the defeated candidates. Voting commenced on Monday and continued on four days over the next week. On the first day O'Connor and Barry established a lead that grew steadily during the week. In some respects polling was conducted in a thoroughly eighteenth-century manner with each new day giving rise to allegations of bribery and intimidation. By the fourth day of campaigning, however, it appeared that the 'anti-Popular' forces had adopted a purely negative strategy that included 'crimping' (kidnapping voters to prevent them from voting). The negative tactics of the Tories were aided (and the situation made more potentially volatile) by the necessity for Catholic voters to swear a qualification oath before they were entitled to vote. O'Connor and his supporters complained bitterly that insufficient magistrates could be found to administer the oath, holding up voting at some booths for hours on end.

By Friday the *Southern Reporter* was lamenting the fact that the Tories were needlessly prolonging the contest in a manner that was 'endangering public peace',[60] but O'Connor also did little to ease the tension despite an increasing assurance of victory. As the week wore on he even orchestrated a measure of ritualised revenge for intimidation and 'crimping' by riding out to greet contingents of voters as they arrived from outlying towns and villages in order to escort them into town past the Tory club-house. As the retinue passed the Tories, O'Connor recalled, he 'gave the word, "DRAW SWORDS" when every man took out his voting paper, held it up in the air, and cheered and cheered again, till the club-house shook'.[61] At the close of voting, O'Connor had topped the poll with 1,837 votes, over 50 ahead of his running mate, and more than 800 in front of his nearest rival. It was a stunning triumph that sent shock waves through the political establishment. 'The landlords', recalled Daunt, 'were unspeakably puzzled to find their influence annihilated.'[62]

How had it happened? There is evidence to suggest that O'Connor's personal style of campaigning, together with his charismatic charm, had won over some who might have normally supported the Tories or at least he succeeded in blunting some of the opposition against him – according to Daunt, some of the 'fox hunting gentry' declared him to be a 'devilish fine fellow'[63] – but O'Connor's core constituency lay elsewhere. The backbone of O'Connor's support was among what one commentator called the 'frieze-coated host' – a reference to the relatively humble attire of a typical tenant farmer – in the southern and western parts of the county. Daunt acknowledged that clerical influence was important in organising these voters, but he argues that by itself it is insufficient as an explanation of why they would so willingly risk 'whatever martyrdom their landlords might think it proper or expedient to inflict'.[64] For Daunt the crucial factor was O'Connor himself: 'He gave life and cohesion to the popular party. He rallied their detached forces, taught them the extent of their power and led them to victory'.[65] O'Connor had succeeded in convincing these electors that he personified their aspirations – that the success of the individual and the nation were inextricably linked. Thus the farmer who attempted to cast his vote 'for Fargus O'Connor and Ould Ireland' was merely articulating the view that would have been shared by many others.[66]

Many commentators felt that O'Connor's victory represented both a milestone in the quest for lost rights and the opening of a new page in Irish political history. 'It is a cheering thing to reflect', Daniel Geran told the crowd at the nomination, 'that what has heretofore been, I may say, the private property of two or three great Landlords – such was their influence in the county, should now be returned to its original appropriation, and become open to the public'. O'Connor, he continued, belonged to the 'modern school of politics'; he was 'of the people', a man of 'democratic principles', 'thoroughly imbued with the enlightened spirit of the times' who will 'carry to a Reformed Parliament the spirit of reform'. O'Connor made a similar point; he was proud, he told the electors, to be the 'first man who had the boldness to rescue from the hands of the Aristocracy your privileges, which they usurped and abused, and in being one of those, who, in despite of all factious opposition, have supported the true democratic principle, that "the people are the source of all legitimate power"'.[67]

Although the end of the electoral power of the landlord had not yet arrived O'Connor's campaign had undoubtedly provided a glimpse of the future. At the very least, in practical terms he displayed talents that were much sought after and demonstrated a model of demotic politics that was worthy of emulation. During the 1832 campaign, O'Connor later claimed, he had assisted several other candidates. By 1834 O'Connor had become an almost ubiquitous presence on the hustings in southern Ireland. Later in the 1840s he gave a detailed account of what he called the 'true history of Irish electioneering' in a series of letters to the *Daily News*. This account included his Herculean efforts on behalf of candidates in Dungarvan, Mallow, Kinsale, Meath, Youghal and the City of Cork, securing victory after victory where none was expected. Nor are we forced to take his word alone for his importance in these contests. Despite their feud that festered throughout the later 1830s and into the 1840s, John O'Connell, son of the Liberator, was fulsome in his praise of O'Connor's skills as a campaigner, and indeed, he was the beneficiary of them at Youghal.[68] Later O'Connor dismissed the younger O'Connell as 'that little nincompoop', but in 1834 he responded to a request for assistance from Daniel O'Connell to come to the aid of his son who was facing a strong challenge from the son of Baron Smith, a prominent Irish judge and Tory politician who had clashed with O'Connell over the issue of tithes.[69] 'Banish your fears O'Connell', O'Connor told him, 'John shall be member for Youghal, if I lose my life by it.'[70]

A constituency based on a small coastal town of the same name, with a population of approximately 9,600 and an electorate of just under 300, Youghal exemplified how little had been achieved by the Reform Act. Describing himself as a 'reformer' O'Connell had won the seat in 1832 without opposition from the seat's patron, the Duke of Devonshire.[71] A place with a reputation for electoral violence – eight men had been shot dead during the 1832 poll – O'Connor arrived to find the streets bristling with military force: in front of the platform 'were stationed the 4th Dragoon Guards, with swords drawn'; behind the hustings were 'two large detachments of infantry', as well as about 700 police. Despite the smallness of the electorate the town was 'literally crammed', O'Connor recalled, 'with the most excited multitude I ever witnessed in my life', a reflection of the fact that the challenge to an O'Connell had much broader significance. Ignoring the advice of the local Roman Catholic clergy, O'Connor mounted the platform and began his speech with bayonets a few feet from his face, taking as his subject flogging in the army. Whether he won over the common soldiers, as he later claimed, or simply bemused them, O'Connor completed the speech without incident and set about organising O'Connell's campaign. According to O'Connell, O'Connor 'tramped about through the ancient and venerable mud of that old fortress town with great industry and éclat'.[72] By his own account O'Connor's activities – 'night and day' – drew on his capacity for physical violence as much as his talent for political rhetoric. In one notorious incident the Tories had despatched a sheriff to evict a man before he could vote; while the officials hammered at the back door, O'Connor and his associates fought their way into the house via the front and conveyed the hapless elector to the polling booth.[73] Every vote was worth fighting for: over the five days of polling the contest was very close. At the last minute, with O'Connell trailing by two votes and his supporters 'in a most doleful mood', O'Connor arrived at the polling booth with five additional voters – whose right to vote he knew to be specious – which ensured that O'Connell was elected by three votes. A parliamentary enquiry subsequently ruled out O'Connor's five electors, together with eight of Smith's, leaving O'Connell the victor by the smallest of margins.[74] Although O'Connor does not even hint at it in his memoir, it is clear that O'Connell's campaign benefited from bribery on a scale that was endemic in Irish (and English) elections. 'Those boroughs are vile places', John's elder brother, Morgan O'Connell, wrote to W.J. Firtzpatrick in April 1835, 'That dirty little town of Youghal was more expensive to me than the County of Meath.'[75]

Despite the heroics at Youghal, O'Connor's most celebrated victory at 'electioneering warfare' – apart from his own triumph in 1832 – was at a by-election in Dungarvan in May 1834. A small port town at the mouth of the Colligan River in County Waterford, Dungarvan was considered to be a pocket borough of the Duke of Devonshire who held a decisive sway over the small electorate of just under 700. Here O'Connor 'effected' the return of the repeal candidate, Ebenezer Jacob, against a 'powerful combination' and despite the wishes of the absentee Whig Duke. According to John O'Connell, O'Connor was, at one and the same time, 'political godfather…speechifier, canvasser, lawyer, gutter agent, [and] mob leader…'[76] According to his own account, O'Connor recognized the difficulty that 'his party' faced in a situation where many voters were 'deprived of the free exercise of the franchise'. He set about the task with characteristic ebullience: 'I remained to a late hour of each night, jigging, dancing, telling stories, and laughing in the different public houses where the voters assembled'. Once polling commenced O'Connor stopped every carriage he could to canvass the electors and, when he found the iron gates at the booth 'guarded by police with fixed bayonets', he resorted to more direct action. 'Many and many a voter did I carry on my back through the streets under the broiling sun', he recalled, 'and many a stand-up fight I had in the streets with respectable parties who endeavoured to smuggle my goods, but I never lost my man.'[77]

O'Connor's most brazen act in the political drama at Dungarvan, however, was an audacious fraud that proved decisive on the final day. According to O'Connell, O'Connor penned a letter that purported to be from the Duke's agent that stated that 'his Grace's tenants have his entire assent to the fullest and freest exercise of their privilege', and, importantly, 'that none would be punished' for voting for the repeal candidate. O'Connor arranged for the forged document to be handed to him during a speech in the town market-place, and by his own account, 'was obliged to read it three times' such was its 'electrical' effect on the crowd. Before its unauthenticity was discovered the fake letter had the desired effect on about 40 voters, sufficient to ensure a narrow victory. In a final act of defiance O'Connor had signed it 'Ebenezer Humbug'. O'Connor freely admitted to the deception to the readers of the *Daily News*, indeed he revelled in it; it was a 'capital dodge' that resulted in a 'glorious triumph for Ireland'.[78] It is perhaps ironic that one who would become well known as an advocate of radical reforms designed to eliminate the abuses that had survived the Reform Act of 1832, had proved so adept at manipulating the corrupt political system for his own ends. In many ways, O'Connor's political skills were more suited to the repertoire of eighteenth rather than nineteenth-century politics.

For all his willingness to exploit the shortcomings of a corrupt political system, as the newly-elected MP for Cork O'Connor was quick to assure his followers that he would not resile from the principles on which he had stood. 'If I am worthy of your choice', he stated, 'depend on my advocacy of the rights of the People in the House of the People. I cannot – I will not – forsake you.' O'Connor also made it clear that he was impatient to begin work: 'The excitement for the sake of my country is so truly pleasurable', he admitted, 'I will hardly know how to pass my time in the month that must intervene before I go to the English Parliament with full freightage of Irish grievances'.[79] Once he got to London, he continued, he would devote every available minute to his parliamentary duties – he would 'sit with the Speaker and rise with the House'.[80] It is not surprising that O'Connor's enthusiasm for the task that lay ahead should be matched by a fierce determination to live up to the pledges he had made on the hustings. Before long he would gain a reputation for an unwillingness to compromise, and even for sheer pig-headedness, and he would be criticised for a lack of tactical imagination, but given the circumstances of the campaign it is hard to imagine how he could have done otherwise. As he travelled across St George's Channel to take up his seat in the House of Commons O'Connor could not have suspected that he had reached the peak of his Irish political career and that his international notoriety in the 1840s would stem for his activities on the British political stage.

Notes

1   'The Life and Adventures of Feargus O'Connor', *National Instructor*, 29 June 1850, pp. 88, 90. See also M. Beames, *Peasants and Power: The Whiteboy Movements and Their Control in Pre-Famine Ireland*, New York, 1983, pp. 42-53.
2   Cited in Beames, *Peasants and Power*, p. 52.
3   'The Life and Adventures of Feargus O'Connor', *National Instructor*, 29 June 1850, p. 88. See also *Hansard* [House of Commons], 22 July 1834, col. 353; 19 March

1835, col. 1218.

4   'The Life and Adventures of Feargus O'Connor', *National Instructor*, 29 June 1850, p. 89.

5   'The Life and Adventures of Feargus O'Connor', *National Instructor*, 29 June 1850, p. 88-9.

6   A. Murphy, 'Agrarian disturbance in West Cork 1822', *Ballingeary and Inchigeela Historical Society Journal*, 2000.

7   'The Life and Adventures of Feargus O'Connor', *National Instructor*, 29 June 1850, p. 90; *Operative*, 5 May 1839. In the letter to his brother, Frank, in September 1843, he is clear that he was not involved. Although it was not until the following year that it emerged that the Home Office had been opening the correspondence of reformers, O'Connor may have been writing with one eye on the censor. For the post-office scandal see F.B. Smith, 'British Post Office Espionage, 1844', *Historical Studies*, April 1970, pp. 190-202. I am grateful to Malcolm Chase for access to the 1843 letter.

8   I am grateful to Iorwerth Prothero for this reference. See also D. Vincent (ed.), *Testaments of Radicalism: Memoirs of Working Class Politicians 1790-1885*, London, 1977, p. 29.

9   'The Life and Adventures of Feargus O'Connor', *National Instructor*, 6 July 1850, pp. 104-5.

10   'The Life and Adventures of Feargus O'Connor', *National Instructor*, 6 July 1850, p. 105. See also T. Frost, *Forty Years' Recollections: Literary and Political*, London, 1880, pp. 175-6. The names O'Connor chose for other characters also had a familiar ring to them. Not only was Cardenio of Andalusia a character in Cervantes, *Don Quixote* (1605), Constantia, sister of Petruccio, was from Beaumont and Fletcher's, *The Chances* (1620). Constantia, a protégée of Lady McSycophant, was also in Macklin's, *The Man of the World* (1764). See E.C. Brewer, *Character Sketches of Romance, Fiction and the Drama*, New York, 1892, vol. 1.

11   'The Life and Adventures of Feargus O'Connor', *National Instructor*, 6 July 1850, p. 105.

12   O. MacDonagh, *The Hereditary Bondsman*, London, 1998, p. 177.

13   In parliament he also stated that he was going to publish two volumes of letters relating to the Orange Order. See *Hansard* [House of Commons], 6 March 1835, col. 615.

14   Frost, *Forty Years' Recollections*, p. 176. Frost cites as evidence O'Connor's serialized novel later published in his *Labourer*, 'which soon lost the thread of his plot'.

15   See D. Read and E. Glasgow, *Feargus O'Connor: Irishman and Chartist*, London, 1961, p. 22.

16   W. Phillips, *The Wild Tribes of London*, 1855, in L. Jackson, *The Victorian Dictionary*, http://www.victorianlondon.org/

17   C. Dickens Jnr, *Dickens's Dictionary of London*, 1879, in L. Jackson, *The Victorian Dictionary*, http://www.victorianlondon.org/

18   C. Dickens, *All the Year Round*, 18 August 1860, p. 453.

19   P. Cunningham, *Hand-book of London: Past and Present* (1850), Wakefield, 1978, p. 210.

20   Cunningham, *Hand-book of London*, pp. 246-8.

21 'The Life and Adventures of Feargus O'Connor', *National Instructor*, 13 July 1850, pp. 121-2.

22 'The Life and Adventures of Feargus O'Connor', *National Instructor*, 3 August 1850, p. 169.

23 W. O'Neill Daunt, *Eighty-five Years of Irish History*, London, 1888, p. 134.

24 Daunt, *Eighty-five Years*, p. 135; W. O'Neill Daunt, *A Life Spent for Ireland*, London, 1896, p. 12.

25 Daunt, *Eighty-five Years*, p. 135.

26 Daunt, *Eighty-five Years*, pp. 139, 142.

27 I. and P. Kuczynski (eds), *A Young Revolutionary in Nineteenth-Century England: Selected Writings of Georg Weerth*, Berlin, 1971, p. 111.

28 Sir B. Burke, *Vicissitudes of Families*, Second Series, London, 1861, p. 40-1; W. J. O'Neill Daunt, *Ireland and Her Agitators*, Dublin, 1845, p. 133. O'Neill Daunt contributed the article for Burke.

29 *Southern Reporter*, 19 January 1833.

30 *Southern Reporter*, 19 January 1833.

31 J. McCarthy, *Reminiscences*, London, 1899, vol. 2, p. 259.

32 Burke, *Vicissitudes of Families*, p. 40.

33 *Southern Reporter*, 3 July 1832.

34 *Southern Reporter*, 3 July 1832.

35 Burke, *Vicissitudes of Families*, p. 42-3; Daunt, *Ireland and Her Agitators*, pp. 137, 140-1; *Southern Reporter*, 19 January 1833.

36 Daunt, *Eighty-five Years*, pp. 142-3; McCarthy, *Reminiscences*, vol. 2, p. 259; Burke, *Vicissitudes of Families*, p. 42-3; *Selected Writings of Georg Weerth*, p. 108. See also D. Thompson, *The Chartists*, London, 1984, pp. 97-8.

37 *Selected Writings of Georg Weerth*, p. 108. See also T. Mooney, *A History of Ireland, From Its Settlement to the Present Time*, Boston, 1846, p. 1395. In September 1843 he told his brother Frank that he was 6' 1" and weighed 14 stone. I am grateful to Malcolm Chase for this reference.

38 A. Rushton, *My Life as Farmer's Boy, Factory Lad, Teacher and Preacher*, Manchester, 1909, p. 64.

39 See J. Epstein, *The Lion of Freedom*, London, 1982, p. 10.

40 *Southern Reporter*, 18 August 1832; Burke, *Vicissitudes of Families*, p. 45.

41 *Southern Reporter*, 18 August 1832. See S. Lover, *The Lyrics of Ireland*, London, 1858, p. 58.

42 According to O'Neill Daunt he announced it days earlier at a similar dinner in Macroom; the representation was discussed at this meeting, but O'Connor confirmed his candidacy at Enniskeane. See *Eighty-five Years*, p. 134.

43 Burke, *Vicissitudes of Families*, p. 46-7.

44 Burke, *Vicissitudes of Families*, p. 48.

45 Burke, *Vicissitudes of Families*, p. 47-8.

46 *Southern Reporter*, 4 September 1832.

47 Cited in I. d'Alton, *Protestant Society and Politics in Cork, 1812-1844*, Cork, 1980, p. 216.

48 'The Life and Adventures of Feargus O'Connor', *National Instructor*, 24 August 1850, pp. 217-8.

49   Burke, *Vicissitudes of Families*, p. 42.

50   Denis Le Marchant's diary, March 1833, in A. Aspinall (ed.), *Three Early Nineteenth Century Diaries*, London, 1952, p. 314.

51   *Southern Reporter*, 18 August 1832.

52   'The Life and Adventures of Feargus O'Connor', *National Instructor*, 17 August 1850, p. 201.

53   *Southern Reporter*, 15 November 1832.

54   Burke, *Vicissitudes of Families*, p. 42.

55   Read and Glasgow, *Feargus O'Connor*, p. 28. They say it also contained O'Connor's claim that he had protected the Lord Lieutenant during a Dublin riot.

56   'The Life and Adventures of Feargus O'Connor', *National Instructor*, 24 August 1850, pp. 217-18.

57   *Southern Reporter*, 24 December 1832.

58   *Southern Reporter*, 24 December 1832.

59   Daunt, *Eighty-five years*, p. 137.

60   *Southern Reporter*, 20 December 1832. According to Thomas Mooney, 'Blood from both parties had besmirched the earth'. See Mooney, *A History of Ireland*, p. 1396.

61   'The Life and Adventures of Feargus O'Connor', *National Instructor*, 31 August 1850, p. 231.

62   Burke, *Vicissitudes of Families*, p. 51.

63   Burke, *Vicissitudes of Families*, p. 46.

64   Burke, *Vicissitudes of Families*, p. 50. The *Southern Reporter* noted the role of the Cork Trades Association. See *Southern Reporter*, 24 December 1832.

65   Burke, *Vicissitudes of Families*, p. 51.

66   Burke, *Vicissitudes of Families*, p. 50.

67   *Southern Reporter*, 24 December 1832.

68   'The Life and Adventures of Feargus O'Connor', *National Instructor*, 26 October 1850, p. 362f.

69   See *Dictionary of National Biography*, vol. XVIII, pp. 563-4.

70   'The Life and Adventures of Feargus O'Connor', *National Instructor*, 2 November 1850, p. 375.

71   C. Dod, *Electoral facts from 1832 to 1853, impartially stated: constituting a complete political gazetteer* (1853), London, 1972, pp. 360-1.

72   J. O'Connell, *Recollections and Experiences During a Parliamentary Career from 1832 to 1848*, London, 1849, vol. 1, p. 142.

73   'The Life and Adventures of Feargus O'Connor', *National Instructor*, 2 November 1850, p. 377.

74   'The Life and Adventures of Feargus O'Connor', *National Instructor*, 2 November 1850, p. 377. According to Dod the margin was seven votes in favour of O'Connell.

75   Cited in A. Macintyre, *The Liberator: Daniel O'Connell and the Irish party, 1830-1847*, London, 1965, p. 106. According to T.P O'Connor (no relation) the very 'whisper' of an election sent a 'thrill' through the community because of the prospect of a bribe.

76   O'Connell, *Recollections and Experiences*, pp. 98, 104; 'The Life and Adventures of Feargus O'Connor', *National Instructor*, 2 November 1850, p. 378f.

77   'The Life and Adventures of Feargus O'Connor', *National Instructor*, 9 November 1850, p. 391.

78   O'Connell, *Recollections and Experiences*; pp. 98-102; 'The Life and Adventures of Feargus O'Connor', *National Instructor*, 9 November 1850, pp. 391-3.

79   *Southern Reporter*, 5 January 1833.

80   Cited in Burke, *Vicissitudes of Families*, p. 51.

4: ENGLAND

O'Connor took his seat in the House of Commons early in 1833. He did not record his first impression of the imperial parliament but we know from other testimony that the chamber often failed to live up to the expectations of those visiting Westminster for the first time. Referring to the ancient chamber that would be destroyed by fire in October 1834, James Grant recalled, 'I shall not soon forget the disappointment which I experienced on the first sight of the interior'. Although he had been warned that it 'ill accorded with the dignity of what has been termed the first assembly of gentlemen in the world', Grant was, he admitted, 'not at all prepared for such a place as I then beheld. It was dark, gloomy, and badly ventilated, and so small that not more than four hundred out of the six hundred and fifty-eight members could be accommodated in it with any measure of comfort'. It was, he concluded, 'a second edition of the Black Hole of Calcutta'.[1] From other recollections we know that the atmosphere in the House was no more hospitable than the conditions. 'Nothing more forcibly strikes an Irishman, upon his entrance into and first acquaintance with the House of Commons', recalled John O'Connell, 'than the discourteousness among themselves of his brother-members, or at any rate most evidently, of those belonging to England ... A set of village school boys could not be more unceremonious with each other.'[2]

There was no more testing political stage for a young man who had not yet reached forty years of age. The first mention of O'Connor in Hansard's record of parliamentary debates did not augur well – listing him incorrectly as Francis O'Connor – and despite his enormous reservoir of self-confidence he knew that he had a lot to learn. 'I was a constant attendant upon my parliamentary duties', he later recalled, 'and a minute observer of the mode of action pursued by the respective political leaders in the House.'[3] Quickly he made his mark. According to James Grant's account of the post-Reform parliament written in 1837, O'Connor was a 'fluent and graceful speaker' who had quickly earned recognition as a 'man of more than respectable talents'.[4] Previous historians have paid scant attention to O'Connor's numerous contributions to debate during his first period in Westminster, but it is an archive worthy of detailed consideration.

O'Connor is recorded as giving his first speech on 8 February 1833. It contained all the themes that would characterise his first period in the House. First, he pleaded the cause of the Irish poor. 'They were told', he fumed, 'that the clergy were under necessity of selling their carriages and horses', but they were never told 'of the manner in which the last blanket was stripped from the widow and the orphan.' Second, O'Connor warned against coercion: the government had 'already driven the people of Ireland to madness, and now they were feeling the reaction resulting from their own conduct'. Rather 'than coerce the people of Ireland', he pleaded, 'redress their grievances'. Related to this theme, O'Connor expressed the growing disillusionment with the Whig government that had come to office on a tide of popular expectation. 'They had waited for two years for redress of grievances from the present Ministry; and he would ask if they had to wait for ever', he noted with a rhetorical flourish. Rising to his task, O'Connor introduced a third theme by levelling the charge of hypocrisy at the Reform Ministry and British reformers in general. 'There was sympathy for the Pole when he rose against his great northern oppressor. He was a hero, as was also the Belgian', O'Connor reminded the House, 'but the Irishman who rose against oppression was stigmatised as a traitor.'[5]

Almost as an afterthought to his accusation, O'Connor introduced the possibility of Repeal: 'If it was not to be a Union, the sooner it was severed the better', he concluded. This point allowed him to introduce his own experience into the debate. Responding to the Secretary of State for Ireland's declaration that he would rather be bayoneted or shot than agree to Repeal, O'Connor stated that 'rather than see his country oppressed', he 'would expose himself to pistols, guns, bayonets, or blunderbusses'. The coda to the speech showed that O'Connor had quickly recognised that there was an English audience for his remarks. What was done to Ireland today, he warned, might be done to the people of England tomorrow.

Betrayal, hypocrisy, self-sacrifice and unity were themes that O'Connor revisited and developed over the next twenty-seven months. Although he never left any doubt that he had witnessed appalling hardship in Cork and that 'since boyhood' he had been anxious to 'support a measure for the relief of the poor',[6] O'Connor's speeches were not filled with heart rending descriptions of Irish poverty. Ireland's malaise he attributed to misgovernment, or more properly to prejudicial government. Take the economy for example. The nation's prosperity, he argued, had been squandered because those in charge of economic policy were interested only in the British economy: Ireland had become a 'beggar at Britain's gates' because her governors had failed in their responsibility. The case was even stronger in relation to the compulsory payment of tithes to support the protestant church in Ireland. No policy, O'Connor felt, was more certain to 'revolutionise' Ireland than the tithes. In Cork, he told the House in February 1834, there were two parishes 'in which there was not one Protestant' that faced an annual tithe bill of £1,000. The cost to the government of collecting a nine penny arrears was £2 or £3. 'There was something so ridiculous in this plan', he quipped, 'that, vexatious as it was, he could keep his temper and laugh at it.'[7] It was, moreover, a situation that would not be contemplated for England. 'Suppose his Majesty's Ministers were to send a body of Catholic priests into Lancashire', he asked, 'and to state to the people that a Papal bull had been issued directing that they, the people, should support them by tithes, what would result? The attempt would, of course, be indignantly resisted.'[8]

The collection of tithes often resulted in violence and bloodshed; in fact, for O'Connor the different treatment afforded to Ireland was most glaring in relation to the administration of law and order. As a local member he often raised local cases of alleged abuse by the military, calling for investigations and Courts Martial, and, at a more general level, he consistently opposed the measures adopted by the Whig government to restore law and order in Ireland.[9] In March 1833 for example, a month after his first speech, O'Connor told the House that the Suppression of Disturbances (Ireland) Bill was a 'mockery of justice' and he would oppose it 'in every stage of its progress'. Referring to the many anti-tithe rallies which the government cited as a justification for the action he added with a note of bitter irony: 'Why not suppress such meetings when they occurred here, and threatened the State with ruin?'[10] This concern reached a peak in December 1834 when troops fired on a crowd in the parish of Gurtroe in Cork. The troops had been assisting in the collection of tithes from Widow Ryan in the village of Rathcormac; the crowd had gathered to assist her and in the resulting melee more than 70 shots were fired, a dozen were killed and over 40 were wounded.

O'Connor was in Cork following the dissolution of parliament and he had been actively fomenting a campaign of civil disobedience in the form of a tithe strike for more than a month. Early in November he proclaimed in a public letter that the 'HOUR IS COME !!!…I SHALL PAY NO TITHES!!!' Promising to 'travel through every part of this great County' to support the campaign O'Connor made it clear that he expected the people to join his strike: 'Let us be united, and persevere in evincing our disgust to tithes by all legal and constitutional means in our power'.[11] Whether Widow Ryan was inspired by O'Connor's example is unclear but once news of the attack reached Cork he rushed to the scene, acting as 'counsel' to wounded victims and their families. It was a situation tailor-made for his charismatic style of leadership. According to his own account, his speech at the funeral for some of the victims reduced even the soldiers to tears. Once parliament reconvened O'Connor was determined to prosecute the case on the floor of the House. Contravening precedent and scandalising legal authorities on both sides of the House, he sought to canvass the issues in debate and he called on the government to institute Courts Martial for the troops involved.[12]

For O'Connor bloody coercion was symptomatic of the complete failure of reform in Ireland. During the campaign to reform the House of Commons, he insisted, the 'voice' of Irish protest had been 'music' to ears of the Whigs. The people of Ireland, he claimed, had tipped the balance in favour of Reform and their expectations had been raised to fever pitch. But, 'just as the cup of hope and of affection had been raised' to Ireland's 'lips', it had been 'dashed from her hands' and 'she was told, that the misgovernment of unreformed ages was to be established and confirmed by the first Reformed Parliament'.[13] Many Irish members, he told the Commons in April 1834, had been prepared to support the Whig government, 'believing that it was likely that the benefits of a Reformed Parliament would supersede the necessity of domestic legislation. But all their hopes on that head have been blasted…'.[14] 'The Government had come in upon a cry of Reform', he concluded, 'and had not redeemed a single pledge they had previously made.'[15] Worse still, he stated on another occasion, as 'soon as the agitation for the Reform Bill had passed over, the Ministers had the audacity to come before a Reformed Parliament and ask them to stifle liberty in its infancy'.[16] Characteristically, O'Connor personalised Ireland's plight by linking it to his own sense of betrayal. He had been 'fool enough to assist the Government through thick and thin with their Reform Bill', he stated.[17]

The failure of Reform led inexorably to Repeal. He had never invested much hope in a united parliament but what little there was quickly dissipated. Referring to the government's first coercion act in March 1833 O'Connor insisted that the 'more brutal, bloody, and despotic it was, coming as it did from the first Reformed Parliament, the better, as it would show the people of Ireland what they had to expect from them'.[18] By July 1833 O'Connor was arguing in the House that the Union 'had done all for England and nothing, worse than nothing, for Ireland', and that Repeal was the 'only thing that could set matters right'. With a brashness that had already brought him to the attention of his parliamentary colleagues he concluded his speech with a challenge to the government to 'meet him foot on foot' on the merits of the Union.[19] By April 1834 O'Connor was revelling in the mantle of 'traitor' and leaving no room for compromise: 'This House may pass enactments – may fill volumes with enactments – but, so long as I have life, I will agitate the Repeal of the Union'.[20]

Given his subsequent career it is important to note that he did not seek Repeal in order to merely return to an Irish parliament as it had existed prior to the Union. In a speech in April 1834 O'Connor made it clear that although the Irish

Parliament had rendered in a few short years more service 'than had been for centuries before', it was 'corrupt and treacherous' and he did not seek to simply re-establish it. There were several reasons for this he suggested, but the most important was that the Parliament of 1782 'could not be considered as the fair representation of the people, who were altogether excluded from any participation in its concerns'.[21] The reforms that he would later advocate so passionately for the British parliament he also considered axiomatic for a restored Irish parliament. This put him at odds with many in the Repeal movement.

As irritating as O'Connor's calls for Repeal undoubtedly were to government members, they were more galling to many Irish politicians, in particular Daniel O'Connell. O'Connell's strategy, culminating in the Lichfield House compact that was agreed with Lord John Russell in February 1835, was to trade Irish votes on the floor of the House for government concessions. This was more than political horse trading for its own sake; the Liberator clung to the belief – or hope – in the early 1830s that justice for Ireland could be achieved from an English parliament. Ireland might even become West Britain if it were allowed to share in the benefits of good government and justice from Westminster.[22] O'Connor's intransigence on the question of Repeal directly threatened both the strategy and the potential outcome. In his 1822 pamphlet on the state of Ireland O'Connor had not directly called for Repeal, demanding instead 'at least an EQUAL participation of justice',[23] but by the early 1830s he was unequivocally committed to Repeal, a fact he made abundantly clear during the election. Many other Irish reformers, including O'Connell himself, had committed themselves to Repeal of the Union on the hustings, but were more open to compromise by the time they got to London. In this sense O'Connell and O'Connor were on a collision course from the outset. 'I had not long taken my seat', O'Connor later recalled, 'when I discovered that O'Connell was a political trickster and juggler.'[24]

Within weeks of his arrival in Westminster O'Connor began to press O'Connell to introduce a motion for Repeal. O'Connell was particularly reluctant to test Repeal in the House early in the session as this would demonstrate how little support it enjoyed and weaken his bargaining position, and he made the valid point that the introduction of the coercion act would even stifle demonstrations of public support in Ireland. By the middle of 1833, however, O'Connor had decided to bring the matter to a head by announcing his intention to introduce a Repeal motion himself. According to numerous reports, O'Connell repeatedly spoke to O'Connor but his legendary charm and powers of persuasion did not deter O'Connor, who was determined to put his case, in the first instance, before a meeting of Irish MPs. O'Connell also welcomed the caucus as an opportunity to silence his young associate. 'We – the Irish Members – meet on

Monday', he wrote to a supporter in Dublin, 'to overrule Fergus [sic] O'Connor in his folly of bringing on the question of repeal at a time when it is impossible to do it any service.'[25] At the meeting held early in June in the King's Arms Hotel in Palace Yard O'Connell offered a compromise: if O'Connor would desist in his plan for the present session O'Connell would guarantee to introduce a motion for Repeal within the first three weeks of the next. O'Connor was not convinced and a division followed which produced a narrow victory – of twelve votes to ten – for O'Connell. *The Times* delighted in pointing out to its readers that eight of Dan's own family had helped to rescue him from an ignominious defeat, but actually nothing had been settled. O'Connor refused to accept the decision of the first caucus, and only a second meeting and a more emphatic margin convinced him to stay his hand.[26] He did not, however, remain silent. On 10 July he presented three petitions in favour of Repeal with a blunt warning: 'In short, nothing but domestic legislation would ensure to the Irish domestic happiness'.[27] Early in the new session O'Connor renewed the warning: 'It was quite in vain to make any endeavour to smother the demand for Repeal', he told the House, 'the whole nation was in a flame; and no power could put it out'.[28]

In April 1834 O'Connell eventually kept his commitment and introduced a motion for a select committee to inquire into the effects of the Union. He did so reluctantly. According to Daunt, the Liberator told him he 'felt like a man who was going to jump into a cold bath, but I was obliged to take the plunge'.[29] O'Connor followed two days later with a long speech. The 'question which we are now to decide upon', he proclaimed, 'is, whether Ireland shall henceforth be an independent kingdom, the right arm of Britain, or whether she shall be a coerced and impoverished province, a disgrace to herself, a shame to her representatives, a drag-chain on British industry, and a beggar at Britain's gates'.[30] The speech contained a detailed exposition of Irish history but at its heart was an appeal to democracy: 'Will the people allow you to continue to legislate for Ireland? I say no. You may despise the power of the people, but recollect that public opinion has repealed many of your statutes and laws, and that there are others which you dare not carry into effect.' 'Will you', he asked rhetorically, 'despise the united voices of 8,000,000 of people?'[31] O'Connell's speech was regarded as flat, O'Connor's speech was attacked as 'discursive and declamatory' and even his friend Daunt lamented that it lacked logic and 'did not touch the marrow of the subject'.[32] The motion was resoundingly defeated by a margin of 523 to 38.

Why had O'Connor provoked this crisis in the ranks of his parliamentary colleagues? First, it is important to remember that he had the support of a sizable minority of the Irish MPs and the backing of sections of the Irish nationalist

press in Dublin as well as in his Cork stronghold. His action was neither a whim
nor a unilateral adventure. Secondly, and most importantly, O'Connor believed
that he had no option but to keep faith with his constituents and fulfil the pledges
that he had made during the campaign. Had he not assured the people of Cork
that he would not forsake them? 'One of the greatest checks upon the conduct
of Members', he reminded the House in February 1834, 'was to be obliged to
return to their constituents…'[33] Although, as noted previously, O'Connor's political skills were often better suited to the political practices of the eighteenth
century rather than the nineteenth, on the issue of representation he adopted
a modern stance. The traditional notion of representation that was still upheld
by many in the political class in the first half of the nineteenth century had
been outlined famously by a leading Whig Parliamentarian, Edmund Burke,
in 1774. '[Y]our representative owes you, not his industry only, but his judgement', Burke told his constituents in Bristol, 'and he betrays instead of serving
you, if he sacrifices it to your opinion.'[34] For O'Connor there was little scope for
judgement; a representative's actions must be in accordance with the views of
his constituents; he was a delegate; an instrument of the majority. He was, he
told the House, 'an avowedly pledged advocate'.[35] The Chartists that O'Connor
would later lead shared this broad commitment to direct democracy.

Moreover, it is important to note that O'Connor invariably ignored the strict
limits within which his constituency was defined. When one member attacked
his right to speak on behalf of the Cork gentry O'Connor agreed: he did not represent the Cork gentry; on the contrary, he represented the 'poorer freeholders'
of Cork, the people, most of whom did not have a vote.[36] This attitude is worth
lingering over both for what it tells us about O'Connor and what it reveals
about the development of democracy in the early nineteenth century. On the
one hand, O'Connor was sustained and replenished by contact with the people.
'He had lately attended nearly twenty public meetings', he told the House early
in 1834, 'at some of which there were more than 40,000 persons present, and all
unanimous in asking for a Repeal of the Union.'[37] His activities in Cork in the
winter of 1834 provide a template for his later strategy as a Chartist leader. As
the author of his political portrait enthused, O'Connor's 'powers of locomotive
agitation are wonderful – his energies are sleepless; wherever popular passion
was to be fed, or popular grievances to consoled, there he was'.[38] His acute sense
of political dramaturgy rarely failed him. At Bantry in January 1834 O'Connor
was mobbed by the 'assembled thousands' at what was described with understandable exaggeration as the largest parochial meeting ever held in southern
Ireland. It was O'Connor's fourth 'appearance' in eight days upon what he, significantly, called 'the theatre of Repeal and no Tithes'. Therefore, he warned the
crowd, 'you may naturally anticipate a repetition of the week's performance'.

After Bantry it was on to Skibbereen where the local journalist enthused: 'If ever a popular Representative had reason to be satisfied with his reception by his constituents, Mr O'Connor had'.[39] No matter how isolated he became in the House, or later among the radical leadership, O'Connor could always draw sustenance and comfort from his symbiotic relationship with his followers at large. This was a form of democracy that was intuitive and emotional rather than cerebral or theoretical. It would later come to be a key element of his Chartist leadership. Second, it is important to recognise that O'Connor's willingness to submit to public opinion – broadly defined – in order to give practical effect to democracy in an undemocratic age was breaking new ground in the way political activity was understood. Historians and political scientists usually identify 1867 for the transition from the politics of interest to the politics of electoral pressure.[40] O'Connor's relationship with his supporters allows us to glimpse the future.

Paradoxically, equally important for O'Connor was his 'independence'. He was a friend of the people but beholden to no one; an intuitive democrat who was an individual beyond the influence of any man. O'Connor entered public life at a time when his gentlemanly status – let alone his 'royal' pretensions – gave him the right to speak. In a system that was built on patronage and rife with bribery, financial independence was highly valued as a political characteristic even among radicals. Despite the fact that he would go on to lead a movement committed to the payment of MPs, O'Connor always insisted that he never took a penny for his services. This contradiction resurfaced repeatedly throughout O'Connor's public life. It was never resolved, not even in death; as we shall see, it is inscribed in stone at his grave.[41] During his first stint in the House of Commons O'Connor was particularly keen to show his independence from one man in particular: Daniel O'Connell. 'He certainly entertained a very high respect and esteem for his honourable and learned friend', O'Connor told the House in February 1835, 'but to be a slave to him, or any other man he would never submit. Slave, indeed!' [42]

Many commentators interpreted O'Connor's stance on Repeal as a direct challenge to O'Connell's leadership. Daunt, for example, was convinced that his friend had 'conceived the idea of supplanting O'Connell in the leadership of the Irish people'.[43] In his memoirs, Daunt recalls that as early as 1833 or 1834 O'Connor showed him a draft of a pamphlet that attacked the Liberator. 'I told him that he could only injure himself by printing it', Daunt wrote, but his entreaty merely delayed the publication until 1836-7 when it appeared as a series of public letters.[44] O'Connor was not afraid of O'Connell but in important respects he was given little alternative other than to speak out. In November 1833 the two men had shared a platform in Cork at a dinner in O'Connell's honour. O'Connell had encouraged the meeting, which he used to challenge the government to undermine the nascent Repeal campaign with concessions. The audience was bemused; O'Connor, who had repeatedly interjected during the guest of honour's speech, used his own remarks to compare O'Connell to Dr Frankenstein who 'seemed to tremble at the very recollection of the monster you had created'. 'Ah, Liberator (said Mr O'Connor, turning to Mr O'Connell), did you hear the echo of the mere lisping of your offspring? We can now judge what the tone of the full grown giant would resemble (cheers)'.[45] In April 1834 O'Connor pointedly told the House of Commons that if 'there is not another man to be found to agitate the question of the Repeal of the Union, I will do so'.[46] Despite his annoyance at Feargus's unilateral declarations O'Connell was slow to recognise any challenge. In February 1834 he told one of his lieutenants in Dublin that there never 'was a more foolish falsehood than the statement that Fergus [sic.] O'Connor meant to attack me'. 'He is daily attacking all my enemies', the Liberator continued, 'and there is not one of the Irish members more heartily cordial with me than he is.'[47] By early 1835 O'Connor was able to enumerate various grounds on which he disagreed with O'Connell but even at this late stage he referred to O'Connell as his 'friend'. It could be argued that this language was merely the mellifluous politeness that characterised some parliamentary exchanges, but there is other evidence that the two men enjoyed friendly relations – dining together, sharing carriages, sitting together in the House – long after they had begun to fall out publicly.[48] It was only after the Lichfield House agreement that committed O'Connell and his 'tail' to support the Whigs had been concluded in February 1835 that O'Connor became his intractable opponent.[49] Within a couple of months O'Connor had left parliament and the bitterness and rancour that characterised his later exchanges with O'Connell was conducted through the prism of the press.

Although he was irrevocably committed to Repeal of the Union O'Connor was acutely aware of the failure of reform more generally and he increasingly levelled the charge of betrayal at the Whigs for their policies on either side of St George's Channel. 'The Government had come in upon the cry of Reform', he stated bluntly, 'and had not redeemed a single pledge they had previously made.'[50] The record of the Whigs was appalling: from flogging in the army and unnecessary government expenditure to restrictions on the freedom of the press and the persecution of trade unionists. Early in his parliamentary term O'Connor became concerned about the treatment meted out to the press. 'There have been more prosecutions under this Government to endeavour to put down the liberty of the press', he noted in February 1834, 'than under any Administration.' Soon, he concluded, there would need to be a new prison built for newspaper editors.[51] No one bothered to challenge his assertion. It is instructive to examine how O'Connor's interest in this issue developed as it is very much a microcosm of his political trajectory during the 1830s. Understandably, many of his contributions to debate, particularly earlier in his parliamentary career, were concerned with Irish issues. Even general discussions were almost invariably a vehicle for an Irish refrain, much to the chagrin of some members. When, for example, during a debate on taxation in February 1833, a disgruntled member complained of parochial references to Ireland being introduced, O'Connor shot back that he 'deprecated the idea that no allusion to Ireland should be mixed up with debate on other matters'.[52] Similarly a debate on the state of public health in towns was an opportunity to speak about conditions in Dublin.[53] Even a debate on the oppression of the Poles and the Greeks was not allowed to pass. 'For himself', he stated, 'he should be ever ready to advocate the cause of the distressed, to whatever county they might belong', but at the same time his parliamentary colleagues needed to look to 'their sister-country' 'closer to home'.[54] Everything, in this sense, was an Irish question.

O'Connor became interested in the treatment of the press from a similar starting point: he first rose in February 1834 to protest at the prosecution of the nationalist Dublin newspaper, the *Pilot*.[55] In July, however, he spoke passionately in defence of Patrick Grant and John Bell, editors of the radical London journal, the *True Sun*. These men, he argued, were victims of Whig hypocrisy. 'There was scarcely a man in the country ignorant of the fact', he argued, 'that the party of the present Ministers were, when out of power, most strenuous advocates for the liberty of the Press; the country now had a specimen of the manner in which their professions were acted upon.'[56] O'Connor's charge was familiar – hypocrisy – but on this occasion Ireland was not mentioned. It is notable, and perhaps ironic, that O'Connor's increasing isolation as an advocate of Repeal that would separate Ireland and England occurred at the same time as he became increasingly vocal about British issues.

This trend was exemplified by O'Connor's involvement in the case of those who became known as the Tolpuddle Martyrs. Early in 1834 the government decided to try to stem the rising tide of trade and political union activities by prosecuting six farm labourers from the village of Tolpuddle in Dorset for administering 'unlawful oaths'. Despite no evidence of any seditious purpose on the part of the hapless labourers, at their trial in Dorchester they were treated very harshly receiving the maximum sentence of transportation for seven years. All this was too much for O'Connor. The Dorchester Unionists had 'erred without a knowledge of the law' he insisted during a withering attack on the government in April 1834, but they were not the real criminals. 'Earl Grey, Lord Brougham, the noble Lord, the Paymaster of the Forces, and the right hon. The Secretary of State for the Colonies, should be on board the hulks in place of those men', he told the House, 'for they had been the prime movers and ac-tors in all the transactions which had for their object the promotion of political change by means of unions of the working classes.' The Whigs were, 'in short, accessories before the fact'.[57] The prosecution was a monstrous hypocrisy. This allegation would reach a crescendo during the Chartist years when the failing Whig administration ruled out any further instalments of political reform, but it came easily to O'Connor's lips from the outset. Characteristically his sense of betrayal was personal, even visceral. The people of Ireland and Britain had been betrayed but so had he; he had been 'fool enough to assist the Government through thick and thin with the Reform Bill',[58] and they had let *him* down.

One consequence of this attitude that had a bearing on the rest of O'Connor's public life was his refusal to differentiate between Whigs and Tories. His con-stituents, he admitted in May 1835, would regret to see a Tory Government,[59] but for him there was little to distinguish the two parties in practice. If there was any difference it was one of expectation. 'The Tories never promised us anything – they did not give us much, to be sure, but they did not promise more than they gave', he argued. On the other hand, 'the Whigs have never given the people of Ireland anything which they have promised'.[60] To support this point he quoted from George Canning's *New Morality*:

> Give me the avow'd, the erect, the manly foe,
> Bold I can meet – perhaps may turn his blow;
> But of all plagues, good heaven, thy wrath can send,
> Save, save, oh! save me from the Candid Friend![61]

Perhaps, he mused, there was a difference of substance after all. Speaking about the Coercion Act O'Connor argued that during 'the entire period of nearly a century, for which the Tories held the reigns of this Government, they never ventured to pass such laws or enactments as have been brought forward by the Whigs'. One of his first speeches to the radicals of London was devoted to an excoriation of the 'dark, designing, treacherous Whigs'. Sentiments such as this quickly earned O'Connor the sobriquet 'Tory-Radical', a charge that gained pace after he fell out with O'Connell and would continue to put him at odds with many moderate radicals. The characterisation is misleading. O'Connor's sense of politics was intensely personal and immediate. In 1817 his enmity was aimed squarely at the Tories who plundered Ireland and persecuted his father; in 1833 his gaze had shifted to the Whigs who coerced Ireland and taunted him in the House. 'He had no confidence…in the present Administration', he stated in March 1835, 'nor in any Administration. His confidence was in the pressure from without.'[62] A few months previously in an public letter published in Cork he had warned his supporters to be wary of the 'machinations of Whig, Tory, and mock Radical'.[63] Only he was to be trusted.

For O'Connor the failure of Reform and the treachery of the Whigs were symptomatic of a crisis in the political system. Second only to Irish issues, O'Connor spoke most often during his first period in the House on the dysfunction of the parliamentary system. As early as May 1833, for example, he gave notice that he intended to move a resolution condemning ministers for their absence during the presentation of petitions. This was 'an insult to the House of Commons', he insisted, 'and an injustice to the people of England'. Asking rhetorically why members should bother to go through the 'farce' of presenting petitions to any empty chamber O'Connor returned to a familiar theme: 'The only benefit the people had obtained from the Reformed Parliament was to have their petitions thrust into a bag under the Table'.[64] It is easy to forget the importance of petitioning at a time when there were few legitimate means for the expression of opinion open to those outside the political nation. The first decades of the nineteenth century had seen an exponential growth in the number of petitions being submitted to parliament (commensurate with the growing demand for reform) and by the 1830s both major political parties were looking at ways to stem the flow. Early in 1833 Grey's Whig government established a committee to examine petitioning which, goaded on further by Peel on behalf of the Tories, recommended a procedural revolution to dramatically curtail the role of petitions in the parliamentary schedule. Under O'Connor's leadership the Chartists would later show that despite the new rules petitioning could still be an effective tactic, but in the short term he and others (including Daniel O'Connell and William Cobbett) strained against the new regulations that restricted the opportunities for MPs to present petitions and removed their right to speak to them.[65]

O'Connor's response was to go on the offensive. His principal weapon, he soon discovered, was not to move resolutions condemning the government (this required a seconder), but to call the Speaker's attention to the state of the House. Parliament – then as now – was often without a quorum. The Speaker was only required to ensure that the requisite 40 MPs were present at the commencement of the sitting; thereafter he would only ask for the House to be counted if prompted to by a member. If members did not then make a quorum the sitting was adjourned. Whether the MPs were in the dining room or in what one commentator called London's 'hells and casinos', or in the library or the committee rooms, forcing them to make a quorum was incredibly disruptive to the rhythm of parliamentary life. Undoubtedly this earned O'Connor many enemies but apparently he cared little. In February 1834 he threatened to 'fill the House every day' until ministers started attending the early sittings of the House when petitions were presented. No part of the 'public business', he insisted, was 'more important than the petitions of the people'.[66] At the core of this concern over the treatment of petitions was his growing conviction that nothing short of a radical reform of the political system would do. Far from ignoring public opinion, he argued that the government should 'depend upon it as their best support'; his 'confidence was in the pressure from without'.[67] 'I was a constant attendant upon my Parliamentary duties', O'Connor wrote in 1836, '…and I came to the deliberate opinion, that, however we may appear liberal, the extension of the suffrage was the only means to secure our remaining so.'[68]

The case for reform that he advocated with increasing vigour was a general one, applicable to England as well as Ireland, and it began to earn him respect among British radicals both inside and outside the House. In June 1834 William Cobbett published a letter in the Cork press commending O'Connor's parliamentary conduct and encouraging him further. According to England's greatest journalist the best way for Irish members to fight the enemies of Ireland 'is to take a prominent and decided part in matters which affect England only'.[69] At the same time as his increasing interest in English grievances and his growing commitment to a general case for political reform, O'Connor began to find allies among British radicals for his Irish objectives. Whereas in 1833 he was convinced that the English people knew nothing of Ireland; in 1834 he speculated that support for Repeal was growing among the people of England; by early 1835 he was welcoming the 'growing disposition on the part of both the people of England and Scotland to do Ireland justice'. The 'Reformers of England', he insisted, were 'beginning to see that the people of Ireland had real grievances to complain of, and wrongs that required redress.'[70]

O'Connor's clash with O'Connell and his increasing interest in general issues did not harm his chances of re-election. 'With the single exception of Mr O'Connell, what Irish Member was so ardent, so enthusiastic in their cause, as Mr Feargus O'Connor', asked the editor of a Cork nationalist newspaper with a rhetorical flourish on the eve of the election in January 1835: 'Was he not always at his post, endeavouring to secure some advantage for his Country, and labouring to expose the heartless tyranny by which it was ruled'.[71] O'Connor was content to stand on his record; as he told the crowd at the nomination: 'I have now served you for two years and a half: it is for you to say whether faithfully'.[72] He offered a simple sketch of his political creed which was remarkably similar to his manifesto of two years earlier: the total abolition of tithes, appointment of Magistrates by the people, short parliaments, the ballot and universal suffrage. Again his skill as a platform orator stood him in good stead. For one commentator, O'Connor's speech at the poll 'carried everything before it like a torrent. For two hours did he pour forth an unceasing flood of eloquence and argument.'[73] When the voting was over O'Connor had again topped the poll. With his personal mandate renewed he again reaffirmed his mission. 'Standing clear of both parties', he wrote in a public letter of thanks, 'I shall redeem my every pledge and vote for every measure calculated to serve Ireland, and against every measure injurious to our common country'. Moreover, he would continue to practice democracy in an undemocratic age: 'I shall continue to tender my resignation at the close of each session', he promised, 'and shall be ready to resign my trust at any other time when called upon'.[74]

Shortly after he returned to Westminster, however, O'Connor's parliamentary career was in ruins. Suggestions that he had financial problems were already circulating among the political class long before the election. Feargus O'Connor is 'very poor', recalled one commentator. Invited to share a simple meal of beef and potatoes with the O'Connells, he had, according to Maurice O'Connell, replied: 'I shall be delighted for that is just what I had ordered at home, *barring the beef*'.[75] Such anecdotes obviously encouraged his opponents in Cork and within weeks of his victory a petition was lodged challenging his election on the grounds that he lacked sufficient property to meet the qualification that was required of members of parliament at that time. In April the House of Commons established a select committee to examine O'Connor's qualification and proceeded to rake over his financial affairs in minute detail. Initially O'Connor dismissed the challenge but, not surprisingly, the committee subsequently found that he did not have the £600 annual income that was required and, in June 1835, his colleagues voted to disqualify him.[76]

During his three years in the House of Commons O'Connor had become increasingly isolated. In his memoir he claimed that the government whip had attempted to buy his silence by offering him a post. Not even the Governor-generalship of India or the Lord Lieutenancy of Ireland, he responded, 'would catch a vote of mine'.[77] We only have O'Connor's word that this exchange took place. The evidence that does exist suggests that the government sought to silence him by another well-trodden route: scorn and abuse. In parliament, he told Daniel O'Connell in 1836, he 'discovered that an honest man, belonging to no party, was like a tell-tale or mischief maker at school, tossed from one set to the other...'[78] Hansard's record of the parliamentary debates shows that O'Connor's speeches were often interrupted and in his reports to his constituents and other public speeches he often referred to the abuse, taunts and invective that he endured at the hands of his parliamentary colleagues. Within months of taking his seat, for example, he told a meeting of London radicals that 'he was one of those men who had been the butt for the ridicule and sport of those infamous Whigs', a fate that he attributed to doing his duty.[79] There were many occasions when he undoubtedly got under the skin of both sides of the House and he was vociferous and visible enough to draw the leading figures of the day into debate. The fact that Peel even bothered to attack him speaks volumes.[80] If his own account is to be believed, the pressure inside the House was more than matched outside. In his memoir O'Connor provides the details of a duel he fought in 1834 over an insult to a fellow Irish member. Later, he would claim, he sought satisfaction on the field of honour from the Home Secretary and future Prime Minister, Lord John Russell, Sir John Easthope, the owner of the *Morning Chronicle*, and J.A. Roebuck, the radical MP for Sheffield. Roebuck was certainly convinced that O'Connor was 'resolved upon deeds of blood', but, apart from this, we only have O'Connor's word for these episodes.[81] Their tenor is, however, entirely in keeping with his combustible personality and his previous violent habits: O'Connor's cousin, Daunt, provides details of two duels fought by Feargus in Ireland.[82]

It is clear that O'Connor's experience as an MP deepened his radicalism. Not only did it convince him of the need for radical reform of the political system but also it fired his contempt for the political class. Many radicals were unimpressed by their first visit to the Imperial Parliament. 'What a scene was this to be enacted by the "collective wisdom of the nation"', reported Samuel Bamford,

> Some of the members stood leaning against the pillars, with their hats cocked awry; some were whispering by half-dozens; other were lolling upon their seats; some, with arms a-kimbo, were eye-glassing across the house; some were stiffened immovably by starch, or pride, or both; one was speaking, or appeared to be so, by the motion of his arms, which he shook in token of defiance, when his voice was drowned by a howl as wild and remorseless as that from a kennel of hounds at feeding time.[83]

The scene was sufficient to leave Bamford yearning for the 'stamp of stern old Oliver on this floor', a reference to Cromwell's famous injunction to the MPs, 'Begone; give place to honester men'. For O'Connor, a frequent victim of the 'babel howl', the problem was less behaviour than motive. '[N]ot only the majority, but nearly all [MPs]', he wrote, 'base their votes upon patronage.'[84] He too was moved to offer a quotation from Britain's past invoking the words of Queen Elizabeth's Lord Chancellor, Lord Burleigh: 'England would never be destroyed but by a parliament'.[85] O'Connor quickly recognised that the value of a parliamentary speech was not in the effect it had on his fellow members, or indeed on government policy, but how it resonated in the nation at large. His opponents knew, he later wrote, 'that words spoken earnestly, and conveying great truths, fell heavily, when reported as coming from that house'.[86] He never forgot that a parliamentary speech would be in the hands of thousands by Saturday morning.[87] As we read the reports of his parliamentary speeches we must never forget that their intended audience was almost always outside the House.

Once the decision to unseat him was announced O'Connor's first inclination was to fight to regain Cork. 'Do they think or hope to keep me out of Parliament? If so they are mistaken', he boasted in a public letter. 'I shall attend every registry in the county of Cork, and marshal my forces for the next battle...I beat them before – I'll beat them again, for I will never surrender', he promised.[88] It was soon clear, however, that the next battle would not be in Cork. On the one hand, the property qualification remained a substantial impediment. The select committee had found that O'Connor had property worth about £300 a year, a long way short of the £600 required. How could he double his income? Secondly, with the Lichfield House compact in place, he must have known that he would struggle to retain support in Ireland against the full force of O'Connell's political machine. No sooner had the idea of re-contesting Cork begun to recede than he publicly toyed with idea of raising an Irish brigade to fight for the infant queen of Spain, Isabella II, against the Carlists.[89] As seductive as the idea of a foreign adventure (that had taken his brother Frank to South America) undoubtedly was it too soon faded.

Instead he resolved to build a career for himself in English radical politics. This was to be an extra-parliamentary career. 'He thought that a man might be just as useful without as within the House', he told a meeting of London radicals. 'He was delighted after the dull plodding labour of Parliament, to find himself again on the public stage, where there was fair play to all.'[90] Within weeks, however, he was embroiled in a by-election in Oldham that was occasioned by William Cobbett's death in June 1835. O'Connor was already known to radicals in the capital, but this would be his first foray into what would become his heartland – the north of England. The Oldham by-election is sometimes held up as an example of O'Connor's unfitness to lead. It was, for J.T. Ward, a mere 'adventure'; for Donald Read and Eric Glasgow it was a 'maladroit intervention'.[91] Nor did his involvement earn him many friends among moderate radicals. John Fielden, the radical manufacturer and Cobbett's fellow member for the seat, believed that he had cleared the way for the election of Cobbett's son (and his future son-in-law), John Morgan Cobbett. Even some disinterested radicals were dismayed by the outcome. As we shall see, O'Connor's candidature effectively split the liberal-radical vote and allowed a Tory victory. Why did he do it?

To understand his motivation we must look more closely at the contest. Oldham was one of the few jewels in the radical crown. As John Foster has shown, an extensive system of 'exclusive dealing', the name given to the practice of patronising or boycotting shops and small trading establishments according to the political activities of their proprietor, had returned radical MPs in successive elections.[92] In an undemocratic age it was one of the few boroughs in England where a radical could aspire to election. Moreover, Cobbett's death, following as it did the death of 'Orator' Henry Hunt in February 1835, had deprived the radical movement of two of its iconic leaders. Ostensibly, there was an opportunity here not merely to fill a parliamentary vacancy but to claim the mantle of leadership of the movement at large. Although O'Connor was in no doubt about his ability to replace either or both Cobbett and Hunt he went to Oldham with his eyes open. Firstly, he can have hardly failed to notice that Oldham's radicals were already seriously divided over the issue of the separation of church and state. In January 1835 the *Poor Man's Guardian* carried a report of a bitter division in Oldham involving the formation of a faction of 'Radical Dissenters' who were appalled that their MP had 'declined to support a separation of Church and State, or the admission of Dissenters to the Universities'. Suggesting that the dispute threatened the 'utter annihilation of all future friendship between the parties', the article went on to make it clear the seceeders were contemplating standing a candidate against Cobbett himself at the next election.[93] Cobbett's death changed nothing. On the morning that O'Connor arrived during the campaign the *Manchester Guardian* reported that the 'radical part of constituency' was 'divided by various shades of opinion on certain points into several sections'.[94]

Within hours of his arrival O'Connor added fuel to the flames. In a lengthy speech he indicated that he was 'an advocate for the separation of church and state' and 'for the redress of all the grievances of dissenters, and giving them all the rights and privileges and a lot more besides'. In a speech delivered with devastating force O'Connor stated that he was for universal suffrage, the ballot and annual parliaments as well as an 'equitable adjustment of the national debt'. He was for taxing the aristocracy instead of the working classes and for reforming the House of Lords ('full-bellied fools' and 'natural idiots') to make it an elective body. Magistrates should also be elected by the people. The Dorchester Labourers should be restored to their homes and Lords Althorp, Grey and Russell transported in their place; the malt tax should be repealed and free trade implemented 'all over the world'.[95]

For John Cobbett, who was away burying his father, there was little he could say to match this and, given the sensitivities that his father had excited, even less room to manoeuvre. When Cobbett returned a couple of days later he only made the situation worse by refusing to give clear and direct answers to questions on the issues that had riled the radical dissenters in the first place. By polling day Cobbett had not only lost them to O'Connor, his support among the largely working-class Huntites and many of the organised trades had also evaporated. At the nomination O'Connor reiterated his radical agenda; Cobbett pointedly mocked O'Connor's claim to royal ancestry (he 'could claim no higher descent than from a day labourer'), and accused him of breaking an assurance, supposedly given to Fielden, not to stand. O'Connor had already spoken and could not deny the charge, but, according to one report, he later 'enlivened the election in the Irish fashion' by taking steps to challenge Cobbett to a duel.[96] A show of hands confirmed O'Connor as the winner and a poll was demanded on behalf of the defeated candidates. O'Connor remained in the contest for the first morning; the 32 votes he received in that time was enough to ensure that the Tory candidate was elected ahead of Cobbett (the eventual margin was a mere 11 votes).[97] The oracle of liberalism in Lancashire, the *Manchester Guardian*, summed up what must have been the feelings of many liberals and moderate radicals when it lamented the relevance of the adage that political extremes meet. Cobbett failed, the editor complained, 'because he was suspected of moderation'. It also suggested that O'Connor's supporters had been seen celebrating with the Tories in the aftermath. It is clear that if O'Connor was responsible for a 'radical' defeat, he did not act alone. Indeed, the question is not so much why he became involved in the by-election but rather why he allowed himself to become a pawn in an internecine radical dispute? The answer is that O'Connor and those who encouraged his candidacy were not prepared to accept a moderate radical purely to preserve unity. O'Connor had made it clear, as he had in parliament, that he would not differentiate between Tories and Whigs and that he would not fall into line to support Whigs, liberals and liberal-radicals merely in order to keep out the Tories. In Oldham he found men of like mind. The episode that O'Connor would later describe as his 'English political birth place' was something of a watershed in English politics more generally.

At the declaration of the poll O'Connor claimed, with apparently no sense of self-consciousness, that it was he that had been treated unfairly by the other candidates, and with characteristic ebullience he promised that having used his influence to secure Cork for a supporter of Repeal he would return to Oldham to contest the next general election.[98] He then left the town for Manchester in an open carriage drawn by four horses. Later in the day he would promise a crowd of several thousand in the shock city of the industrial age that he would 'fill up the vacancy caused by the death of Henry Hunt'.[99] The carriage that had carried him from Oldham had sported a flag on which was depicted a 'figure in armour and inscribed "Roderick O'Connor, Monarch of Ireland"'.[100] The symbolism of the gesture is worth noting as it summarises the rest of his public life. O'Connor was heading to a career in English radical politics but he was not leaving Ireland behind him.

Notes

1   J. Grant, *Random Recollections of the House of Commons, from the year 1830 to the close of 1835, including personal sketches of the leading members of all parties,* London, 1837, pp. 1-2.

2   J. O'Connell, *Recollections and Experiences During a Parliamentary Career from 1832 to 1848,* London, 1849, vol. 1, pp. 47-8.

3   'The Life and Adventures of Feargus O'Connor', *National Instructor,* 23 November 1850, pp. 425-6.

4   Grant, *Random Recollections,* p. 366.

5   *Hansard* [House of Commons], 8 February 1833, col. 452-4.

6   *Hansard* [House of Commons], 19 March 1835, col. 1218.

7   *Hansard* [House of Commons], 20 February 1834, col. 600.

8   *Hansard* [House of Commons], 2 May 1835, col. 442.

9   See *Hansard* [House of Commons], 18 February 1833, cols. 899-900; 19 February 1833, col. 954; 1 March 1833, col. 19; 13 March 1833, col. 586; 18 June 1833, cols. 979-8; 4 March 1835, col. 523; *Southern Reporter,* 19 January 1833.

10 *Hansard* [House of Commons], 8 March 1833, col. 400; 15 March 1833, col. 682-3.

11 *People's Press and Cork Weekly Register,* 8 November 1834.

12 *Hansard* [House of Commons], 4 March 1835 col. 524; 'The Life and Adventures of Feargus O'Connor', *National Instructor,* 27 July 1850, p. 151-4; 23 November 1850, p. 425; D. Read and E. Glasgow, *Feargus O'Connor: Irishman and Chartist,* London, 1961, p. 36.

13 *Hansard* [House of Commons], 15 March 1833, col. 682; 24 April 1834, cols. 1334-1352.

14 *Hansard* [House of Commons], 24 April 1834, col. 1334.

15 *Hansard* [House of Commons], 21 June 1833, col. 1024.

16 *Hansard* [House of Commons], 28 February 1833, cols. 1346-7.

17 *Hansard* [House of Commons], 7 July 1834, col. 1232.

18 *Hansard* [House of Commons], 15 March 1833, col. 683.

19 *Hansard* [House of Commons], 10 July 1833, col. 472.

20 *Hansard* [House of Commons], 24 April 1834, col. 1350.

21 *Hansard* [House of Commons], 24 April 1834, cols. 1340-1.

22 See O. MacDonagh, *The Emancipist: Daniel O'Connell, 1830-1847,* London, 1989, pp. 121-2.

23 F. O'Connor, *A State of Ireland, Shewing the Rise and Progress of the Present Disaffection, with an Address to the Irish People,* Cork, [1822?], p. 22.

24 'The Life and Adventures of Feargus O'Connor', *National Instructor,* 3 August 1850, p. 169.

25 O'Connell to P.V. Fitzpatrick, c.6 June 1833, *The Correspondence of Daniel O'Connell,* edited by M. R. O'Connell, Dublin, 1972, vol. 5, p. 38.

26 *Southern Reporter,* 15 June 1833; 9 July 1833; 20 July 1833.

27 *Hansard* [House of Commons], 10 July 1833, col. 472.

28 *Hansard* [House of Commons], 14 February 1834, col. 352.

29 Cited in MacDonagh, *The Emancipist,* p. 98. See also T.C. Luby, *The Life and Times of Daniel O'Connell,* Glasgow, n.d (1872), p. 535. According to Luby, a

Fenian leader, O'Connell was forced into action by 'eccentric, half-mad' Feargus O'Connor.

30 *Hansard* [House of Commons], 24 April 1834, col. 1334.

31 *Hansard* [House of Commons], 24 April 1834, col. 1351.

32 *Hansard* [House of Commons], 24 April 1834, col. 1352; W. O'Neill Daunt, *Eighty-five Years of Irish History*, London, 1888, p. 156.

33 *Hansard* [House of Commons], 18 February 1834, col. 454.

34 Quoted in P. Kelly, 'Constituents' instructions to Members of Parliament in the eighteenth century', in C. Jones (ed.), *Party Management in Parliament 1660-1784*, Leicester, 1984, p. 170.

35 *Hansard* [House of Commons], 14 February 1834, col. 353.

36 *Hansard* [House of Commons], 26 February 1834, col. 833.

37 *Hansard* [House of Commons], 18 February 1834, col. 454.

38 *Southern Reporter*, 19 January 1833.

39 *Southern Reporter*, 16 January 1834.

40 The *locus classicus* of this view is M. Ostrogorski, *Democracy and the Organisation of Political Parties*, London, 1902.

41 See P.A. Pickering, 'The Chartist Rites of Passage: Commemorating Feargus O'Connor', *Contested Sites: Commemoration, Memorial and Popular Politics in Nineteenth-Century Britain*, Aldershot, 2004, pp. 101-126 and chapter 8 below.

42 *Hansard* [House of Commons], 27 February 1835, col. 456.

43 Daunt, *Eighty-five Years*, p. 156.

44 W. O'Neill Daunt, *A life Spent for Ireland*, London, 1896, p. 14; F. O'Connor, *A series of letters from Feargus O'Connor, Esq., Barrister at law, to Daniel O'Connell, Esq., M.P. containing a review of Mr. O'Connell's conduct during the agitation of the question of Catholic emancipation, together with an analysis of his motives and actions, since he became a member of Parliament*, London, 1836.

45 *Freemans' Journal*, 7 November 1833; MacDonagh, *The Emancipist*, p. 98; 'The Life and Adventures of Feargus O'Connor', *National Instructor*, 28 December 1850, p. 504. O'Connor misremembered it as 1834.

46 *Hansard* [House of Commons], 24 April 1834, col. 1350.

47 O'Connell to P.V. Fitzpatrick, 26 February 1834, *The Correspondence of Daniel O'Connell*, vol. 5, p. 107.

48 In addition to O'Connell's letter of February 1834 see 'The Life and Adventures of Feargus O'Connor', *National Instructor*, 14 December 1850, p. 473; *Cork Southern Reporter*, 22 June 1833; Denis Le Marchant's diary, March 1833, in A. Aspinall (ed.), *Three Early Nineteenth Century Diaries*, London, 1952, p. 314. On the other hand, Thomas Mooney believed that there was a 'mutual dislike' between them from the outset. See T. Mooney, *A History of Ireland, From Its Settlement to the Present Time*, Boston, 1846, p. 1397.

49 O'Connor did suspend hostilities and gave strong support to O'Connell during his trial and imprisonment in 1844. See *Northern Star*, 6 July 1844.

50 *Hansard* [House of Commons], 21 June 1833, col. 1024.

51 *Hansard* [House of Commons], 21 February 1834, cols. 638-9.

52 *Hansard* [House of Commons], 20 February 1833, col. 996.

53 *Hansard* [House of Commons], 21 February 1833, col. 1058.

54   *Hansard* [House of Commons], 1 March 1833, col. 19.

55   *Hansard* [House of Commons], 25 February 1834, col. 815.

56   *Hansard* [House of Commons], 23 July 1834, col. 401.

57   *Hansard* [House of Commons], 16 April 1834, col. 861.

58   *Hansard* [House of Commons], 17 July 1834, col. 1232.

59   *Hansard* [House of Commons], 25 May 1835, col. 43.

60   *Hansard* [House of Commons], 24 April 1834, col. 1348.

61   *Hansard* [House of Commons], 24 April 1834, col. 1348. Canning's *New Morality* was published in 1797; O'Connor quoted lines 207-210.

62   *Hansard* [House of Commons], 12 March 1834, cols. 892-3.

63   *People's Press and Cork Weekly Register*, 8 November 1834; *Southern Reporter*, 1 April 1834.

64   *Hansard* [House of Commons], 17 May 1833, col. 1344; *Poor Man's Guardian*, 23 March 1833.

65   See P.A. Pickering, 'And Your Petitioners &c: Chartist Petitioning in Popular Politics 1838-48', *English Historical Review*, vol. CXVI, no. 466, pp. 368-388.

66   *Hansard* [House of Commons], 28 February 1834, col. 956-7. See also 18 February 1834, cols. 454.

67   *Hansard* [House of Commons], 27 July 1834, col. 402; 12 March 1835, cols. 892-3.

68   O'Connor, *A series of letters to Daniel O'Connell*, p. 4.

69   *Southern Reporter*, 26 June 1834.

70   *Hansard* [House of Commons], 27 February 1835, cols. 455-6; 6 March 1835, cols. 615-6.

71   *People's Press and Cork Weekly Register*, 10 January 1835.

72   *People's Press and Cork Weekly Register*, 20 January 1835.

73   *People's Press and Cork Weekly Register*, 24 January 1835.

74   *People's Press and Cork Weekly Register*, 31 January 1835.

75   Le Marchant's diary, March 1833, Aspinall (ed.), *Three Early Nineteenth Century Diaries*, p. 314.

76   *People's Press and Cork Weekly Register*, 11 April 1835; *Southern Reporter*, 11 June 1835; *Journals of the House of Commons*, vol. 90, 26 May 1835, p. 287; 5 June 1835, pp. 320, 322.

77   'The Life and Adventures of Feargus O'Connor', *National Instructor*, 17 August 1850, p. 200.

78   O'Connor, *A series of letters to Daniel O'Connell*, p. 4.

79   *Poor Man's Guardian*, 23 April 1833.

80   See *Hansard* [House of Commons], 25 April 1834, col. 91.

81   R.E. Leader (ed.), *Life and Letters of John Arthur Roebuck*, London, 1897, p. 196.

82   'The Life and Adventures of Feargus O'Connor', *National Instructor*, 28 September 1850, p. 298; W. O'Neill Daunt, *A Life Spent for Ireland*, London, 1896, p. 329.

83   S. Bamford, *Passages in the Life of a Radical* (1844), Oxford, 1984, pp. 26-8. See also J. Pearce (ed.), *Life and Teachings of Joseph Livesey*, London, 1885, pp. lvii-lviii; B. Harrison and P. Hollis (eds), *Robert Lowery: Radical and Chartist* (1856-7), London, 1979, p. 140; P.A. Pickering and A. Tyrrell, *The People's Bread: A History of the Anti-Corn Law League*, Leicester 2000, pp. 166.

84 'The Life and Adventures of Feargus O'Connor', *National Instructor*, 17 August 1850, p. 200.

85 O'Connor, *A series of letters to Daniel O'Connell*, p. 4; *Hansard* [House of Commons], 8 March 1833, col. 400; 12 June 1833, col. 602. The quotation is from Blackstone's *Commentaries*, chapter 2. Like O'Connor, William Cecil (Lord Burleigh) had attended Gray's Inn.

86 F. O'Connor, *The Land and Its Capabilities* (1842), reprinted in G. Claeys (ed.), *The Chartist Movement in Britain 1838-1850*, London, 2001, vol. 2, p. 456.

87 *Nottingham Review*, 30 July 1847.

88 *People's Press*, 13 June 1835.

89 *Dictionary of National Biography*, vol. XIV, p. 846.

90 Cited in J. Epstein, *The Lion of Freedom*, London, 1982, p. 21.

91 J. Ward, *Chartism*, London, 1973, p. 85, Read and Glasgow, *Feargus O'Connor*, p. 45.

92 J. Foster, *Class Struggle and the Industrial Revolution*, London, 1974, pp. 52-6.

93 *Poor Man's Guardian*, 10 January 1835. The article originally appeared in the *Morning Herald*. The editor of the *Poor Man's Guardian* suggested that the dispute would be resolved in time to prevent a division in the liberal vote.

94 *Manchester Guardian*, 27 June 1835.

95 *Manchester Guardian*, 27 June 1835.

96 *Manchester Guardian*, 4 July 1835.

97 *Manchester Guardian*, 11 July 1835.

98 *Manchester Guardian*, 11 July 1835.

99 *Manchester and Salford Advertiser*, 11 July 1835; Epstein, *Lion of Freedom*, p. 24.

100 *Manchester Guardian*, 11 July 1835.

5: CHARTISM

The next phase of O'Connor's public life is the best known. Over the next decade he became a household name in Britain, adored by hundreds of thousands, and feared and loathed by many more. Lauded as the 'Lion of Freedom' of the labouring poor this was also the period when, as he put it so vividly, his name 'actually stank' in the noses of the middle class.[1] He took pride in both outcomes. In the immediate aftermath of his adventure in Lancashire O'Connor returned to London. He was no stranger to the capital. As we have seen, he had spent extended periods living there in self-imposed exile and as a student, and during his years in parliament he had divided his time between Cork and the imperial capital. O'Connor already had a well-established network of contacts, a process that had begun during his first visit as a teenage runaway when he had knocked on the door of his father's friend, Francis Burdett, arguably the most famous London radical at that time. Subsequently he had been in contact with his father's political associates, and later, during his time in the House, he had set about establishing his own network among the ranks of London radicalism. He settled in Hammersmith, to the west of London on the northern bank of the Thames. A bustling and rapidly growing area, Hammersmith combined opulence – De Loutherberg had lived there, Queen Caroline had died there – with industry (an extensive iron-foundry and forge and two large breweries) and suburban agriculture in the form of numerous nursery gardens.[2]

By September 1835, a few short months after he was forced from his Irish seat in the House of Commons, O'Connor had helped to establish the Great Radical Association at Marylebone. He was joined in this enterprise by a group of experienced and committed activists, including veterans of the National Union of Working Classes, the campaign for a free press, and London's Owenite, trade union and cooperative schemes. Meetings of the Association were dominated by concern over the government's recent amendments to the laws that governed entitlements to poor relief and the demand for the repatriation of the Dorchester labourers. O'Connor, who had championed the labourers' cause in parliament, even led a delegation to see Lord John Russell.[3] The core of the programme – 'true radical principles' – is not surprising: universal suffrage, vote by ballot, annual parliaments, equal representation and no property qualification for members of parliament.[4] As James Epstein has noted, this declaration pre-dated the People's Charter drafted by the London Working Men's Association, and it was for this reason that most Chartists saw O'Connor as the 'founding father' of their movement.[5]

More important than the chance of a place in radical history, the new associa-tion gave O'Connor a mandate. According to his letter of introduction, Feargus O'Connor was a delegate of a 'great radical association' in London, with a 'mis-sion' to form 'others of a similar character and for similar principles'. Armed with these credentials O'Connor headed north on an extensive tour that took him to many of the towns and cities of Lancashire and Yorkshire. The reports of his visit to Manchester show him at work. His first meeting with the Manchester radicals took place at the Albion Mills Tavern in Tib Street, a regular radical haunt in the heartland of the working-class New Cross district. O'Connor pre-sented himself as the 'leader of a new radical party' but his audience was made up of hardened political veterans; they were fiercely independent radicals not sycophants waiting for instructions. Accordingly his reception was welcoming but searching. Why, asked one radical, had O'Connor supported the retention of the corn laws (repeal had long been part of the radical programme) when in parliament? O'Connor insisted that he had voted to protect the Irish peasantry from ruin – an argument widely accepted among Irish politicians of all stripes – but with an ideological flexibility that, for some, would characterise his later career, he willingly agreed that he would now vote to repeal them.[6]

Apart from promoting the cause of radical reform and the virtues of organi-sation a recurrent theme of many of O'Connor's speeches was the advantages of a National Convention of radical delegates elected by the people to meet in London and proclaim the cause of reform beneath the walls of the parliament. He also mused over the benefits of securing a small group of committed radical MPs. Epstein is correct to point out that what O'Connor coveted was the bal-ance of power that, he believed, had been squandered by O'Connell.[7] Encour-aged by his words at least one group of radicals in Glasgow urged O'Connor to stand for election in their city early in 1836, but this came to naught.

By any measure O'Connor's tour was very successful: over 50 radicals asso-ciations were established in three weeks. In many cases the infrastructure of these associations was already in place and the grievances and demands of their members had long been drawn up. O'Connor's genius was to generate a sense of common purpose, the feeling of being part of something bigger. He engen-dered almost paradoxical feelings of intimacy and community. O'Connor ac-complished this – much as he had done in Cork – through the sheer force of his physical presence. He was, as Francis Place would later observe, 'the constantly travelling dominant leader', a recognition of the importance of his punishing program of public meetings.[8] By addressing several meeting in one day – in halls, pubs, market squares, on street corners, on upturned carts, in open fields – O'Connor managed to give the impression to all who heard him that not only was he speaking to them personally, but also that thousands of others were being simultaneously given the same message. O'Connor provided a physical link that nourished and sustained the radical movement and the network of supporters that he established during this first tour would remain loyal to him throughout the remainder of his public life. The nature of that loyalty was, as we will see, never unconditional or uncritical.

O'Connor was less successful in his efforts to build the radical movement in the metropolis. Late in 1835 he had played an important role in melding the remnants of the National Union of the Working Classes – an important organisation in the early 1830s – with the Radical Associations and the supporters of the unstamped press, but with the reduction of the newspaper stamp in 1836 the movement lost momentum. By the middle of 1836 O'Connor was attempting to drum up support for a new initiative, a Universal Suffrage Club, which combined the cause of radical reform with educational objectives. This venture was overtaken by the establishment of the London Working Men's Association in June 1836 with similar objectives. By the end of the year O'Connor had become an 'honorary' member of the organisation that would produce the People's Charter but he played little part in its affairs. O'Connor had built a base among London's artisans and trade unionists that would grow and develop over the coming years, but not surprisingly he had failed to unite all reformers in the metropolis. As he reflected on the fissiparous and factionalised ranks of the movement in his adopted home, the industrial north must have seemed all the more alluring.

1836 was also the year when his relationship with Daniel O'Connell degenerated into a vicious public brawl. As he had done in Parliament, O'Connor frequently devoted his time on the platform to attacks on the Whig administration. The growing unpopularity of the amendments to the poor laws, as well as the on-going campaign in support of the Tolpuddle martyrs, was grist to his mill. The Whigs were now O'Connell's parliamentary allies and the Liberator felt compelled to defend them. In August he used a speech in Dublin to denounce the 'extraordinary' actions of English radicals that he believed gave succour to the Tories and he identified O'Connor as one of Ireland's 'heroes' who had encouraged this folly. O'Connor, insisted Ireland's Liberator, had 'conducted himself in a manner that disentitles him to public confidence'.[9] Casting doubt over O'Connor's status as a radical, O'Connell urged the people of Cork 'not to have anything to do' with their former MP. As for Feargus, he should, O'Connell concluded, 'stick to the radicals of England'. O'Connor protested indignantly, but he must have been delighted. O'Connell's complaint was against many English radicals, but he had singled out O'Connor for personal attention. 'It seems that the thought of me haunts this Dictator', O'Connor mused.[10] By individualising his grievance O'Connell gave O'Connor an opportunity to repeatedly employ his favourite pronoun: I.

O'Connor's response was quick, belligerent and effective. Published in October 1836, his series of open letters to O'Connell combined a detailed self-justification with a manifesto and a blistering indictment. The first letter was actually addressed to O'Connell's allies in the Whig government in which he repeated the charge of hypocrisy that he had often levelled in parliament: 'It would appear as if you held power with no other view than to induce a comparison between the promises of men out of office and the acts of the same men in office'.[11] In the subsequent letters O'Connor charged O'Connell 'with every species of political delinquency' from accepting Catholic emancipation 'with the disenfranchisement of thousands and tens of thousands of Irish voters' to falling in 'with political economists...and the monied men of England'. O'Connell was not the Liberator but a 'whimsical dictator' bent on the accumulation of personal power and wealth.[12] The most controversial allegation in the Letters was that O'Connell had been bribed by a group of Manchester manufacturers to alter his position in relation to the regulation of child labour, voting for an amendment that would allow twelve year olds to work longer than eight hours a day.[13] Whatever the merits of the case, this was an indication of the depths to which the relationship had sunk. It was a position from which there was no way back, and his final letters contain a realisation that O'Connell's popularity in Ireland would make it difficult for him to pursue political aspirations in his native land in the foreseeable future. 'In your generosity you have bestowed me on the English radicals', he wrote, 'I hope to make myself worth their acceptance.'[14] But if his future was now inextricably linked to the fortunes of British radicalism, O'Connor had not given up on Ireland. The cause of the Irish people would not be neglected: 'I am serving them here – you know I am – they know I am...', he insisted. And, when 'the herald shall proudly proclaim the triumph of knowledge in Ireland', he warned, 'then the people will call upon me, and, however long our separation, the first advance shall be the signal for a renewal of affection'.[15] O'Connor would cherish this dream for the remainder of his public life.

O'Connell responded to the Letters by insisting that his former protégé was 'playing into the hands of the Tories' and that by 'unmasking' himself as a 'Tory-radical' O'Connor had 'put it entirely out of his power to do any injury' to Ireland.[16] As a parting salvo O'Connell's description of O'Connor struck a chord. When, for example, the Tory favourite, Sir Robert Peel, was inducted as Lord

Rector of Glasgow University in January 1837, one member of the crowd called for 'A cheer for Feargus O'Connor' which was followed by 'Great laughter'.[17] Nevertheless, O'Connor had succeeded in establishing himself as a prominent and implacable critic of the Whigs and the attacks on him merely added to his notoriety. O'Connor intuitively understood the value, in some circumstances, of polarising political opinion, or perhaps he was just lucky. Either way, the sharper the divisions within the ranks of reformers, the more his star rose with those who regarded themselves as radicals.

For much of the time that the dispute with O'Connell was unfolding O'Connor was on the road. In the second half of 1836 he undertook another extensive tour that included his first visit to Scotland and to Nottingham, the city he would later represent in the House of Commons. By any standards his speech was an extraordinary one that must have lived long in the minds of those that heard him. As a sample of his developing ideology it is worth detailed consideration. He began, as so often, by musing over the failure of reform. 'Contumely and tyranny, insult and oppression we have previously borne', he told the large audience in Nottingham's Exchange, 'They have been wreaked upon us by our enemies: but since the passing of the Reform Bill we have suffered these from our friends'.[18] The behaviour of both 'factions', he continued, constituted a denial of the rights bestowed upon Britons by their history: 'Up to the reign of Henry the Sixth', he insisted in a thumb nail sketch of the British past, 'we had universal suffrage'. Despite the inclusive use of 'we' when speaking of Britain, O'Connor was soon tempted to introduce Ireland into the discussion. Turning to the 'accursed topic' of coercion ('here the speaker could scarcely contain his emotion'), O'Connor suggested that the Irish experience allowed them to glimpse what was in store for England in the form of a 'rural police'. The speech also anticipated many of his later concerns, most notably, with the land. 'No constitution that was ever framed has denied, or can deny, the right of the poor to an inheritance in the land'.

The heart of the speech, however, was a discourse on tactics. The premise of his strategy was twofold: first, it was based on the well-rehearsed assertion that there was no difference between Whig and Tory – 'The Tories would hang us all up at once', he argued, 'the Whigs would throttle us gradually, and strangle us with promises' – and, second, that the 'factions' could be drawn into 'bidding for the people'. Fanciful as it might seem in hindsight O'Connor sketched out the alluring scenario of Lord John Russell and Sir Robert Peel locked in a bizarre popularity contest with the prize the support of the people:

Russell offers a £10 suffrage, Peel proposes a qualification of £9 only; Russell again outbids him – £8 are offered; – Going! Going! Peel proffers a £7 rental, Russell bids down to £6; and so on…through all the other figures, 5, 4, 3, 2, 1.

And so the scene develops: in 'desperation' Russell offers 'universal suffrage', and throws the ballot 'into the bargain'. At this point Peel might be driven to top the Whig offer by conceding shorter parliaments. This strategy, O'Connor insisted, was based both on principle and on expediency: 'We can be bought by either party at a fair and equitable price, and at that only – universal suffrage'.[19] O'Connor concluded his speech with an attack on the sitting Whig MP for Nottingham, John Cam Hobhouse, the man he would later defeat in order to make a triumphant return to the House of Commons.

The speech in Nottingham also contained an attack on the iniquities of the government's new poor law. The 1834 Poor Law Amendment Act, or the 'Whig starvation law' as it widely became known, had first been implemented in the south of England and it was not until late in 1836 that the assistant commissioners began to appear in the midlands and northern counties. Everywhere they went they excited a fierce protest movement that reached its apogee in 1837-8 in south-east Lancashire and the west riding of Yorkshire. Here was a campaign ideally suited to O'Connor's declamatory style. O'Connor spoke at his first anti-poor law meeting in Huddersfield during January 1837. He arrived in an open carriage drawn by four horses with an escort of radical banners and bands of music.[20] According to the titular head of the campaign, Richard Oastler, Ireland's loss was England's gain: O'Connor was a 'Radical Patriot, who is banished from his native land, by the most rapacious beggar that ever stole a potato from a starving Irish pauper'. Oastler went on to congratulate the people for accepting 'Ireland's "Present," so worthily'.[21] For his part O'Connor evoked the heart-rending image of children being separated from their parents and confined to 'prison-houses and bastilles' by a malevolent government that was clinging to power by a 'pitiful majority'.[22] For all his skill at describing the overflowing 'cup of suffering', O'Connor never strayed far from a radical agenda: grievance was invariably linked to a political solution. As James Epstein has noted, O'Connor was adamant that 'injustices such as the new Poor Law were merely part of a larger system of oppression and exploitation which would only be ended when the working class had political power'.[23] The way to change the world was to change the composition of the House of Commons. Universal suffrage, O'Connor told a crowd in Wakefield, was 'the right above all others…with that right he thought other rights would be obtained, without that he thought it was impossible to obtain anything worth having'.[24] In July 1837 he stood for the late Henry Hunt's seat of Preston. According to one report O'Connor had stood merely to have the chance of addressing the 'vast' crowd

from the hustings – 'which he did at great length, and with much ability'.[25] Although he did not contest the subsequent poll O'Connor resoundingly won the
show of hands, an important index of his growing popularity. Here indeed was
a man who could assume Hunt's mantle.

The second half of 1837 provided O'Connor with a further charge in his indictment against the Whigs: the persecution of the Glasgow cotton spinners. It
also marked the occasion of a further deterioration of his relationship with the
moderate radicals of London. The Glasgow spinners were on trial for administering secret oaths and conspiracy during a strike that had been precipitated
by a substantial reduction in wages. O'Connor threw himself into the defence
of the spinners, portraying it as a struggle for the protection of labour 'against
the domination of capital',[26] and even travelling to Glasgow to attend the trial.
A comparison with the statements he made in defence of the Dorchester Labourers shows a significant development in his thinking: two years of touring
the industrial districts of northern England and Scotland had sharpened his
awareness of class. O'Connor recognised that he had learned much. 'If you recollect some two years ago…from this spot I showed you my infant Radicalism',
he told a meeting in Leeds early in 1838, 'Now my friends, I stand before you
upon different principles, and I may say that I am a new a[nd] prouder man. I
showed you the infant *then*, *now* behold it a monster grown to gigantic size…'
'Since he had come amongst them', he continued, 'he found that he had come
to a good school where he could learn many useful lessons, and indeed where
he had already obtained much valuable information.'[27] He was not the first – or
last – 'friend of the people' to be further radicalised by a close encounter with
the reality of industrial Britain.[28]

The Glasgow spinners' case was also the pretext for O'Connor's increasingly
sour relationship with William Lovett and others in the London Working Men's
Association. Strategy played a part. Despite a fierce sense of independence and
awareness of class Lovett's preferred *modus operandi* was to work in alliance
with middle-class extra-parliamentary reformers of various stripes and with a
small group of parliamentary radicals (including O'Connell) in order to pressure parliament from within and without. To O'Connor this appeared to be a
vehicle for compromise. When O'Connell intervened in the Glasgow spinners'
case by calling for a parliamentary enquiry into the activities of trade unions
(including the Dublin trades) it seemed to confirm the worst fears of many radicals. Lovett was in an invidious position but his decision to support the enquiry
– even taking a paid position in order to better facilitate it – exacerbated the developing schism and afforded his opponents an opportunity that was too good
to miss. Detailing his efforts in the cause of the Glasgow spinners – he travelled
day and night for over 2,000 miles, he boasted – O'Connor dismissed those

he called the 'London sham radicals and their parliamentary pets' as unfit for public confidence.[29] Class played a part too. Lovett and his colleagues had kept O'Connor at arms length precisely because he was not a working man; now it was his turn to play the class card. When O'Connor suggested that the London Association was complicit in the establishment of the enquiry that was a thinly veiled attack on the trades an exasperated Lovett penned a vitriolic public letter accusing O'Connor of setting himself up as the 'great I AM' of radicalism.[30] O'Connor responded by inviting 'real working men', 'those with unshorn chins, blistered hands, and fustian jackets', to note the occupations of the principals of the London Association. 'The greater part of those gentlemen who addressed me belong to the Fine Arts', he sneered, 'and with the exception of perhaps the gentlemen compositors, I do more real work in a week than they perform in a year.'[31] This was the first occasion on which he used what was to become his well known aphorism – a Chartist trinity that would come to define his leadership – and he did so with great effect. He was not turning his back on London – there were many radicals there who agreed with his critique of Lovett's Association – but he was appealing to a nascent sense of class that was far more common among the industrialised communities in the north. He was not a working man – and nor did he ever seriously claim to be one – but for many he was, paradoxically, the personification of the cause of working men. Like O'Connell before him Lovett had played into O'Connor's hands by singling him out for personal attack; this was politics on his terms.

By this time O'Connor had relocated to Leeds, the industrial capital of west Yorkshire, and become the proprietor of the *Northern Star and Leeds General Advertiser*. The idea for a new radical newspaper based in the north of England had first been mooted early in 1837 among the network of radicals with whom O'Connor had forged links on his first tours over the preceding months. From this group (which included the paper's first editor, William Hill, and its printer, Joshua Hobson) a campaign to raise funds generated £690 which, together with a financial contribution from O'Connor, was sufficient to get the venture off the ground.[32] His financial contribution was probably less than he implied but certainly more than his critics – then and now – allowed. In any case the financial question was of secondary importance: O'Connor's role in the establishment of the newspaper and his influence on its shape went well beyond the depth or otherwise of his pocket. O'Connor was well aware of the power of the printed word; it was, he believed, part of his heritage. His father, Roger O'Connor, had been a prolific writer of books, pamphlets and public letters, as well as editing a short-run nationalist newspaper, the *Harp of Erin*, in 1798; his uncle, Arthur O'Connor, had added to his glowing reputation as an Irish patriot by editing another radical journal during the magical 1790s. 'While I can find one single plank of the scattered rights of my country to stand on', wrote Arthur O'Connor upon taking up the editorship in 1797, 'I will fix my eyes upon the PRESS, as the polar-star which is to direct us to the haven of freedom.'[33] Feargus also attributed to his uncle a central role in the establishment of another newspaper of the United Irishmen in Belfast called the *Northern Star* that was suppressed in 1797.[34] Although Feargus had previously published letters and pamphlets and had been a vocal defender of the radical press in the House of Commons, he got his first serious taste of journalism in 1837 when he became an associate editor of John Taylor's *Glasgow Liberator*, a role he fulfilled for eight months.[35] Clearly the Glasgow experience further inspired his involvement in the proposed newspaper but at the same time there was never any doubt in his mind that he was carrying on a family business: he had printer's ink in his veins. The name he chose for the newspaper provided, he believed, a palpable link to his country and his family and he invited direct comparison: 'Oh! That the breath of our *Northern Star* may but equally raise the cause of liberty and freedom', he enthused.[36]

Quickly the *Northern Star* became one of the most important and successful radical newspapers of the first half of the nineteenth century. At one level, as R.G. Gammage, the first historian of the movement, noted, the *Star* owed its success to the fact that it became a 'complete record of the movement'. Chartists from all points of the compass could see their speeches in print, their resolutions listed, their principles enunciated. It also promoted a sense of solidarity among its readers, of which there were many. As O'Connor later boasted to the Chartists, the *Star* was a 'universal press': 'Have you not fifty-five columns weekly, to yourselves, of yourselves, for yourselves?'[37]

For O'Connor the *Star* complemented perfectly his constantly travelling style of leadership. Almost invariably an issue of the *Star* contained a long epistle from his pen that, interspersed between his regular personal appearances, must have made him seem ubiquitous. O'Connor's letters became part of the rhythm of Chartist activity. W.E. Adams, for example, recalled 'gathering in a humble kitchen' in Cheltenham where Larry the shoemaker 'made his appearance every Sunday morning, as regular as clockwork, with a copy of the *Northern Star*, damp from the press, for the purpose of hearing some member of our household read out to him and others "Feargus's Letter"'.[38] There were many similar 'humble kitchens'. Georg Weerth, a young German socialist, recorded a vivid image of carts overloaded with bundles of the *Northern Stars*, such was the voracious appetite of an extensive readership. The weekly circulation quickly grew from an average of 11,000 in 1838 to 36,000 in 1839. By April 1839 the *Star* boasted of a weekly readership of 400,000, a ratio of about ten readers for every copy.[39] O'Connor later claimed that there were as many as 100 readers for every issue.[40] Weerth identified the *Star* as an almost unique organ of mass communication, but he also recognised the intimacy of Feargus's letter. On the one hand, they were addressed collectively – and famously – to the 'fustian jackets, blistered hands and unshorn chins' (and later 'my children', or the 'old guards'), and written to be read aloud in pubs, meeting rooms, and a multitude of 'humble kitchens'. At the same time, the letters were personal communications that could have been read by any Chartist (woman or man, despite the gendered salutation) as though they had been addressed to them in person. The voice was conversational, friendly, direct, immediate, emotive, active, and inclusive; the prose is full of intimate pronouns: I, you, we, our, us.

The *Star* gave O'Connor access to a huge weekly audience and it attracted a legion of critics keen to suggest that he was abusing the platform that it gave him. Predictably, O'Connell led the chorus of criticism of his erstwhile lieutenant. 'Upon my word, this paper of Feargus's is a literary curiosity', he quipped, 'The first page is filled with praise of Feargus; second page, praise of Feargus; third page, ditto; fourth page, ditto; and so on all through till we come to the printer's name'.[41] Attacks of this sort were not only inaccurate – the editorial reins were relatively lightly held – but they also fundamentally misunderstood the nature of O'Connor's political style. O'Connor's critics did not have to look far for an outlet for their views. In fact the *Northern Star* often published (or reprinted) attacks on O'Connor in full – broadcasting them to a far wider audience than they would have otherwise reached – in order to give him the opportunity to refute them.[42] Denigration, as much as adulation, was the fuel that drove his public life. O'Connor relished criticism because it strengthened his claim that he personified the radical cause beset as it was by powerful interests on all sides.

Despite the unprecedented reach of the *Northern Star* O'Connor did not rest on his laurels. The wider the circulation of his newspaper the more he adopted the same technique he had employed in Cork: constant travelling. Weerth later asked rhetorically, 'whether any one in the whole wide world can be busier than this Feargus O'Connor?'[43] The following is only one amongst many reports of his whistle-stop tours around Britain:

From the 18th of December to the 15th of January, I have attended in London, Bristol, Manchester, Queenshead, Bradford, Leeds, Newcastle, Carlisle, Glasgow, Paisley, and Edinburgh, 22 large public meetings, and have travelled over 1,500 miles...[44]

After more than a decade of fulfilling this punishing program O'Connor boasted to a Manchester audience, with some justification, that he had 'attended more public meetings than any man that ever lived'.[45] As the Chartist agitation

gathered pace during 1838 so did the frequency and size of the meetings, culminating in a series of 'monster meetings': 150,000 people at Glasgow in May;
200,000 at Birmingham in August; 250,000 at Kersal Moor, Manchester, in September; and 300,000 at Peep Green in Yorkshire in October. O'Connor was an
ever-present figure on these mass platforms. His participation at Peep Green is
typical. At the beginning of proceedings O'Connor nominated a local leather
cutter to the chair – after all, he pointed out, 'this was a meeting for the benefit
of working men'. Having set the tone O'Connor waited until several others had
spoken to the vast gathering before again rising to his feet.

   He began by employing a metaphor; they were travelling a road, a 'constitutional road' he called it, that was 'stopped up' with 'foul barriers', a point he
reinforced by paraphrasing Byron. Their way was blocked, O'Connor stated,
'With fragments of things that should pass away/ With remnants of laws made
by creatures of clay'.[46] What lay at the end of the road? The specifics came easily to his lips: once the People's Charter had been enacted, the factory should
'surrender some hours from slavery to domestic enjoyment and social comfort';
the 'bloody Bastille should close, and forever, its jarring gates against the cap-
tive'; the 'children of freemen should graduate from the mother's breast to the
father's knee, from the cottage to the national school, and from the school to
take his station in the commonwealth as part partaker of those fruits of which
he had been part producer'. In old age, O'Connor continued, this same person
might visit the 'national savings bank in which in youth he had freely depos-
ited' in order to provide 'for comforts in after life'.[47] Books, banks, and burials
might sound commonplace to modern ears but in 1838 in west Yorkshire they
were akin to a light on a hill. Not surprisingly it elicited 'Tremendous and long
continued cheering'.

   Rasing the emotional temperature even further O'Connor declared the Charter to be a 'prize to fight for – a prospect worth living for, and for the chance
of its accomplishment worth dying for...' He then proceeded to emphasise the
closeness of his personal relationship with his audience, referring to them as
'my political children': 'Were they not his political children? (cheers and 'we
are') Aye deny it who could.' At the same time O'Connor drew attention to the
fact that he was a 'stranger, an alien in language and blood', a comment that
apparently caused a 'great sensation' among the crowd. His reason for sound-
ing a potentially discordant note was to introduce Ireland into the discussion.
'Freedom for England, if Ireland were not incorporated', he insisted, 'would for
her be increased tyranny'; their task was to 'consider how best this national agitation could be made to serve the universal cause of freedom.'[48] '[T]hey could
have Ireland with them; they must have Ireland with them; they should have
Ireland with them', he thundered. The idea of a union of working people across

the Irish Sea was never far from O'Connor's thoughts, and underscores the fact that it is unhelpful to think of his long public life as being divided into discrete Irish and British phases.

O'Connor concluded his address by imaging his own death – 'they may drag me to the dungeon, and thence to the scaffold, and then shed my blood – (exclamations, and no, no, never, they shan't) – but from every drop of the martyr's blood will spring ten thousand patriots to avenge the martyr's death'. It was an effective, if histrionic, conclusion but it did not deflect the meeting from the 'constitutional road' on which they travelled. The purpose of the spate of meetings in the later months of 1838 was the adoption of a National Petition calling on parliament to enact the People's Charter and the election of delegates to a national meeting in London, grandiloquently entitled the General Convention of the Industrious Classes, to oversee its presentation to parliament.

The Convention opened with a burst of enthusiasm in February 1839. O'Connor was ill – exhausted from months of travelling and speaking – and according to some reports he was close to death (even O'Connell expressed concern for his former lieutenant: 'I am, after all, sincerely sorry for his premature fate', he wrote to a colleague, 'May the great God be merciful to him!').[49] Rumours of O'Connor's imminent demise proved baseless, but the episode provides one of the first glimpses of the 'delicate health' that would increasingly disrupt the remainder of his public life. At a dinner for the delegates on the opening day of proceedings O'Connor appeared, despite the advice of many of his fellow delegates, and made a short speech from the chair.[50] 'Politically speaking', he told them, 'he had spent two of the happiest days of his life in Marylebone', the day the Radical Association was formed in 1835 and the opening of the Convention earlier that day. Although his speech was 'unusually short' it was long enough to get to the heart of the issue that would confound delegates over the coming months. 'I have heard that others intend to Petition again if the National Petition should be rejected this time', he mused, 'however, for my part, I am willing to try a petition on paper now, but if I ever do it again, ____ me.'[51] It was not a sour note and it did not dampen the festivities, but it did portend the future. Every session of the Convention over the next eight months would be shaped, in one way or another, by this question. The delegates were divided roughly into two camps: those who believed that the Convention's role was to oversee the presentation of the petition and that it should consider no action other than this; and those who believed that the they ought to contemplate 'ulterior measures' for the day that the petition was rejected. The attitude of the latter group was summarised in the compelling phrase first coined in the United States, the home of republicanism and revolution against the Empire, 'peaceably if we can, forcibly if we must'.[52]

O'Connor had advocated a Convention for a number of years and was keen to see it act as an analogue of the House of Commons, providing an alternative source of leadership for the nation. After all, these were the 'real' elected representatives of the people. Equally, O'Connor's position was based on a sober assessment of their likely success in convincing the government to embrace reform. As he pointed out in one of his first contributions from the floor of the Convention: 'For himself he had no hesitation in saying that all the craft, all the artifice, all the ingenuity, all the courtesy of that Convention would not gain a single Member of the House'.[53] For all the energy that he invested in the Convention however, O'Connor carefully maintained a direct link with the rank and file, interspersing sittings in London, and later Birmingham, with numerous public appearances and whirlwind tours that allowed him to commune directly with the people. In this respect he treated the Convention much as he had done the House of Commons.

From the outset O'Connor supported the discussion of ulterior measures. 'The strongest impression the Convention could make', he told the delegates, 'would be by taking their petition in one hand, and their ulterior measures in the other.'[54] It is important to stress that this stance was neither novel – it had been, for example, at the core of the campaign for the Reform Bill – nor peculiar to the Chartists at the time. The leading parliamentary spokesman for the corn law repealers, C.P. Villiers, believed that 'the brickbat argument is the only one that our nobles heed', a strategy later described by a pro-League newspaper as a form of 'salutary terrorism…that convinces spiritual and temporal Lords that concession is much more safe and more salutary than repression'.[55]

The question of ulterior measures provoked numerous resignations from the ranks of the Convention and resulted, following the overwhelming rejection of the petition in July, in the abortive general strike or National Holiday in early August and the tragic uprising in Newport at the beginning of November. O'Connor had been absent when the Convention finally committed itself to the strike – he was in court in York answering charges of sedition – but he was on hand to second the motion to cancel it a few days later. The view of the majority of the delegates was that the rank and file would not support the strike; their bluff had been called. In September, however, O'Connor insisted that the Convention had not failed and he called for another body to be elected to continue its work. Other Chartists took the government's rejection of their prayer as the cue to plot revolution and sharpen pikes. O'Connor was again absent at the crucial moment, a fact that his critics subsequently latched on to. According to Lovett, Feargus was 'apprehensive of being called upon to set an heroic example, in those rising times, [and] thought it a timely opportunity of visiting Ireland'.[56] R.G. Gammage, another Chartist with a personal axe to grind, later concluded: 'there is not a single man, whose judgement is worth one minute's consideration, but will without hesitation admit that the pretext was about as flimsy a one as could have been devised'.[57] In fact there is no direct evidence that O'Connor knew anything of the plans that were being developed. At the Convention he had not been the leader of the so-called 'physical force' Chartists – rather he had played a conciliatory role between the two factions and, as noted, he had acted decisively to call off the general strike. Epstein is correct to conclude that O'Connor's strategy of open intimidation was designed to avert revolution.[58]

Moreover, his visit to Ireland was not a 'flimsy' pretext. He went home for a combination of personal and political reasons. He had not been to Fort Robert since 1836 and his property had suffered from his neglect. The principal reason for his visit to Ireland was to attempt to establish a Chartist movement. This was no whim: it was a manifestation of O'Connor's passionate commitment to the creation of political unity between the people of Ireland and England. 'Universal suffrage is the battle that your order in England and Scotland are now fighting', he told a meeting of several thousands at Enniskeane near Fort Robert on 13 October, 'and it is the next battle that you must fight, and you shall fight with me at your head.'[59] No reader of the Convention debates could have been surprised that O'Connor headed for his native Cork at an early opportunity in order to expound this message. Early in the life of the Convention he had introduced Ireland into the debate, insisting that 'the grievances of the Irish are not a question of religion, but, as I shall prove, a question of the franchise'.[60] By August the Convention had resolved to send 'missionaries' to promote the cause in Ireland. The original intention was to send O'Connor and Bronterre O'Brien but in the end Robert Lowery and R.J. Richardson went in place of the 'Irish O's' of Chartism. The rough handling the missionaries received at the hands of O'Connell's supporters in Dublin led many to conclude that Chartism in Ireland 'should be let to work its own way for a while', but O'Connor was undeterred.[61] He had not altered his programme in the four years since he had last spoken to them, O'Connor told his 'political children' in the Catholic Chapel at Enniskeane: he was for universal suffrage, annual parliaments, vote by ballot, repeal of the union, total abolition of the tithes and the appointment of magistrates by the people. This was indeed the platform on which he had won Cork in 1832 and 1835. The only variation to his message was a passionate defence of the working men of England and Scotland – they were 'the best friends of Ireland' – against the attacks of O'Connell. He also lingered on the need to subdivide the land into 'convenient plots', a subject that he would return to many times during the 1840s.[62] O'Connor addressed several other large meetings in Cork but no organisation was generated. Still he was not deterred.

Conveniently or otherwise, the Irish tour took O'Connor out of harm's way as the Newport rising unfolded. No sooner was he back in England than he threw himself heart and soul into the defence of John Frost and his fellow conspirators, organising the nationwide defence fund and petitioning campaign and attending court on a daily basis. Soon, however, O'Connor had to prepare for his own legal battle. His prosecution for seditious libel commenced in March 1840 at York Court House. Nestled in the shadow of the ancient castle at York, the Court House provided O'Connor with an opportunity to re-enact the ordeal endured by his father more than two decades earlier in Trim. Early in the morning of 17 March a large crowd began to 'besiege' the doors of the late seventeenth century building and by 8.00 am the Court was crammed to capacity and a large force of police had been deployed to 'prevent confusion'. A 'greater degree of excitement', commented the reporter from the *Northern Star* with understandable exaggeration, 'was probably never before witnessed'.[63] Shortly before 9.00 the Attorney General, Sir John (later Baron) Campbell, arrived to conduct the prosecution in person, a role reserved for important cases. Campbell was a moderate Whig, known to favour triennial parliaments and the ballot, who had earlier advised against the prosecution of O'Connor (he believed the government would appear harsh and there was a risk of acquittal).[64] O'Connor himself arrived a few minutes later and spent some time looking around the Court before taking his seat.

After the charge against O'Connor was read and his plea of not guilty had been recorded Campbell opened the crown case by accusing O'Connor of fomenting insurrection to 'overturn established institutions by force'. O'Connor then defended himself in a marathon speech of over five hours. O'Connor's oration was part of a longstanding Anglo-Irish tradition of court room addresses from Wilkes and Tooke to Tone and Emmett. Some Chartists, for example, cut their political teeth by learning Robert Emmett's speech at his trial for treason. 'So much did I admire the daring courage of the young Irish rebel that I was never weary of reading his speech', recalled R.G. Gammage, 'I read and re-read until every word was fixed in my then tenacious memory'.[65] The bench mark had also been set by some of O'Connor's fellow Chartists who had already distinguished themselves in the court room. Take Peter Murray McDouall for example. According to William Aitken, an Ashton-under-Lyne Chartist, who sat in the crowded court room gallery, McDouall defended himself 'with a firmness and an eloquence which even his enemies could not but admire. There was no shrinking before that high tribunal from the principles he had advocated...' In a public house the following day, another Chartist, Thomas Dunning, found the special constables 'ordering in jugs of ale and drinking the health of Dr McDouall whose speech had converted them to Chartism'.[66]

As he rose to his feet O'Connor must have felt the weight of expectation upon him. He did not disappoint. Although several thousands words in length the report of the speech in the *Northern Star* is a fragment of the oration; it is nevertheless long enough to provide an understanding of both its content and the manner of its delivery. The content had several elements. First he made it clear that he regarded the Court as irrelevant. Addressing the jury he blithely said: 'I neither court your sympathy, desire your pity, or ask for your compassion'. 'I shall establish my innocence…', he continued, 'if not to your satisfaction, to the satisfaction, I trust, of the rest of the world.' This was a crucial point. Much as he had done in the House of Commons (and the Chartist Convention) he spoke not primarily to those within the institution but to the nation beyond it. The people were his jury. Who were the people? Including himself, he told the court, we 'have but six men in England and Scotland in our ranks above the order of working men'. To emphasize the importance of class in his conception he listed 'powers arrayed against them': 'The Monarch – the House of Lords – the House of Commons – the church – the army – the navy – the aristocracy – the middle classes – the local authorities – traitors – hired spies and informers'.[67] Moreover, O'Connor was acutely aware that the court provided him with a national platform to advocate Chartism that was not to be missed. The authority of the court could be flouted. As he later quipped 'Tis worth while to suffer a little imprisonment to get their Court House to meet in'; he had turned every day of the trial into a Chartist meeting 'with a judge in the chair'.[68]

Notwithstanding his opening denial of the authority of his prosecutors O'Connor then proceeded to devote a considerable part of his defence to legal argument. Whatever its legal merits, O'Connor conducted a wide ranging meditation on the law of libel, displaying his erudition by drawing on sources as diverse as Glanvill's twelfth century *Treatise on the Laws and Customs of England* and Blackstone's eighteenth century *Commentaries* to the trials of previous radicals such as Tooke and his father's colleague, Burdett. O'Connor buttressed his juridical argument with a history lecture. On the one hand he invoked the historic right to a free press guaranteed by the venerable Constitution. At the same time he made a bold claim for the sanction of history to the Chartist cause itself. How could he be guilty of sedition when what he was calling for was a 're-establishment of the Constitution' he asked? His persecutors, those who administered the Constitution, were acting against its principles. 'We have six points', he remarked, 'five of which are part and parcel of the constitution of England'. 'Universal suffrage', he continued, 'was the constitution itself up to the seventh year of the reign of Henry VI'; sessional parliaments 'were part of the constitution in the following reign'; equal representation was 'only broken into by successive Monarchs' to 'increase royal prerogative'; no property qualification had also existed and payment of members 'did not cease till the reign of Charles I'. In short, he concluded, 'we ask for no more than that which our ancestors possessed'.[69]

O'Connor was not the author of this radical interpretation of British constitutional history and he was not the only Chartist to advance it. Whatever the interpretation lacked in historical veracity, it wanted for nothing in rhetorical force. In fact, most Chartists claimed rights that they believed had been lost. Historians, such as James Epstein, have suggested that the court room environment imposed constitutional language on the defendants, forcing them to temper their revolutionary views and argue their defence within the limits of the system.[70] In O'Connor's case, however, there is no reason to believe that his constitutional position was not entirely genuine as it differed little from his other statements, before and after. The same is true of O'Connor's attitude to monarchy. O'Connor repeatedly insisted that he was a democrat, but not a republican and he was not changing his story to suit the circumstances. On this point he quoted from one of his own speeches. 'I am for a Monarchy, and an hereditary one', he had said on the hustings in Glasgow some months previously, 'provided the power behind the throne is greater than the throne itself'. In supporting a limited monarchy, which some Chartists called 'mild monarchy', O'Connor was speaking for the Chartist majority.[71]

The third element of his defence was a purely political attack on the Whig government. First, he raised the charge that had characterized many of his platform performances: hypocrisy. O'Connor detailed numerous instances during the Reform Bill crisis when members of the government had uttered or sanctioned sentiments similar to those that now saw O'Connor before the court. In order to intensify this line of attack special attention was given to Daniel O'Connell, whose votes the Government relied upon in the House of Commons. Referring to O'Connell as the Attorney's 'master' and the 'rotten prop of his expiring Government', O'Connor read into the court record a string of quotations from his erstwhile colleague which sounded every bit as seditious as anything published in the Northern Star. 'Gentleman, that is moral philosophy, while I am a destructive!', O'Connor stated with mock indignation. O'Connor was careful here to draw attention to the suffering of Ireland as a result of the pact between O'Connell and the Whigs. The 'Attorney General', he continued, 'has not learned to distinguish between the infamy of his supporters and the virtuous indignation which tyranny has brought upon his Government'. 'Gentleman, can I point out error in honied words?' he asked rhetorically, 'If so, teach me how to call adultery fascination; national plunder and universal bankruptcy, commercial distress and tyranny, persecution and prosecution, the necessary exercise of constitutional power.'

The final and perhaps most important element of his defence was his self presentation as a Whig martyr in waiting. For all that O'Connor sought to turn the trial into a Chartist meeting and broaden the agenda into a discussion of the nation's grievances he never let the subject drift far from himself. A court case was ideally suited to this purpose; it was intrinsically about him. In positioning himself as a victim O'Connor advanced a careful admixture of self-deprecation and egotism. '[I]s there such a magic spell in my voice', he asked at one point, 'as to persuade a well-fed people that they are a starving people; a well-clothed people that they are naked; a well-housed people that they are ill lodged; and a well protected people, that they are out of the pale of the law?' Yes and no. 'Am I to be the only man found guilty of libels without the intent being proved' he later asked? Yes and no. As indicated O'Connor began by defying the authority of the court and by daring the jurors to find him guilty. Later O'Connor enlisted the aid of the radical sympathiser and *enfant terrible* of his father's generation, Lord Byron, quoting from *Marino Faliero* to accentuate his earlier stand:[72]

> They never fail who die
> In a great cause; the block may soak their gore;
> Their heads may sodden in the sun; their limbs
> Be strung to city gates and castle walls –
> But their spirit still walks abroad.

The popular image of the Venetian Doge executed in 1355 in the cause of 'freedom' still lingered in the air when O'Connor addressed his final words to the jury: 'Send me then to my dungeon; that dungeon, with my principles unsullied, will be a paradise'.[73]

When assessing the impact of O'Connor's performance outside the court room it is equally important to consider not only its content but also the manner in which it was delivered. In one sense the published report is inadequate for this purpose. 'Only those who heard the rapid, the manly, the sarcastic, and eloquent appeal of the Learned Gentleman', conceded the *Star*'s correspondent, can 'judge the electrical effect which it had on all present'. Not only was the bar 'astonished' the reporter himself was moved to a significant admission: 'we confess that we did not think him possessed of one half of the power and ability which throughout he displayed'. Even from the truncated report it is nevertheless possible to appreciate the rhythm of the address, interspersing juridical commentary and political polemic with satire, comedy and literary allusions, and we are given glimpses of the range and dramatic force employed, from 'withering scorn' to mockery, mimicry and comedy. At one point, for example, O'Connor apparently noticed that the Attorney General had laid his head upon his hands. Unable to resist the opportunity this presented he interrupted his diatribe against the Whigs to suggest that his prosecutor was, not surprisingly, hanging his head in shame. The report makes it clear that humour was O'Connor's object here: 'the Attorney-General threw back his head, opened his mouth wide as if to join in the laugh, and blushed to his very ears, while the Judge, the Barristers, and the audience were literally convulsed with laughter'. Later O'Connor entertained the court with an anecdote about an Irish peasant boy given a bad shilling to illustrate the government's attempts to prosecute him. The story was greeted with 'roars of laughter' and an effect that the reporter endeavoured unsuccessfully to translate into text: 'It is impossible to give any idea of the effect produced by this Irish anecdote, told, as it was, with the look and in the very dialect of an arch Irish peasant boy'. The court room was the perfect nexus between politics and the theatre.

Not unexpectedly O'Connor (according to his later account) was inundated with letters and messages of congratulation on his marathon oration. Equally unsurprisingly the speech had no effect on the outcome of trial; the jury devoted 'about ten minutes' to deliberation before finding O'Connor guilty. He would get his opportunity to play the role of Whig martyr. The Attorney General asked for an immediate sentencing but O'Connor won a small legal victory by successfully arguing for a delay. Within a week he was using a speech at a large meeting in Manchester to defy his persecutors. 'What mattered it to him', he told the crowd, 'how long or how often they incarcerated him?' The 'only boon he would ask', O'Connor continued in a glib gesture of expiation, was 'that the incarceration of all those poor labourers who had been thrown into prison should be laid upon his shoulders'.[74] It is only with hindsight that these words sound hollow and perhaps even disingenuous; at the time his speech was met with 'renewed and deafening cheers'. Ignoring the fact that he had not been found guilty of a capital crime O'Connor concluded his remarks with a vision of the ultimate sacrifice: 'I leave you now, saying, as I have always said, that if I have to die in this cause, though I be stretched on the rack, I will even there smile terror out of countenance, and die as I have lived – a pure lover of liberty'.[75] Soon, however, the 'Renewed and deafening cheers' that greeted this vision ceased to ring in his ears and he faced the loss not only of his freedom but also of his most effective political weapon: his physical presence. O'Connor well knew that some commentators were already speculating that a custodial sentence would put paid to his political career.[76] Early in May he returned to Court and was sentenced to eighteen months imprisonment in York Castle. He was determined that, like the Venetian Doge, his spirit would still walk abroad.

Notes

1   'The Life and Adventures of Feargus O'Connor', *National Instructor*, 28 September 1850, p. 295.

2   N. Hamilton, *The National Gazetteer of Great Britain and Ireland*, London, 1868, vol. 5, pp. 178-9; E. Walford, *Old and New London: A Narrative of Its History, Its People, and Its Places*, London, n.d. [1878], vol. 6, pp. 529-548.

3   See D. Read and E. Glasgow, *Feargus O'Connor: Irishman and Chartist*, London, 1961, p. 46; *Manchester and Salford Advertiser*, 28 November 1835.

4   *Manchester and Salford Advertiser*, 12 December 1835.

5   J. Epstein, *The Lion of Freedom*, London, 1982, p. 24.

6   *Manchester Times*, 19 December 1835.

7   Epstein, *The Lion of Freedom*, p 33.

8   Cited in H. Jephson, *The Platform: Its Rise and Progress*, London, 1892, vol. 2, p. 223. See also W. O'Neill Daunt, *Ireland And Her Agitators*, Dublin, 1845, p. 139.

9   'The Life and Adventures of Feargus O'Connor', *National Instructor*, 23 November 1850, p. 423.

10 'The Life and Adventures of Feargus O'Connor', *National Instructor*, 9 November 1850, p. p. 394.

11 'The Life and Adventures of Feargus O'Connor', *National Instructor*, 16 November 1850, p. 407.

12 'The Life and Adventures of Feargus O'Connor', *National Instructor*, 30 November 1850, p. 441; 7 December 1855, pp. 455, 456.

13 'The Life and Adventures of Feargus O'Connor', *National Instructor*, 1 February 1851, p. 72f. Epstein notes that it was already current in the radical press. See *Lion of Freedom*, p. 41.

14 'The Life and Adventures of Feargus O'Connor', *National Instructor*, 22 February 1851, pp. 119-120.

15 'The Life and Adventures of Feargus O'Connor', *National Instructor*, 22 February 1851, pp. 119-120.

16 *The Times*, 19 December 1836.

17 *The Times*, 14 January 1837.

18 *Nottingham Review*, 26 November 1836.

19 *Nottingham Review*, 26 November 1836.

20 See J. Knott, *Popular Opposition to the 1834 Poor Law*, New York, 1986, p. 134.

21 R. Oastler, *Damnation! Eternal Damnation to the Fiend-Begotten, 'Coarser Food' New Poor Law*, London, 1837, pp. 4-5. I am grateful to Tina Parolin for bringing this pamphlet to my attention.

22 Knott, *Popular Opposition*, p. 134.

23 Epstein, *Lion of Freedom*, p. 97.

24 *Northern Star*, 20 January 1838.

25 *Manchester Times*, 29 July 1837.

26 *Northern Star*, 20 January 1838.

27 *Northern Star*, 13 January 1838.

28 See O.R. Ashton and P.A. Pickering, *Friends of the People: Uneasy Radicals in the Age of the Chartists*, London, 2002.

29 *Northern Star*, 10 February 1838.

30 W. Lovett, *Life and Struggles of William Lovett* (1876), London, 1967, p. 134.

31 *Northern Star*, 24 February 1838.

32 The extent of O'Connor's contribution is unclear but I agree with Jim Epstein that it must have been substantial.

33 R.R. Madden, *The United Irishmen, Their Lives and Times*, Second Series, London, 1843, vol. 2, p. 303. O'Connor's paper was called the *Press*. Elsewhere he wrote that a free press was the 'best benefactor of mankind' (see Madden, *United Irishmen*, p. 299).

34 R.R. Madden, *The United Irishmen, Their Lives and Times*, First Series, London, 1842, vol. 2, pp. 50-3; Read and Glasgow, *Feargus O'Connor*, p. 56.

35 *Northern Star*, 10 February 1838. This role has not been previously identified.

36 Cited in Read and Glasgow, *Feargus O'Connor*, p. 57.

37 *Northern Star*, 11 July 1840.

38 W.E. Adams, *Memoirs of A Social Atom* (1903), New York, 1968, p. 164.

39 *Northern Star*, 3 April 1839; Epstein, *Lion of Freedom*, p. 86n. See also J. Allen and O. Ashton (eds), *Papers for the People: A Study of the Chartist Press*, London, 2005.

40 *Northern Star*, 8 August 1840. O'Connor's estimation is not too far from other contemporary calculations. As Donald Read has shown the *Manchester Times* and *Manchester Guardian* were reckoned to have between fifty and eighty readers for every copy. See *Press and People 1790-1850*, London, 1961, p. 202.

41 W. O'Neill Daunt, *A Life Spent for Ireland*, London, 1896, p. 25.

42 See G.J. Holyoake, *Sixty Years of An Agitator's Life*, London, 1906, pp. 106-7.

43 I. and P. Kuczynski (eds), *A Young Revolutionary in Nineteenth-Century England: Selected Writings of Georg Weerth*, Berlin, 1971, p. 113.

44 *Northern Star*, 19 January 1839.

45 *Northern Star*, 25 March 1848.

46 *Northern Star*, 16 October 1838. Byron, *The Siege of Corinth*, 1816, verse XVIII, 'Remnants of that that have pass'd away/ Fragments of stone, rear'd by creatures of clay'.

47 *Northern Star*, 16 October 1838.

48 *Northern Star*, 16 October 1838.

49 See O'Connell to FitzPatrick, 11 February 1839, *The correspondence of Daniel O'Connell*, edited by M. R. O'Connell, Dublin, 1972, vol. 6, p. 216; Read and Glasgow, *Feargus O'Connor*, p. 81.

50 *Northern Star*, 9 February 1839.

51 *Northern Star*, 9 February 1839.

52 The expression was coined by Josiah Quincy and used also by Henry Clay.

53 *Northern Star*, 16 February 1839.

54 *Northern Star*, 16 February 1839.

55 See *Manchester Examiner*, 18 March 1848. See P.A. Pickering, 'Peaceably if We Can, Forcibly if We Must: Political Violence and Insurrection in Early-Victorian Britain', in B. Bowden and M.T. Davis (eds), *Terror*, Brisbane, 2007, forthcoming.

56 Lovett, *Life and Struggles*, pp. 198-9.

57 R.G. Gammage, *History of the Chartist Movement* (1854), New York, 1969, p. 265.

58   Epstein, *Lion of Freedom*, pp. 145, 154.

59   *Northern Star*, 19 October 1839; Read and Glasgow, *Feargus O'Connor*, p. 88.

60   *Charter*, 24 February 1839.

61   *Charter*, 8 September 1839; *Northern Star*, 18 September 1839; 5 October 1839.

62   *Northern Star*, 19 October 1839.

63   *Northern Star*, 21 March 1840.

64   F.C. Mather, *Public Order in the Age of the Chartists*, Manchester, 1959, p. 46.

65   W.H. Maehl (ed.), *Robert Gammage: Reminiscences of a Chartist* (1883-5), Manchester, 1983, p. 39.

66   'Reminiscences of Thomas Dunning' reprinted in D. Vincent (ed.), *Testaments of Radicalism*, London, 1977, pp. 137, 140; R.G. Hall and S. Roberts, *William Aitken: The Writings of a Nineteenth Century Working Man* (1869), Tameside, 1996, p. 39. For McDouall's speech see *Manchester and Salford Advertiser*, 24 August 1839.

67   *Northern Star*, 21 March 1840. See also 'The Queen against Feargus O'Connor', J. MacDonell (ed.), *Reports of State Trials*, London, 1892, vol. IV, cols. 1352-1366.

68   *Northern Star*, 21 March 1840; Epstein, *Lion of Freedom*, p. 211.

69   *Northern Star*, 21 March 1840.

70   See J. Epstein, *In Practice: Studies in the Language and Culture of Popular Politics in Modern Britain*, Stanford, 2003, chapter 3.

71   See P.A. Pickering, 'The Hearts of the Millions: Chartism and Popular Monarchism in the 1840s', *History*, vol. 88, no. 290, April 2003, pp. 227-248.

72   Byron, *Marino Faliero*, 1820, Act II, Sc. 2. The story had been painted by Eugenè Delacroix in 1827 and turned into an opera by Gaetano Donizetti in 1835.

73   *Northern Star*, 21 March 1840.

74   *Northern Star*, 28 March 1840.

75   *Northern Star*, 28 March 1840. He was fond of this turn of phrase having used it in 1832. See Daunt, *Ireland and Her Agitators*, p. 132.

76   See Read and Glasgow, *Feargus O'Connor*, p. 89.

6: NO SURRENDER

O'Connor slipped quietly out through the gates of his 'Whig dungeon' on Thursday evening, 26 August 1841, four days earlier than expected and three months prior to the expiry of his sentence, and checked into Etridge's Hotel in Blake Street near the Minster in the heart of the ancient city of York. There, according to the *Northern Star*, 'he was visited by men of all parties and of all ranks in York, congratulating him on his release, and paying him personal respect'.[1] The Chartists were in no doubt that O'Connor's early release was a deliberate attempt on the part of the authorities to upset the elaborate plans that had been laid to celebrate his liberation on the following Monday. If that had been their intention they were to be disappointed. Over the course of the weekend delegates and well-wishers gathered from far and wide in the 'priest-ridden city' to witness O'Connor's liberation, albeit re-enacted.

At one o'clock on Monday 30 August a massive crowd gathered at the prison gate. The walls of the castle were arrayed with many flags and banners and a 'magnificent triumphal car, built and fitted up expressly for the occasion by the good men of York' stood waiting to receive the guest of honour. Drawn by six white horses, with postilions resplendent in the traditional colours of radicalism, green jackets and caps and white breeches, the car was shaped as a conch shell and decorated in pink and green velvet. A symbol that resonates across cultures and time, the conch shell has been variously understood to represent high rank, dignity, to herald battle or auspicious news and reincarnation. The York Chartists did not explain their choice but all of the above possibilities were apposite. The arrival of the carriage prompted the crowd to chant for O'Connor who was 'soon at its side', providing the illusion of release at the appointed hour. According to the report in the *Northern Star* O'Connor's appearance 'was received with a shout, which penetrated into the gloomiest cell' of the gaol 'gladdening the hearts of many of the miserable captives who he left behind him'. The reporter commented, first, on O'Connor's clothing:

> Mr O'Connor was habited, as he had promised, in fustian. He wore a full suit, made out of a piece which had been manufactured expressly for the occasion, and was presented by those who had not only his welfare at

heart, but were imbued with his principles, and with his spirit – the blistered hand and fustian jackets of Manchester.[2]

O'Connor's 'first' words to the crowd were to exhort them to peaceful conduct and to return thanks to 'Almighty God' for 'the graceful and merciful manner, in which, whilst *almost hid from human eye*, he preserved me from the oppressor's toils'. He then proceeded to explain the symbolism of his dress:

> I have appeared, Brother Chartists and working men, amongst you in fustian, the emblem of your order, in order to convince you, at a single glance, that what I was when I left you, the same do I return to you.

These first words represent a critical juncture in the history of Chartism and in his public life: they provide crucial insight into his prison experience and the path that he envisaged for the future (see plates 2 and 3).

O'Connor had entered the Castle at York fifteen months earlier under a cloud of uncertainty. Friend and foe alike were unsure of how he would cope with the loss of his most important political asset: his personal presence. Even before he left London O'Connor had an opportunity to keep his name before the public. According to his own account, he had been taken from the court room to the infirmary of Queen's Bench where his doctors mounted a case that he was too ill to travel. The government rejected the plea and he was transported from London to York and lodged in what was known as the 'hospital' in the Castle. The fact that the rejection of O'Connor's medical appeal became a matter of public controversy gave the authorities adequate warning of what was to come. Soon the conditions of his incarceration made O'Connor fleetingly the centre of public and parliamentary attention. Although prisoners had been detained on the site since the thirteenth century O'Connor was housed in the relatively new male prison that had been built in 1835 according to the ideas about penology that were becoming fashionable at that time. In keeping with the belief that prison reformation was best promoted by constant surveillance the male prison featured the governor's house at the centre of four radial wings. In theory this allowed him the opportunity to supervise all his charges continuously but O'Connor was located at the 'very extremity' of the building, 'quite out of ear-shot, and shut out from human observation, or communication by countless iron gates'. His cell was a large, vaulted stone room that he was permitted to furnish himself.[3] This was one of the privileges usually extended to political prisoners of previous generations, but it was here that the concessions to O'Connor stopped. In most other respects he was to be subjected to treatment that bore the hallmarks of the new 'reformed' prison system designed to 'grind men good'.[4]

According to this regime, O'Connor was forced to wear prison dress and undertake prison labour (scrubbing the floor, for example), and, much to his chagrin, he was fed prison rations. Within days, he later recalled, he was refusing meals – 'I lived upon fury and frenzy'.[5] His treatment differed little from that meted out to a common felon and he was compelled, as one commentator noted, to 'associate with thieves and others convicted of disgraceful crimes'. Moreover, his correspondence was opened and special restrictions were placed on his visitors. Significantly, O'Connor was informed that he was not permitted to write for publication and that any visitor found to have carried a communication from him would be banned from any future visits. 'If ever man or beast was so treated before, I am ignorant of it', O'Connor complained: 'What! SOLITARY CONFINEMENT FOR EIGHTEEN MONTHS? …I am now worse than dead! I am to be buried alive in a stone coffin; at the mercy of every one who pleases to insult me!'[6]

The reaction of the Chartist press to 'barbarous treatment' of their leader was swift and predictably strident. 'It is contrary to reason and to justice, that any political offender, unless he be proved a traitor to society, should be punished as a *felon*!', fumed the editor of the *Star*, 'It is against the principles of our Constitution, that any Briton, convicted of an inferior, should suffer for a superior offence!'[7] Within weeks of his incarceration O'Connor's treatment became a public scandal, earning him sympathy in unlikely quarters. 'One of the most animated conversations of the whole week', opined the editor of the *Spectator*, 'was on the subject of the treatment of Mr Feargus O'Connor, a state prisoner in York Castle'. Dr John Epps, a moderate London reformer and erstwhile opponent of O'Connor, took out a subscription to the *Star* to protest against the harsh treatment of political prisoners.[8] Despite insisting that O'Connor was being treated in accordance with the rules the government hastily dispatched prison inspectors to York and subsequently urged the local authorities to modify some of the conditions of his imprisonment: O'Connor would now be permitted to provide his own food, coal and candles and allocated a turnkey to wait upon him; was to be given a private yard to walk in and permitted unlimited visits from friends; and, he was to be allowed books and newspapers, and pen and paper to write (although not for publication).[9] It was too little too late.

In the House of Commons members from all points of the political firmament – from the respectable London radical, Thomas Duncombe, to the rising star of the Tory backbench, Benjamin Disraeli – pressed the government on the detail of the case and enquired about an apparent change of policy. Duncombe described the treatment of O'Connor as 'outrageous and disgraceful to the country' and pointed to the inconsistency with the rules applied to radicals a few years earlier: 'Mr. Cobbett and Mr. Hunt were allowed to continue to write their papers under similar circumstances, and why should not Mr. O'Connor?' Other members contrasted the treatment of O'Connor with that applied to Sir Francis Burdett in the 1790s. Disraeli drew the point to a powerful conclusion by invoking the proceedings of the notorious Star Chamber of Archbishop Laud in the 1630s. The 'question', he told the House, 'was whether a great change had not taken place in the punishment of political offenders? (Cheers.)': 'The Hon. Member for Finsbury had shown that since the year 1792, no political offenders had been treated as they had been by the present Government. He maintained that in no period, except the worst period of history, had they been so treated.' Even Daniel O'Connell 'could not help raising his voice against the injustice' of the 'hideous' treatment of O'Connor.[10] 'The little amelioration that has been wrung from them', protested the *Star*, 'does but show how deeply rooted is their hatred and their fear'.[11] In a public letter to Lord Normanby, O'Connor brought the argument full circle by comparing his treatment to that meted out to his father and uncle by the Tories in the 1790s: 'Lord Castlereagh violated every pledge, and wilfully misrepresented every occurrence which took place between Government and the state prisoners, but all through there is no attempt to suppress the letters of these prisoners intended for publication'.[12]

Notwithstanding the strain of incarceration, O'Connor must have been delighted: the government had appeared to single him out for harsh treatment (thereby underscoring his claim that he uniquely personified the Chartist cause) and contrived to make him the centre of national attention. The mantle of martyr sat comfortably. Moreover, as a steady stream of communications proved, enforcing the ban on writing for publication was well nigh impossible. Far from being 'buried alive' in anonymity as he feared, his voice, he now boasted, had 'burst the walls of his cell'.[13] Over the next year O'Connor's pen was prolific. Early in 1841 he claimed to have completed a novel entitled *The Devil on Three Sticks* which, he boasted, 'he would fearlessly place in competition with the work of any living author'.[14] Unlike his earlier plays, no clues to the contents of this work have emerged (the title refers to a well known children's carnival game). Other writings were published. First, he gave full reign to his lyrical muse. He was not the only Chartist to explore a poetic form of expression whilst in prison; the irascible Thomas Cooper, for example, composed his masterpiece, *The Purgatory of Suicides*, in Stafford Gaol.[15] Unlike Cooper's deftly crafted and well-received verse, however, O'Connor produced little more than pedestrian abstractions in iambic pentameter:[16]

Let England, Scotland, Erin too,
Join hearts to gain the Charter:

The laws are made but for the few,
Our rights are in the Charter.

Even his most ardent supporters could have found little to recommend these hackneyed offerings. Whatever he lacked as a bard, however, he made up for with an irrepressible self-belief:[17]

Now Daniel, my hearty,
I'll break up your party,
Though muffled and fetter'd and tongue-tied in York;
You cunning old mouser!
How do you feel now, Sir?
When you are no more, I'll be Member for Cork.

On another occasion O'Connor dabbled with the ultimate conceit expressed in the third person:[18]

O'Connor is our chosen chief,
He's champion of the Charter:
Our Saviour suffer'd like a thief,
Because he preached the Charter.

More interesting than the trite poetry was the rubric under which he presented it: a regular column entitled the 'Dungeon Mirror', or 'York Castle Mirror; Feargus O'Connor's Looking Glass'. A decade later he offered a plausible explanation for the title,[19] but it is useful to consider what else he might have meant by it. Given that the contents of the poems provide plenty of evidence of the author's high opinion of himself, it is hard not to see Feargus's Mirror as analogous to Echo's pond that trapped the young Narcissus with a fatal image of himself. O'Connor would undoubtedly have been familiar with Ovid's story as he would with Shakespeare's 62nd Sonnet: 'Methinks no face so gracious as mine,/ No shape so true, no truth of such account,/…But when my glass shows me myself indeed,/ Beated and chopt with tann'd antiquity,/ Mine own self-love quite contrary I read; Self so self-loving were iniquity'.[20] For all that the trope was a familiar one, O'Connor seems to have missed the point.

On the other hand, he may not have intended the Looking Glass to denote a process of self reflection. Rather, he may have seen his Mirror as a contribution to the process of collective introspection that was underway among his audience. The incarceration of numerous national and local leaders had sent the Chartist movement into retreat and provoked earnest discussion of future tactics and objectives. This was a time when countless schemes to reorganise, reorient and revitalise the campaign were tabled. Most importantly these discussions gave rise to the National Charter Association. Established at Manchester in July 1840 the National Charter Association was, commentators and historians since Marx and Engels agree, the 'first working men's party the world ever produced'.[21] From his cell O'Connor enthusiastically promoted this development. As James Epstein has noted, O'Connor's leadership was subsequently 'inextricably associated' with the National Charter Association; he became the 'greatest agitator' in its service, and 'its most prominent spokesman and defender'.[22] Nevertheless, O'Connor was determined to have his say more broadly in what he clearly regarded as an expansive process of purification and renewal. In one intervention, for example, he argued that the movement's salvation could be achieved by the establishment of a daily newspaper. It is surely no accident that O'Connor proposed this at a time when the press was his only conduit to his audience. The project was to be financed by £1 shares paid off in instalments and underwritten by O'Connor himself. The sum required to put the *Morning Star* on the streets, he admitted, would be £20,000.[23] The time was not right and the proposal was, not surprisingly, ignored.

In fact, O'Connor penned hundreds of thousands of words for publication in defiance of the government ban. Often his letters ran to four and five columns, dominating the contents of the *Star* in ways that he had not done previously. Three interventions that dramatically shaped the course of the movement are worthy of note. The first was a plea for purity. During 1840 a tract by William Lovett, former Secretary of the London Working Men's Association where the People's Charter had originated, and John Collins of Birmingham, entitled *Chartism: A New Organisation of the People*, outlined a comprehensive proposal for a National Association for 'Promoting the Political and Social Improvement of the People' through a system of national education. The book (written in prison) was well received. Late in 1840 another group of London based Chartists, including several veterans of the Working Men's Association such as Henry Vincent, Henry Hetherington and John Cleave, issued an Address which identified 'the ignorance and the vices of the people' as the 'chief impediments in the way of all social and political improvement' and called on Chartists to take the teetotal pledge.[24] This initiative was also warmly received. At about the same time a number of Chartist Churches were established in Scotland, Wales, in the West Country, and in the Midlands at Birmingham. These Churches were founded upon a simple premise: 'No man, we believe, can be a true Christian unless he is also a sincere Christian Chartist, for Jesus Christ is the Divine founder of the Christian Chartist Church, and the prime teacher of our political doctrines'.[25] Earlier, in 1840, the Leeds Parliamentary Reform Association had been established to promote co-operation between middle and working class radicals on a platform of household suffrage.

From his prison cell in York O'Connor issued a blistering attack on what he dubbed the 'quadruple alliance' to effectively impose additional qualifications on the suffrage. Describing himself as a 'sober, knowledge-loving Christian, AND A Chartist', he railed against those who sought to establish a 'man's adhesion to any of them, as a political test':

> I object to Teetotal Chartism, because all who do not join it, and I fear there will be many, will be considered unworthy of their civil rights. I object to Knowledge Chartism, because it impliedly acknowledges a standard of some sort of learning, education, or information, as a necessary qualification to entitle a man to his political rights…I object to Household Suffrage Chartism, because it is not Chartism at all.

Rising to his task O'Connor gave full reign to his splenetic wit. Insisting that only those committed to the six points had a right to the name of Chartism he concluded:

> Let them call themselves the Hokey Pokey, New Brummagem, or old Jerusalem, froth and flummerites, and preach Southey and Shelley, and play the Highland bagpipes, as a means of regenerating man, till they are black in the face…[26]

The barrage should not have been unexpected. Even before his cell door had clanged shut behind him O'Connor had composed a plea to the London Chartists to resist the embrace of the middle-class liberals running the campaign against the Corn Laws: 'Join them now, and they will laugh at you; stand out like men, and THEY MUST JOIN YOU for the Charter'.[27] Nevertheless, O'Connor's words rocked the movement to its core. Although few Chartists had dabbled with household suffrage or the Corn Law repealers, many of his close supporters had endorsed other aspects of the 'New Move'. Even William Hill, the editor of the *Northern Star*, insisted that O'Connor's attack was misplaced, a result of being out of touch due to incarceration.[28]

Why was he so vehement in his opposition? For Gammage, O'Connor was only interested in a 'mob, which should conclude every meeting with three cheers for Feargus O'Connor'.[29] Not surprisingly, Lovett felt that the 'lowest passions of the multitude were appealed to, to obtain a clamorous verdict against us'; their plan 'denounced as a "new move", concocted by Hume, Roebuck and O'Connell for destroying his power'.[30] Lovett and others – eighty-seven signa-

tories in all – exacerbated the situation by taking steps to found the National
Association that had been foreshadowed in *Chartism*. Based on the premise that
'no earthly power can prevent an intelligent people from obtaining their rights',
the Association was to be a vehicle to 'rescue' the people 'from the thraldom of
their own vices'.[31] To O'Connor it looked like a crude attempt to establish a rival organisation to the National Charter Association. O'Connor was undoubtedly spoiling for a fight and seized his opportunity to settle some scores in the
movement following up his initial assault by issuing a list of eighty-seven local
leaders – the 'Old list' – he believed worthy of the people's trust: 'I am in the
old, my enemies are in the new; declare for one or the other...'[32] As Lovett later
complained, even some who sought to retract their support of the 'New Move'
as a result of O'Connor's 'storm of vituperation' were rancorously branded as
'rats escaping from the trap'.[33] To Lovett's chagrin O'Connor had succeeded
again in personalising Chartist politics: the argument was about him.

At the same time, O'Connor certainly spoke from a combination of broader
tactical and principled considerations. Behind every offer of common cause
O'Connor saw a trap. Mixing the Charter with other causes would, he believed,
dissipate the people's energy and resolve:

> I look for the Charter to promote Christianity, to insure temperance, to
> inculcate knowledge, and to give the House and *something more*, while the
> use of those several qualifications, as a means to an end, will but place the
> Charter, year after year, farther from our reach.[34]

It would also provide the enemies of the people with an open-ended list of reasons to withhold popular rights. He was clearly exasperated by this prospect.
Soon, O'Connor forecast, the 'humbugs' and 'crotchet mongers' would be back
for more: 'We shall then have washing and cleaning Chartists declaring that
you are too dirty for enfranchisement'.[35] The lesson of the Reform Bill agitation was never far from his mind: 'So believe me, my good and worthy fustian
jackets, blistered hands, and unshorn chins', O'Connor warned, 'that no one of
the crotchet mongers will abate a pin's point of his dogma to carry the Charter'. As we have seen, O'Connor distrusted the strategy of Lovett and others to
work with middle-class radicals (including O'Connell) and he suggested that
their willingness to negotiate reflected the fact that they were not 'real' working
men: their chins were shorn, their jackets made of broadcloth and their hands
smooth. Inevitably they would lead the people to the sin of compromise. The
interconnected themes of class and independence underpinned this intervention as with much of O'Connor's political thinking. Apart from the ceremony
to celebrate his release, O'Connor did not sport a fustian jacket either, but he

was the exception that proved the rule: 'My friends, get your Charter, and I will answer for the religion, sobriety, knowledge, and house, and a bit of land into the bargain'.[36]

O'Connor's second noteworthy intervention was in relation to electoral politics. Independence and class were at its heart also. Invariably, O'Connor's previous electioneering (on his own behalf and on behalf of others) had been characterised by a determination to stand apart from both major parties. In practical terms the beneficiaries of his obdurate attitude had been variously O'Connellite liberals and Tories depending on the seat and the circumstances. In June 1841, however, he urged Chartists to support the Tories in the coming general election. Returning to the theme of his many speeches in the House of Commons – betrayal – O'Connor argued that the Whigs had forfeited any claim to popular support: 'Now, comrades, I thus sum up: for forty-one years the Whigs used you for obtaining political power; for nine years they have held that power... They have insulted you, betrayed you, despised and loathed you!' Again, he was surely referring to himself, a conclusion that is clear from his gleeful vision of the discomfiture of Lord John Russell and Daniel O'Connell that he sketched: 'Just get the Whigs once off the perch, the golden perch, and little Jack and the Big Beggerman will froth at the mouth like mad blood-hounds...'[37]

O'Connor's epistle called forth a torrent of criticism from liberals, moderate radicals and from some Chartists, but the suggestion that he was revealing his true colours as a Tory radical is, in fact, difficult to sustain. On the contrary he could not have been clearer in emphasising his distaste for Tory and Whig alike: 'vote boldly against the devils', he argued, 'by voting for the devils in hell!' Admittedly, the Whigs had been the object of most of O'Connor's public criticism but this is hardly surprising given that they had occupied the 'St Stephen's cockpit', as he put it, for the best part of a decade. The Whigs had unseated and imprisoned him, but his motivation was not merely revenge. For all that it appears fanciful with hindsight, O'Connor's proposal was actually based on a persuasive tactical argument. A Tory victory, he suggested, would put the Whigs 'at the same side of the hedge as you': 'if you get a House of Tories you get a good working Whig-Chartist opposition'. Many radicals supported the Whigs as the lesser of two evils. O'Connor drew exactly the opposite conclusion from this argument: it was reason to vote against them, not for them. 'A Tory minority never will oppose tyranny', he contended, 'a Whig minority must do so to acquire popular support...'[38] O'Connor's approach to the 1841 election was thus based on expediency and tactical considerations, and should not be judged according to principle. In relation to principle his framework remained remarkably consistent. In the month before his release O'Connor opted for an extended sporting metaphor to emphasise the independence of the people for either of the major parties: 'the people have now had quite enough of the great-cricket match between Whigs and Tories', he told the landlords of Ireland, 'The Tories had a long innings, and left a heavy score before they were run out; the Whigs have in turn been bowled out...' Now, he continued, 'we must try a match of all Britain and Ireland against the oligarchy. And believe me, the Britons and Irish will catch the oligarchy out at every ball they strike'.[39]

It is no accident that O'Connor prefaced his electoral advice by invoking a sense of class solidarity: 'In a little more than four months I shall meet you in a full suit of fustian at my prison gates...Let us then, in one dress, and in one mind, be able to embrace and return thanks to God that Chartism has survived'.[40] The significance of his suit of fustian, manufactured in the commonplace cloth of everyday working-class life, was twofold. First, it was a symbol of unity between leader and led. When, for example, the 'Women of Manchester' commissioned a banner to celebrate O'Connor's release they encapsulated this sense of unanimity in the vista they ordered: O'Connor was shown 'dressed in fustian, with the People's Charter in his hand. At a short distance behind him appear a large assemblage of people, the males dressed in fustian'.[41] A similar objective led a Chartist weaver from Preston in Lancashire to write an open letter to enquire about the colour of the suit. Admitting that his 'heart often beats high when I contemplate the pleasure I shall have in seeing you released from your dungeon', he stated: 'if we poor devils are ever permitted to have another new jacket, we could like the same colour'.[42]

If, in this way, the suit represented the solidarity between a popular leader and his followers, it was a symbol that had been negotiated on entirely new terms. Fustian was an unequivocal symbol of working-class life that, as a uniform for public performance, reflected the growing redundancy of 'gentleman' leaders. As William Martin, a Bradford Chartist, stated at the meeting that followed O'Connor's liberation: the people retained confidence in O'Connor because he was an 'honest aristocrat', but they 'were determined to place confidence in men of their own order'.[43] No one understood this better than O'Connor himself. By donning a suit of fustian it could be argued that he was, at one level, merely attempting to forestall an implied threat to his leadership but, at that same time, it is clear that this was a challenge that he welcomed and nurtured. 'My aim and end through life', he wrote in March 1840, 'has been to make you independent of me and all other leaders; and never until you are thrown upon your resources, shall I consider the great cause of freedom likely to be achieved'.[44] His pride in the National Charter Association, as well as his passionate and, at times, destructive, commitment to independent working-class radicalism, were both fired by this aspiration. 'No Surrender' was not a hollow slogan; it summed up his mature thinking. In this way we should regard the suit of fustian as he intended it, as a tribute, a mark of respect that signified what he believed was an important transition in popular politics. At the soirée that followed the liberation parade he made the same point:

> Allow me, in the first instance, to return those delegates, who have come from a distance to attend this meeting, my warmest gratitude and heartfelt thanks, and through them allow me to return thanks to those who sent them here, – (hear, hear.) – the fustian jackets, the blistered hands, and the unshorn chins – the poor, – (cheers,) – those who are, in fact, an ornament to their country.[45]

William Lovett hoped the people would not be duped: the 'working classes', he wrote, 'have got a habit of penetrating below the surface of things. Balderdash and bullying, fustian and yellow silk, may cajole them once or twice. But a reaction of sound sense will come'.[46] He was to be disappointed. For the Chartist majority fustian remained a symbol of the struggle for rights on their own terms, a symbol of class without words.

Having said that, O'Connor's notion of class was capacious; intuitive rather than cerebral, grounded in a compassionate hatred of oppression rather than a theoretical grasp of political economy. In his voluminous writings and reported speeches he identified at least six classes often using characteristically colourful terms for rhetorical effect. There was, for example, not one aristocracy but two: between 'the people and their rights', he told a Manchester audience in 1842, were 'two great ocracies…the sod-ocracy and smoke-ocracy'.[47] The middle class too was divided. 'The manufacturers don't call themselves an aristocracy, but a *middle class*', O'Connor argued, 'Now I call them the smoke-ocracy, and I call the shopkeepers, who are the agents between the consumers and producers, the middle class.'[48] Similarly, as William Lovett and his comrades in London well knew, O'Connor identified a clear division within the working class between the fustian jackets – the real workers – and those he disparagingly called the 'fine arts', a reference to the skilled artisans who predominated in Lovett's organisations. Overlaying this fragmented understanding of society, O'Connor consistently upheld a simple binary division: between the industrious and the idle, those who lived by their labour and those who lived by the labour of others, between 'the people' and their corrupt rulers.

Like many Chartists, however, he did not believe that society was driven by solely economic relationships and his aspirations for working people were not narrowly related to changing the ownership of the means of production.[49] This was the age when a belief in the capacity of politics was almost limitless – changing the composition of the House of Commons could change the world. Consequently, what O'Connor feared was not so much the economic power of the factory bosses but their untrammelled political ascendency. He disparaged the Anti-Corn Law League as a manufacturers' pressure group and he regarded their promise of cheap bread as a thinly veiled disguise for a pernicious desire to reduce wages. But the real danger was the consolidation of middle-class political power which must inevitably follow the repeal of the Corn Laws.[50] Richard Cobden agreed. As he famously wrote to Peel in 1846 in the wake of repeal, it was time to govern 'through the *bona fide* representatives of the middle class. The Reform Bill decreed it; the passing of the Corn Bill has realized it'.[51] Not surprisingly, in the wake of repeal O'Connor advocated an alliance with the aristocracy to ensure that the whole community benefited from free trade not just the factory bosses. Political power was the key: capital was protected by a vote whereas labour was wholly unrepresented.[52]

If O'Connor was guilty of inconsistency in his contributions to the process of renewal which took place during 1840-1, it related, at least ostensibly, to the third intervention that he made from behind the locked gates at York. At the beginning of his incarceration O'Connor penned a long letter to James Leach, a Manchester cotton operative and fierce O'Connor loyalist who was soon to be elected as the inaugural President of the National Charter Association. The letter contained the essential elements of a plan that he would advocate for the remainder of his public life: rural resettlement. O'Connor's gift for communication was never put to better effect than in relation to the benefits of rural resettlement. 'Formerly society was divided into small rural communities, so closely allied in interest, and so mutually dependent on each other for companionship as to make them resemble a large family,' he told Leach:

Suppose seven hundred to constitute the village population. They were masters and men reciprocally depending on each other for everything. The stamp upon each man's fabric bore the sterling representation of each man's value in the community. They possessed a sufficiency, but none either extravagantly or exclusively.

These rural communities had required few of the institutions of modern life: no police; no Commissioners of Poor; no spies; no informers. 'The civil power, consisting of the whole population, with the exception of the offender, was the law's only staff and the law's best protection…Drunkenness and immorality seldom occurred because they set an indelible brand upon the vicious.' 'Every man', he continued, 'was known to his neighbour, and every man's character was of value to his neighbour, and vice was hunted from the society.' O'Connor believed that rural life was superior in every respect. The casual use of the past tense in the descriptive passages did not denote a reactionary impulse. O'Connor saw himself as a pragmatic man, interested in what he fervently believed to be realistic solutions. Moreover, the benefits of the plan would not only be enjoyed by those relocated in the countryside. '[T]he reduction of the surplus population working for the tyrants', he predicted, 'would at once throw the balance of power into the hands of the operatives. The dead weight would be taken off them. The unemployed reserve would no more remain at the disposal of the master; and, as the terror of the slave.'[53]

From the very beginning O'Connor's land scheme was nothing if not ambitious. 'I want five millions of acres at any rent', he told Leach, 'to take off seven millions of wretched slaves from the slave market.' Obtaining the five million acres was not seen as a problem. Emphasising again his belief in the capacity of politics O'Connor suggested that the government would provide the funds – a loan – although he would quickly rethink this aspect of the plan. His wonderfully simple solution for the curse of national poverty, he lamented bitterly in August 1841, was dismissed as 'too visionary!' by the political class ('if two hundred millions of pounds were required for a speculation to build a floating-bridge across the Atlantic, or to make a tunnel form Dover to Calais...every angle in a fascinating drawing by some happy draftsman would be scanned, and all FOOLISH objections overruled'[54]). Even at this stage he urged Leach to use land as the basis of the Chartist organisation by forming 'Five Acre Associations', or 'Chartist Agricultural Associations', which would 'let the whole people know what we expect from Universal Suffrage'. The campaign for rural resettlement, he told Leach, was 'a new, a sure, a wholesome channel'.[55] The fact that it appeared to gainsay his missives about mixing the campaign for the suffrage with other objectives was not lost on many commentators; the fact that behind it lurked a deeper contradiction in his thinking was surely also apparent.

O'Connor returned to the theme of rural resettlement in a series of public letters to the landlords of Ireland that were published as a tract entitled the *Remedy for National Poverty and Impending National Ruin* in what turned out to be the final month of his sentence.[56] Describing himself as a 'Barrister at Law and a Prisoner' in the 'Condemned Cell' at York Castle he issued the landlords with a stark warning: revise the way you manage your estates or lose them to English manufacturers. His argument was simple: 'either the Corn Laws must be repealed, or you must render their immediate repeal unnecessary'.[57] On the one hand, O'Connor appeared to genuinely believe that he could convince the Irish landlords to join with 'the people' ('for I have left you' he told them, 'and become part and parcel of the people'[58]) in resisting the domination of English capitalists. All they had to do was sell fifteen million acres of surplus land at a fair price (to be repaid over 20 years) to the people who, under his guidance, would effect a root and branch transformation of agricultural practices. Why were 'the eyes of all...eternally directed to other countries for what we could better, more freshly, more conveniently, more profitably, more abundantly, and more comfortabl[y] supply from under our noses?' Did no one else 'observe the striking anomaly' of this he asked? [59] Utopia was within easy reach.

Even without a debate about the capacity of Anglo-Irish agriculture the notion that the landlords would willingly participate in this venture was only slightly less absurd than the idea that the politicians at Westminster might finance the transaction from the coffers of the Treasury. Again, O'Connor would soon revisit the *modus operandi* for the implementation the scheme. On the other hand, the landlords merely provided O'Connor with a pretext to articulate his broader vision of a genuinely productive and happy nation that was framed by a quotation (that he used frequently) from Corin, the humble shepherd in Shakespeare's *As You Like It*: 'A true labourer earns that he eats; gets that he wears: owes no man hate; envies no man's happiness; glad of other men's good; content under his own privations; and his chief pride is in the modest comforts of his condition'.[60] This, he insisted in a carefully weighed assonance, was Chartism 'in all its *Destructive* simplicity': 'I have explained the modest results anticipated from its success, and the great national advantages to be derived from its substitutions for the present pauperizing, sterilizing, brutalizing, degrading, peace-destroying, hatred creating system'.[61]

These were the 'rays of knowledge' that had begun 'to shine through my prison bars'; they would, O'Connor was in no doubt, 'spread their benign influence abroad over the whole face of the earth'.[62] A month later in his suit of fustian O'Connor indicated that he intended to turn his back on York Castle and 'pass over what has happened as a dream'. 'I forget the past', he told the crowd gathered to celebrate his release, 'and I shall devote my mind to the future'. The past was not forgotten. On the contrary, by adding the land to his agenda he completed a secular trinity that he would advocate for the rest of his public life: repeal of the union, the vote, and the land.[63] The idea that linked them all was not democracy, freedom or nationalism; it was independence.

Having put the land on the agenda it became a regular refrain. According to his own account O'Connor lectured and wrote continually on the subject of the land following his release in August 1841.[64] In March 1842 he published a lecture that he had only days before given in the Hall of Science in Manchester entitled *The Land and Its Capabilities* that neatly summarises his thinking at this time. The content would have been unsurprising to any reader of his letters from York. These were, he insisted, 'principles to which I have long been wedded'.[65] In relation to the question of how the people were to get the land O'Connor advanced a familiar instrumentalist view of politics: the Charter would 'strip the land of its representative power'; 'take away the power of the aristocracy to legislate solely for themselves, and if they fail to make £200,000,000 a-year by class legislation, they will be glad to take the £10,000,000 which, under the small farm system, they would get by their land'.[66] He followed this pamphlet with a series of letters in the moderate London journal, the *English Chartist Circular and Temperance Record*, which he later regarded as his most cogent account of his proposal.[67] By the middle of the year self-congratulation was in order. 'I may, without vanity', he wrote, 'congratulate you and myself upon the rapid progress that the question has made. This day twelve months [ago], not one in one hundred thousand of the working classes knew anything whatever of the land, its capabilities, and value; whereas now, many – very many, have a good notion of the subject, and ninety-nine in every hundred are thirsting for knowledge upon it.'[68]

The development in O'Connor's thinking at this time was not ideological but tactical. In May 1842, following the rejection of the second Chartist national petition by an obdurate House of Commons, he outlined two alternative paths to salvation for the people. The first was an alliance with the middle classes. This was a period when the Anti-Corn Law League invested considerable effort into building what Cobden called a 'working class party of repealers'.[69] Moreover, many middle-class reformers had responded warmly to the teetotal, Christian and 'knowledge' initiatives, and the Birmingham Quaker radical Joseph Sturge had proposed a national campaign for 'complete suffrage' as the basis of an alliance between the middle and working classes.[70] O'Connor had praised Sturge ('I esteem and value Mr. Sturge more than the whole party with which he is mixed up', he argued[71]) and, in August 1842, he had strategically intervened in a parliamentary by-election in Nottingham where Sturge was taking on the local Tory establishment. In a scene described famously by Thomas Cooper, O'Connor backed up the Quaker reformers' words with his fists. As the temperature of the election meeting rose steadily:

Mr. Sturge, with Vincent, and the rest of Mr. S's friends, quitted the wagon; and it was wise of them to do so. It was not our part, however, to retreat. Feargus waited until the Tory lambs got nearer, and then, throwing his hat into the wagon, he cried out 'Now my side charge!' and down he went among the crowd... It was no trifle to receive a blow from O'Connor's fists; and he 'floored them like nine-pins', as he himself said. Once, the Tory lambs fought off all who surrounded him, and got him down, and my heart quaked, – for I thought they would kill him. But, in a very few moments, his red head emerged again from the rough.[72]

For all that he was prepared to lend his arm to Sturge's (unsuccessful) campaign O'Connor wanted nothing to do with the Complete Suffrage Union. 'They wish to make our movement auxiliary to their movement', he argued in a familiar refrain, 'it is up to you to decide whether or not, after ten years' trial of, and as many years affliction under, one Reform Bill, you will now waste your energies by confirming the power in the hands of those who alone were benefited by the former measure.'[73] His position was clear: 'No surrender'.

If the middle class embrace must be resisted at all costs, how must the people proceed? Now O'Connor suggested that rural resettlement might actually provide a means to achieve the Charter. Recognizing that under the existing system the ownership of land was the key to the suffrage O'Connor mused over the possibility of the Chartists enfranchising themselves by purchasing the very soil of the nation.[74] This was not a novel idea. Following the passage of the Reform Bill the future Tory Prime Minister, Robert Peel, had argued that the 'battle for the British constitution would be played out in the registration courts'. Coincidentally with O'Connor's epiphany, in February 1842 Cobden had called for an analysis and classification of 'all the boroughs in the kingdom' as a prelude to the establishment of Electoral Committees in each borough 'to look after the registration'. 'Register! Register! Register!' became a catch-cry that contributed to the reputation of the League as a formidable political machine.[75] For O'Connor the idea was not an opportunity lost; the typical Chartist did not have deep pockets, certainly not deep enough to buy the House of Commons in forty shilling freehold blocks.

O'Connor's next attempt to promote the land scheme began in April 1843 with the publication of a series of letters in the Chartist press addressed 'To the Producers of Wealth, and All Those who live by Industry on the Land'.[76] Again, much of the content of these letters would have been familiar to readers, with an important exception. Now O'Connor proposed 'a *practical illustration* of the successful result which must follow the fulfilment of my plan...'[77] No less than 5,000 families (25,000 people) would be resettled into some forty small farming communities dotted throughout the British countryside. He would organise the finance to obtain 20,000 acres of land for the experiment to commence within a year. Who was O'Connor hoping to convince by such a demonstration? Not the government, but the 'tamely starving operatives' in the industrial towns and cities must be convinced.[78] O'Connor was a shrewd politician and he realised that he was skating close to the edge of political heresy by promoting a scheme that might undermine the belief in the efficacy of politics. 'In thus propounding the scheme for your consideration,' he insisted, 'you are not for one moment to suppose that in my most sanguine moments I anticipate from it more than the means of making your teeth water for *your Charter*.'[79] On the contrary, without the protection of the Charter, he argued, tyrants would 'watch the first fitting opportunity to dispossess you' of your land.[80] In other words the land and the Charter could only go forward together like 'Siamese twins'.[81]

O'Connor's lengthiest contribution to the agricultural question was not only a honed polemic but also a collection of homespun farming tips. Published in 1843, and again in 1845 and 1846, *A Practical Work on the Management of Small Farms* was firstly an attempt to educate. Agriculture was, he wrote, 'a science of which the English working classes are, shame to their rulers, wholly ignorant'.[82] Accordingly many of the 200 pages in the book are set aside for a didactic compendium of handy hits for budding farmers: from how many barrow loads of manure to use per crop ('Much ignorance prevails upon the subject of manures'[83]) and what to feed cows (warm drinks, bran and water with a little salt mixed in[84]) to the pros and cons of wheat, potatoes, turnips, mangel wurtzel (a 'valuable root'), carrots, vetches, cabbages and clover. There is more than a touch of William Cobbett in these passages. England's greatest journalist had often appeared in public dressed as a gentleman farmer and some of his writings had given vent to his enthusiasm for agriculture in the form of practical guidebooks that are remarkably similar to O'Connor's tract. O'Connor would have known that copies of Cobbett's *Cottage Economy* (1824) and *The English Gardener* (1833) adorned the shelves of many working-class homes and would have expected the brisk sales that he enjoyed.[85]

Intermixed with O'Connor's practical observations are some insights into his core values – 'When I see a man with his foot upon his spade, I think I recognise the image of his God', he wrote[86] – and many anecdotes from his own days as a farmer – 'my frequent experiments' – which he obviously remembered with fondness and pride. No reader of the tract could mistake the tinge of longing to return, like Quinctius Cincinnatus, to the happy piles of excrement in Fort Robert; nor will they miss the note of regret that he could not discourse on digging and dung without being 'hemmed in and hampered on all sides by the mysterious science of politics', as he had earlier put it.[87]

The *Practical Work* also contained a detailed iteration of his plan to establish the small farming system. By now O'Connor was reconciled to the idea of a subscription – 'clubbing of the pence of the poor'[88] – as the way for the people to inaugurate the millennium themselves an acre at a time. Thus with every version O'Connor came closer to confronting a contradiction at the heart of his conception. 'The question may here arise then, as to which of the changes that I contend for should have priority: – the establishment of the small farm principle – or the enactment of the People's Charter', he demanded.[89] Moreover, if peace and plenty might be attained by a weekly subscription; if the people might 'buy...their liberties', was the Charter even necessary? His answer to these questions varied. Sometimes O'Connor argued that political power – the Charter – was a necessary precondition for the implementation of the land system: 'I defy you to get an Act of Parliament to cause a subdivision of the land into profitable allotments; while I fearlessly contend that you can get the Charter'.[90] On other occasions, he argued that the Charter without the land would be meaningless – 'Lock up the land to-morrow, and I would not give you twopence for the Charter the next day, because you would have deprived it of its jewel'[91] – and that rural resettlement was 'Real Chartism'.[92] On other occasions still he displayed an uncritical ability to uphold both sides of the argument simultaneously.[93] He had been conceiving it too long.

Critics, inside and outside the movement, were quick to latch onto this inconsistency. James Bronterre O'Brien, a leading Chartist who had formally been one of O'Connor's closest allies, composed a withering satire worthy of O'Connor himself:

> But the strangest of all is, that the philanthropic Feargus should have dragged millions of people after him to torch-light meetings, demonstrations, &c., all attended with great sacrifice of time and money, and caused the actual ruin of thousands through imprisonments, loss of employment, and expatriation, when all the while he had only to establish a "National Chartist Co-operative Land Society" to ensure social happiness for us all…[94]

Looking back in 1851 William Linton, a London Chartist, recalled that the promulgation of the land scheme marked the transition from Chartism to 'O'Connorism' when the people 'almost lost sight of the Suffrage through looking for allotments of unprofitable land'.[95] It was easy to offer a disparaging assessment with the benefit of hindsight; at the time O'Connor's Arcadian vista struck a chord with many urban workers who had lived their lives in the shadow of the 'dark satanic mills' of the industrial Britain. For one Chartist from Aberdeen, for example, 'thousands – tens of thousands' of his fellow operatives saw in O'Connor's land plan a chance to realise a world that had been described by Robert Burns 'where a ripened field and azure skies, call forth the reapers' rustling noise'.[96] To this Chartist O'Connor's purpose was a religious one that was, at least in part, summed up almost verbatim in the words of the 23rd Psalm: 'To lead poor peasants and half starved operatives from the close, unhealthy, pestiferous atmosphere of the hell-born factory, and "make him lie down in green pastures, and lead him beside the still waters"'.[97]

Critics were also quick to point out that many of those attracted to rural resettlement hardly knew 'wheat from barley or a plough share from a pruning hook',[98] but this could not be said of O'Connor himself. He claimed the right to speak on agricultural subjects, firstly, on the basis of practical experience. After all, he reminded Leach, he had been the best farmer in Cork.[99] For him life on the land was a better life, more natural. As we have noted, O'Connor believed that he had made the transition from idle to industrious when he got mud on his boots at Fort Robert.[100] O'Connor also undoubtedly drew on his family heritage. The idealised communities he wrote about were remarkably similar to those described by his father in the *Chronicles of Eri*. In 1798 his uncle, Arthur O'Connor, published a tract that advocated small farms as the solution to Ireland's grievances (O'Connor republished it in 1843). Moreover, his exiled uncle had made a life in central France in a small agricultural community. As noted, Arthur O'Connor reinforced Feargus's appreciation of rural life; his 'little commune' in Loiret, which he cultivated with his workforce of '450 souls', and helped to shape his vision of the Chartist land colonies in important respects.[101] 'I have seen poor working men walking through my uncle's demesne, in France,' he told a crowd in Manchester in 1842, 'one to his half acre, another to his rood, his own, and no price would induce him to part with it. There's a better working-ocracy for you.'[102]

Finally, O'Connor's passion for rural resettlement was sustained by cultural values and national aspirations that animated many Irish hearts. He embraced a sense of connectedness to the land that is captured in the Gaelic word '*dùth-chas*';[103] he did not use the term but he surely understood its meaning. The *Eri* of his father's imagination was a land of small farms. O'Connor's particularly Irish sense of dispossession also helps to explain why, unlike many English radicals, he was not at all interested in collective ownership of the land. The socialist communities founded by followers of Robert Owen, he wrote, were better than the 'the present system' but 'I very much prefer' a co-operative system based on 'individual responsibility and possession'.[104] Individual proprietorship was the most effective way to guarantee independence, a crucial precondition for a healthy democracy. 'Living from hand to mouth destroys the independence and energy, and patriotism of man', he told Leach; 'having a stake in the country makes him a noble being. I seek to give him that stake.'[105] What O'Connor did share with many radicals on both sides of St George's Channel was an abiding belief in the productive capacity of the land. '30,000,000 may be an over population for a country badly governed', he told a Manchester audience in 1842, 'whereas 80,000,000 might be supported in comfort and plenty in the same country, under a different state of things.'[106]

For O'Connor, the land was the bridge between his Irish and his British careers, and (every bit as much as the suffrage) was a panacea, a key to understanding his world view. In fact, it is the key to understanding his economic policy in general. For example, O'Connor had often eloquently detailed the problems caused by machinery but he did not wish to destroy, tax or otherwise regulate it.[107] Rather he saw that the way to make machinery a 'benefit' rather than a 'curse' was to create a 'natural labour market' on the land. O'Connor had often argued for a fair remuneration for factory labourers; this too could be secured by rural resettlement. Reducing what Marx would later call the 'reserve army' of the unemployed would increase, at a single stroke, the bargaining power of those who remained in the cities. Similarly, the complex debates about free trade, protection, repealing the Corn Laws and opening the ports that absorbed interminable hours of discussion in parliament and millions of words in the public prints during the first half of the 1840s, could be swept aside with ridiculous ease. Why import wheat, O'Connor asked, when more than sufficient could be grown at home?[108]

The land plan also provides an important opportunity to understand his attitude to women. O'Connor consistently used gendered language in a pejorative way – those who 'betrayed' the people by advocating compromise, for example, were 'unmanly' – and he consistently advocated an idealised masculinist vision of domestic life. This was never clearer than in relation to rural resettlement. 'Think of the mother', he told Leach in May 1840, 'rising when she felt that duty and nature called, and the children called, according to their nature and constitution.'[109] In his Manchester lecture O'Connor painted a more detailed canvas. Addressing operatives 'working fifteen or eighteen hours a day, vainly endeavouring, by competition with machinery, to earn a comfortable livelihood', O'Connor suggested that they ask the 'small farmer' how he lived:

I have a comfortable house for a family of seven; we eat beef, mutton, pork, bread, butter, honey, eggs, and poultry; work ten hours a day and 280 a year; (playing on holidays and rainy weather,) my wife is the housewife to prepare meals, to wash, to brew, and look after my comforts, and the education of my children...[110]

Some historians have suggested that, if not a misogynist, O'Connor was at least guilty of instantiating the idea of 'separate spheres' in working-class politics.[111] He was. As Anna Clark has put it, Chartists, with Feargus at their head, manipulated 'the ideology of separate spheres for their own ends', demanding 'entry into the public sphere for working men' and 'the privileges of domesticity for their wives'.[112] For Clark the link between citizenship and masculinity came at a high cost: the genuinely egalitarian activism of the previous generation of radicals (women as well as men) was lost. It was. For the student of O'Connor, however, it is worth noting that his views about women and family life were essentially hypothetical. O'Connor never married and had few, if any, long-term domestic relationships with women. Nor did women feature centrally in his account of his youth. His mother died before he was a teenager; he never even mentions her by name in his autobiography. Whatever else might be said (or speculated), it is clear that O'Connor had not experienced the idealised domestic family life that he so passionately advocated for others. The people were his family; he knew them intimately but not personally.

O'Connor entered prison determined not to lose the intimate relationship with the people that he had established over the preceding decade. By treating him as a common felon the government had managed to make him the centre of national attention and the object of sympathy; from the moral high ground O'Connor found a way for his voice to breach the walls of his cell. When he exited his cell he offered a tribute to his followers by dressing in a suit of working-class fustian. It was symbol that summed up his commitment to independent working-class radicalism, free from compromise. A month later the *Northern Star* published a poem ('the composition of a Welsh Chartist woman', according to Thomas Cooper[113]) that reciprocated the tribute with a hymn of praise:

The Lion of Freedom comes from his den;
We'll rally around him, again and again:
We'll crown him with laurel, our champion to be:
O'Connor the patriot: for sweet liberty![114]

As Cooper quipped, 'the popularity of this song may serve to show how firmly O'Connor was fixed in the regard of a portion of the manufacturing operatives...'[115] Another erstwhile ally, William Hill, even invented a term for the symbiotic relationship between Feargus and the Chartist majority: 'Lionism'.[116] In important respects, however, the 'Lion of Freedom' does not tell the whole story. The devotion of O'Connor's followers was never unconditional; it was dependent on his principles. He had little room to manoeuvre. Moreover, from his prison cell O'Connor had started to promote in earnest another panacea for the nation's ills: rural resettlement. As he told readers of the Chartist press early in 1843, 'my solution is the land'.[117] By the end of 1841 the 'Lion of Freedom' was determined to become the 'People's Bailiff'.[118]

Notes

1   *Northern Star*, 4 September 1841.
2   *Northern Star*, 4 September 1841. See also P.A. Pickering, 'Class Without Words: Symbolic Communication in the Chartist Movement', *Past and Present*, no. 112. August 1986, pp. 144-162.
3   *Northern Star*, 6 September 1840.
4   See M.E. DeLacy, 'Grinding Men Good? Lancashire's Prisons at mid-Century' in V. Bailey (ed.), *Policing and Punishment in Nineteenth Century Britain*, London, 1987, pp. 182-216; M. Foucault, *Discipline and Punish: The Birth of the Prison*, London, 1977.
5   'The Life and Adventures of Feargus O'Connor', *National Instructor*, 7 September 1850, pp. 247-8.
6   *Northern Star*, 6 June 1840, 11 July 1840.
7   *Northern Star*, 6 June 1840.
8   *Northern Star*, 6 June 1840; 20 June 1840.
9   *Hansard* [House of Commons], 2 June 1840, cols. 908-913.
10 *Northern Star*, 18 July 1840; *Hansard* [House of Commons], 27 May 1840, cols. 647-56; 2 June 1840, cols. 908-13; *Hansard* [House of Lords], 4 June 1840, cols. 917-22.
11 *Northern Star*, 13 June 1840.
12 *Northern Star*, 8 August 1840.
13 *Northern Star*, 11 July 1840.
14 *Northern Star*, 16 January 1841; *Dictionary of National Biography*, vol. XIV, p. 846.
15 Another example of an important Chartist poem produced in prison was George Binns' *The Doom of Toil*. See S. Roberts, *Radical Politicians in Early Victorian Britain*, Lampeter, 1993, pp. 46-9. I am grateful to Stephen Roberts for bringing this to my attention.
16 *Northern Star*, 4 July 1840.
17 *Northern Star*, 11 July 1840.
18 *Northern Star*, 4 July 1840.
19 'The Life and Adventures of Feargus O'Connor', *National Instructor*, 7 September 1850, p. 249. O'Connor claimed that the column took its name from the fact that he used the back of a hand mirror to smuggle the first article out from prison. It was more meaningful as a literary allusion than what we would nowadays call an in-joke. See also T. Frost, *Forty Years' Recollections: Literary and Political*, London, 1880, p. 179.
20 Sonnet 62, *Complete Works of William Shakespeare*, London, 1994, p. 619. See Philippa Kelly, 'Surpassing Glass: Shakespeare's Mirrors', *Early Modern Literary Studies* 8.1, May, 2002, 2.1-32 <URL: http://purl.oclc.org/emls/08-2/kellglas.htm> I am grateful to Philippa Kelly for a helpful discussion of the mirror as a trope in English literature.
21 F. Engels, 'A Working Man's Party' (1881), reprinted in K. Marx and F. Engels, *Articles on Britain*, Moscow, 1978, p. 376; T. Rothstein, *From Chartism to Labourism* (1929), London, 1983, p. 68; D. Thompson (ed.), *The Early Chartists*, London,

1971, p. 28; J. Epstein, *Lion of Freedom*, London, 1982, p. 220f.

22   Epstein, *Lion of Freedom*, p. 233.

23   *Northern Star*, 18 July 1840.

24   *Chartist Circular*, 19 December 1840.

25   *Chartist Circular*, 29 August 1840.

26   *Northern Star*, 3 April 1841. Presumably he meant flummeries.

27   *Northern Star*, 4 April 1840.

28   *Northern Star*, 3 April 1841. See also P.A. Pickering, *Chartism and the Chartists in Manchester and Salford*, Basingstoke, 1995, chapter 7.

29   R.G. Gammage, *History of the Chartist Movement 1837-1854* (1854), New York, 1967, p. 197.

30   W. Lovett, *Life and Struggles of William Lovett in His Pursuit of Bread, Knowledge and Freedom* (1876), London, 1967, pp. 207, 210.

31   Lovett, *Life and Struggles*, p. 204.

32   *Northern Star*, 24 April 1841.

33   Lovett, *Life and Struggles*, p. 207.

34   *Northern Star*, 3 April 1841. Original emphasis.

35   *Northern Star*, 3 April 1841.

36   *Northern Star*, 3 April 1841.

37   *Northern Star*, 19 June 1841.

38   *Northern Star*, 19 June 1841. Defending his stance a couple of weeks later, O'Connor indicated that, in addition to a tactical judgement, he had also been drawn into the contest from a desire to assist a number of Chartist candidates already in the field, including Henry Vincent, Peter McDouall and William Sankey, whom he praised as 'open, frank, straightforward, and honourable' men. See *Northern Star*, 26 June 1841.

39   F. O'Connor, *The Remedy for National Poverty and Impending National Ruin* (1841) reprinted in G. Claeys (ed.), *The Chartist Movement in Britain 1838-1850*, London, 2001, vol. 2, pp. 354-5. Later, in 1846, he argued that the only distinction which mattered was between 'THE RICH OPPRESSOR AND THE POOR OPPRESSED'. See *Northern Star*, 22 May 1846.

40   *Northern Star*, 19 June 1841.

41   Pickering, *Chartism and the Chartists*, p. 171.

42   *Northern Star*, 21 August 1841.

43   *Northern Star*, 4 September 1841. See also: *Northern Star*, 10 May 1845.

44   *Northern Star*, 28 March 1840.

45   *Northern Star*, 4 September 1841.

46   *National Association Gazette*, 30 April 1842.

47   F. O'Connor, *The Land & Its Capabilities* (1842) reprinted in G. Claeys (ed.), *The Chartist Movement in Britain 1838-1850*, London, 2001, vol. 2, p. 432.

48   O'Connor, *The Land & Its Capabilities*, p. 437. See also J. Walton, *Chartism*, London, 1999, p. 52. On another occasion O'Connor argued vehemently that 'small shopkeepers and tradesmen' were part of the 'industrious classes'. See F. O'Connor, *A Practical Work on the Management of Small Farms* (1843), reprinted in G. Claeys (ed.), *The Chartist Movement in Britain 1838-1850*, London, 2001, vol. 4, p. 173.

49 As Nev Kirk has noted, O'Connor's economic critique 'did not embrace revolutionary socialist goals, but it was, nevertheless, saturated by notions of class pride and class exploitation'. See N. Kirk, 'In Defence of Class: A Critique of Recent Revisionist Writing upon the Nineteenth-Century English working-class', *International Review of Social History*, vol. xxxii, 1987, p. 31.

50 *Northern Star*, 11 November 1843.

51 Reprinted in J. Morley, *The Life of Richard Cobden*, London, 1903, p. 395.

52 *Northern Star*, 18 December 1847; F. O'Connor, *The Employer and the Employed: The Chambers' Philosophy Refuted* (1844), reprinted in G. Claeys (ed.), *The Chartist Movement in Britain 1838-1850*, London, 2001, vol. 3, pp. 418-19. See also *Northern Star*, 11 November 1843.

53 *Northern Star*, 16 May 1840.

54 O'Connor, *The Remedy for National Poverty*, p. 354

55 *Northern Star*, 16 May 1840.

56 *Labourer*, vol. 4, 1849, p. 56.

57 O'Connor, *The Remedy for National Poverty*, p. 336.

58 O'Connor, *The Remedy for National Poverty*, p. 337.

59 O'Connor, *The Remedy for National Poverty*, p. 343.

60 O'Connor, *The Remedy for National Poverty*, frontispiece and p. 355. Actually it was a misquotation from Act 3, Scene 2: 'Sir, I am a true labourer: I earn that I eat, get that I wear; owe no man hate, envy no man's happiness; glad of other men's good; content with my harm; and the greatest of my pride is to see my ewes graze and my lambs suck'. See *Complete Works of William Shakespeare*, p. 146.

61 O'Connor, *The Remedy for National Poverty*, p. 355.

62 O'Connor, T*he Remedy for National Poverty*, p. 353.

63 He later said as much. See *Northern Star*, 24 November 1849.

64 *English Chartist Circular*, vol. 2, no. 117, p. 257.

65 O'Connor, *The Land & Its Capabilities*, p. 429; *English Chartist Circular*, vol. 2, no. 67, p. 57; no. 117, p. 257.

66 O'Connor, *The Land & Its Capabilities*, p. 446.

67 *English Chartist Circular*, vol. 2, no. 117, p. 256.

68 *English Chartist Circular*, vol. 2, no. 76, p. 93.

69 See P.A. Pickering and A. Tyrrell, *The People's Bread: A History of the Anti-Corn Law League*, Leicester, 2000, chapter 6.

70 See A. Tyrrell, *Joseph Sturge and Moral Radical Party*, London, 1982, chapter 10.

71 *English Chartist Circular*, vol. 2 no. 58, p. 21.

72 T. Cooper, *The Life of Thomas Cooper* (1872), Leicester, 1971, pp. 157-8.

73 *English Chartist Circular*, vol. 2, no. 58, p. 21.

74 A.M. Hadfield, *The Chartist Land Company*, Newton Abbot, 1970, p. 16. See also D. Read and E. Glasgow, *Feargus O'Connor: Irishman and Chartist*, London, 1961, chapter 11.

75 Cited in Morley, *Life of Richard Cobden*, vol. 1, p. 228. See also Pickering and Tyrrell, *The People's Bread*, chapter 1.

76 The series appeared in the *Northern Star* between 15 April and 27 May 1843.

77 *Northern Star*, 15 April 1843.

78 *Northern Star*, 22 April 1843.

79   *Northern Star*, 22 April 1843. Original emphasis.

80   *Northern Star*, 22 April 1843.

81   See Hadfield, *The Chartist Land Company*, p. 17.

82   O'Connor, *A Practical Work*, p. 195. He urged Chartists to meet to discuss it, p. 199.

83   O'Connor, *A Practical Work*, p. 126.

84   O'Connor, *A Practical Work*, p. 131.

85   O'Connor, *A Practical Work*, p. 201. Later he quoted Cobbett. See F. O'Connor, *What may be done with three acres of land*, London, 1848 (copy in the *Goldsmiths'-Kress library of economic literature*, no. 35579.16, National Library of Australia).

86   O'Connor, *A Practical Work*, p. 117.

87   O'Connor, *The Remedy for National Poverty*, p. 352.

88   O'Connor, *A Practical Work*, p. 167.

89   O'Connor, *A Practical Work*, p. 94.

90   *English Chartist Circular*, vol. 2, no. 76, p. 94.

91   O'Connor, *The Remedy for National Poverty*, p. 344.

92   *Northern Star*, 2 September 1843; 16 September 1843.

93   See O'Connor, *A Practical Work*, p. 94. See also *Northern Star*, 1 November 1845.

94   Cited in Gammage, *History*, pp. 268-9.

95   *English Republic*, 1851, p. 82.

96   *Labourer*, vol. 3, 1848, p. 23; Burns, *The Vision*, 16 (1786).

97   *Labourer*, vol. 3, 1848, p. 23. 23rd Psalm: 'He maketh me to lie down in green pastures: he leadeth me beside the still waters'.

98   J. Layhe, *Tenth Report of the Ministry of the Poor*, Manchester, 1844, pp. 20-1.

99   *Northern Star*, 16 May 1840.

100 *Labourer*, vol. 2, 1847, p. 147.

101 A. Condorcet O'Connor, *Monopoly the Cause of All Evil*, Paris and London, 1848, vol. 1, pp. 294, 300.

102 O'Connor, *The Land & Its Capabilities*, p. 446; O'Connor, *A Practical Work*, p. 185. French agricultural workers had practical liberty, he argued, as opposed to the English who enjoyed theoretical liberties.

103 See *Fonn's Duthchas: Land & Legacy*, Highland 2007 Exhibition outline: 'Duthchas can mean a hereditary right to the place of your birth', http://www.fonnsduthchas.com/learning/resources/fonns_exhibition.pdf See also *Scotsman*, 10 February 2005.

104 O'Connor, *A Practical Work*, p. 178. See also *Northern Star*, 9 November 1844; 17 May 1845; *Labourer*, vol. 3, 1848, pp. 54-5.

105 *Northern Star*, 16 May 1840.

106 O'Connor, *The Land & Its Capabilities*, p. 435.

107 O'Connor, *The Land & Its Capabilities*, p. 432; O'Connor, *The Employer and the Employed* pp. 454, 468 and part 2 *passim*.

108 O'Connor had argued that it was better to grow wheat than import it (see O'Connor, *The Employer and the Employed*, p. 439) but like Peel his hand was forced by the famine and he supported the opening of ports. See *Northern Star*, 27 December 1845.

109 *Northern Star*, 16 May 1840.

110 O'Connor, *The Land & Its Capabilities*, p. 433.

111 See A. Clark, *The Struggle for the Breeches: Gender and the Making of the British Working Class*, Berkeley, 1995, chapter 13; T. Koditschek, 'The Gendering of the British Working Class', *Gender & History*, vol. 9, no. 2, 1997, p. 343. Dorothy Thompson has argued persuasively that the increasing 'modernisation' of working-class politics as seen in the development of more formal institutions, was one of the key reasons for a decline in women's participation. See 'Women and Nineteenth-Century Radical Politics: A Lost Dimension', in J. Mitchell and A. Oakley (eds), *The Rights and Wrongs of Women*, Harmondsworth, 1976, pp. 137-8.

112 Clark, *The Struggle for the Breeches*, p. 247.

113 Cooper, *Life of Thomas Cooper*, p. 160.

114 Cooper, *Life of Thomas Cooper*, p. 175; *Northern Star*, 11 September 1840.

115 Cooper, *Life of Thomas Cooper*, p. 176.

116 *The Life Boat*, 30 December 1843.

117 *English Chartist Circular*, vol. 2, no. 116, p. 255.

118 *Northern Star*, 6 November 1847; A. Somerville, *Conservative Science of Nations*, Toronto, 1860, p. 228.

7: UNCONQUERABLE PRIDE

By his own estimation, O'Connor devoted a considerable amount of his energy following his release to promoting rural resettlement but there were many other demands on his attention. Time would soon become his enemy. 1842 was marked by violence and the real possibility of further incarceration. In March he arrived in Manchester to deliver a lecture at the Hall of Science on the repeal of the Irish Union. He had hardly uttered a word before a dispute with supporters of Daniel O'Connell saw the meeting descend into a wild fracas. He had been ambushed. As one of the orchestrators, Edward Watkin, noted gleefully in a private report:

> – desks – chairs – gas pipes – were used as weapons & the result is something like as follows – 'The lion' – the king of Chartism – F. O'C – knocked down 3 times – has he says 7 wounds – six he can tell the position of – the 7th. was I believe inflicted as he was running away – wh. he did after fighting about two minutes.[1]

O'Connor later recalled that he had feared the worst:

> During the fray, Duffy, who had been voted to the chair, caught hold of my collar to knock me off the platform, where a ruffian of the name of Price, a butcher, with a hatchet in his hand, and who had been offered a reward of five pounds by the free traders, if he would cut my head off, was watching the opportunity to earn his honourable fee.[2]

The sequel in court suggests that O'Connor did as much fighting as he did fleeing although surely, at age forty-six, his best brawling years were behind him.[3] Nevertheless, as we have seen, O'Connor had barely sufficient time for his bruises to fade before he was involved in another serious fight during an election rally in Nottingham. It was a bad few months. O'Connor returned to Manchester in August for a Chartist Conference only to become embroiled in the massive industrial unrest known as the Plug Plot riots. O'Connor arrived on 15 August from London to find the streets of Manchester crowded with thousands of working people – women as well as men – from Manchester, Salford and many surrounding towns and villages in south-east Lancashire. They were in the streets because they were on strike.

For more than a week, industrial action, that had begun in the Staffordshire Potteries, had been spreading through the midlands and across the north of England until it finally reached the 'shock city' of the Industrial Revolution where it had quickly brought the heart of the nation's cotton industry to a standstill. O'Connor was in Manchester not to meddle in the strike but to attend a Chartist conference and the inauguration of a monument to the leader of the previous generation of radicals, Henry Hunt, which was scheduled to take place in Ancoats on the anniversary of the Massacre of Peterloo. O'Connor had often assumed Hunt's mantle and he revelled in the opportunity to bathe in the reflected glory of the venerated hero. He was disappointed. Soon after the commencement of the strike the 'very unexpected excitement of the town' forced the organising committee to abandon the planned procession from central Manchester to Ancoats; the authorities completed the disruption of events soon afterwards by banning the unveiling ceremony.[4] The Chartist Conference, however, did proceed in Scholefield's Chapel in Ancoats and, on the morning of 17 August, O'Connor took his place among about forty delegates gathered there under the watchful eye of the Manchester police.

Soon a fierce debate broke out about how to respond to the events taking place all around them. Some Chartists (notably William Hill, editor of the *Northern Star*) argued that they should repudiate the strike as a conspiracy concocted by the Anti-Corn Law League to use the people to force the government into repeal. Others, such as Thomas Cooper and Peter McDouall, argued that it was the Chartists' duty to lead the strike, consolidating its aim as the enactment of the Charter. O'Connor was in two minds. He had publicly warned that the League was planning a lock out to use a starving people as a weapon against the government but he was also reluctant to let others direct the strike. The Chartist Executive issued an inflammatory placard which employed apocalyptic language – the 'God' of 'battles' was invoked – and called on Chartists to do whatever they could to extend the strike throughout Britain. The Executive Address sent a frisson of alarm through the ranks of polite society and led to a spate of arrests. O'Connor had been present for part of the time when the wording of the placard was discussed but as he was not on the executive it did not carry his name.[5] This meant that he escaped immediate arrest, but the period of grace would not last long. By the end of September he and 58 others had been charged with various counts of sedition, conspiracy, tumult and riot.

Before the time came for him to again defend his liberty, O'Connor played a crucial role in the Complete Suffrage Conference organised by Joseph Struge.

Whereas in August he had gone to Nottingham to try to ensure Sturge's election
to the House of Commons, in December he went to Birmingham to finally
wreck Sturge's dream of a unified middle and working-class campaign for the
suffrage. The fact that the Complete Suffrage movement originated from within
the ranks of the Anti-Corn Law League late in 1841, and for several months its
promoters were unclear about their commitment to a radical programme in
total only added to the suspicion of O'Connor and his supporters. To O'Connor
it was nothing short of 'Complete Humbug'.[6] The movement had, however,
attracted some Chartist support, particularly among erstwhile supporters of the
'New Move' and, although a first conference had failed to resolve the status of
the Chartist programme, let alone its name, Sturge was encouraged to convene a
second Conference to be held in Birmingham in December. In April O'Connor
had organised a rival assembly and carped from the fringe, urging the people to
remain true to 'YOUR CHARTER AND YOUR ORDER;[7] in December he was
determined to attend and force the middle-class radicals to accept the Charter,
'the whole hog, bristles and all', or expose them as hypocrites. The National
Charter Association was careful to ensure the election of plenty of sympathetic
delegates – Feargus himself was elected to represent three towns including
Sturge's home town of Birmingham – but O'Connor could not have expected
the proceedings to go as well as they did. In an attempt to forestall division
and convince the Chartists of their sincerity Sturge and his associates had put
together a 'People's Bill of Rights', that embraced all of the six points. All that
was left out was the name. It was a crucial miscalculation that brought William
Lovett into the fray on O'Connor's side. In fact, in a remarkable turn around,
Lovett moved, and O'Connor seconded, a resolution that the People's Charter
be the basis for discussion. For once O'Connor was undoubtedly delighted to
let someone else lead. The motion was supported by a substantial majority,
forcing Sturge and his associates to withdraw from their own Conference.[8] For
historians the significance of the Complete Suffrage episode has been that it
marked the consolidation of O'Connor's dominance of the Chartist movement
which was itself now much more clearly defined by class, but in fact it was,
ironically, the last time O'Connor asserted the primacy of an exclusive form
of Chartism. As we have seen, he was already undermining his proscription
against adjuncts with his advocacy of the land plan.

As he left Birmingham O'Connor would have been entitled to walk with a
spring in his step and smirk on his face at the way his opponents had managed
to defeat themselves. The only dark spot on the horizon was the prospect of
imprisonment: how long would he be free to enjoy his triumph? Earlier *Punch*
had entertained its readers with an image of O'Connor as a 'modern' Milo
attempting to chop down a tree inscribed 'British Constitution' with his bare

hands (see plate 4). Like his ancient namesake, Milo of Croton, Feargus's hands are stuck in the trunk and a lion (with a judge's wig for a mane) is about to devour him. The trial of Feargus O'Connor and 58 others commenced in the Nisi Prius Court in the ancient city of Lancaster on Wednesday, 1 March 1843. The trial, as one commentator enthused, 'was looked forward to with the most intense and thrilling interest by men of every shade of politics throughout the country' and among the dense throng of spectators he drew special attention to the presence of many women: 'On either side of the bench an array of beauty and fashion presented itself such as we have seldom seen gracing a court of judicature'.[9] O'Connor's reputation for grand theatricality in such situations – the certainty that he would put on a good show – was obviously sufficient to overcome the 'moral repugnance' with which he was usually regarded by members of polite society.[10] As with O'Connor's previous trial, the Crown was represented by the Attorney General. Unlike his Whig predecessor, Sir Frederick Pollock was keen to outshine the principal defendant, telling the jury in his opening address that the evidence against O'Connor was 'as good evidence as could possibly be given'.[11] In fact the hubris of the eminent Privy Councillor and Lord Chief Baron of the Exchequer soon got him into trouble. Pollock left London claiming, at least this is what was reported in the press, that he was heading to Lancashire to prosecute the 'leading and most important offender', but later denied he had used these words; allowing O'Connor to make much of the unreliability of newspaper reports.[12]

O'Connor's defence against the charge contained two interconnected strands. On the one hand he dismissed it as a political trial. All the major political players had been busily blaming each other for the outbreak, but '[h]ere is an extraordinary thing; six parties on the field; lords and commons charge five different sources with being the cause of these disturbances; but no one, except the Attorney-General, charges the Chartists'. O'Connor followed this by conjuring an amusing image of the Attorney as an 'old hunter', whose favourite horse had died, tramping around the manufacturing districts looking for another to fit his favourite saddle: 'He tried it upon the League; but finding the Chartists had the broadest shoulders, and that it fitted them best, he placed the saddle upon their backs and gathered it fast up on them'.[13] Readers of the Chartist press might have had every expectation that O'Connor's defence would revolve around demonstrating the culpability of the Anti-Corn Law League and scoring some political points in the process. The list of witnesses he subpoenaed – including a number of leading Leaguers who simultaneously held public office – confirms this, at least in part, but he clearly changed his mind when the weakness of the case against him became apparent. Unlike his trial in 1839 his remarks were not framed by a heroic appeal to the court of public opinion; O'Connor clearly believed that he could beat the charges.

His strategy was to expose the farcical nature of the Crown case, in particular the absurd proposition that he had engaged in a conspiracy – by definition a secret act – in the full glare of public attention, including in print.[14] The Attorney General had offered the Jury a 'melo-dramatic performance', O'Connor asserted, 'but he could not see the scenery, the masks or the daggers to stage it'. In a tone dripping with sarcasm O'Connor teased the Attorney much to the amusement of the court. The fact that he had arrived in Manchester in the dead of night, for example, was not evidence of his furtive intentions as had been implied, but a consequence of the train timetable. Hadn't the Home Secretary, Sir James Graham, sitting in court that day, arrived in Manchester on the same train, he asked? As one commentator recalled, '[t]his portion of Mr. O'Connor's address was delivered in a subdued but perfectly audible tone of voice, analogous to what is usually termed, "a playhouse whisper," and well adapted for exhibiting the ludicrous character of the charge of conspiracy'.[15] One can imagine a hushed courtroom with the audience on the edge of their seats; their heads inclined forward hanging on every word. The comparison to the theatrical arts is apt: O'Connor was engaged in a performance in every sense of the word. He answered the government's melodrama with a farce: the comment most often recorded by the reporter during his address was 'laughter'.

O'Connor spoke for two hours and twenty minutes in his own defence and, in fact, he was rarely off his feet for long during the eight days of the trial. Almost every witness was extensively cross-examined – he was particularly effective in discrediting the evidence of two hapless Chartists who had agreed to go into the witness box rather than the dock.[16] He had succeeded in entertaining the courtroom and newspaper readers up and down the country and by the end of the trial there was speculation that his persistence had had an impact on the bench. In the event the Judge's summation drew attention to the weaknesses in the government case and few were surprised when the jury acquitted many of the defendants on most of the charges in the indictment. O'Connor was found guilty on only the fifth of nine counts against him, the relatively minor charge of endeavouring to incite disaffection by unlawfully encouraging a stoppage of labour.[17] For the Attorney General even this meagre victory was snatched from his grasp when it was revealed that the original indictment contained errors in law and none of the defendants was ever called for sentence. For O'Connor, who lavished praise on the 'just judge', it was a signal victory. Later he claimed that what he called the 'Lancaster triumph' had made prosecutions for sedition unfashionable.[18]

True to his stated intention O'Connor spent a lot of time in 1843 and the early months of 1844 promoting the land plan, including the publication of his self-help guide to agriculture, *A Practical Work on The Management of Small Farms*. He also toured extensively with Thomas Duncombe, the Radical MP for Finsbury, promoting membership of a revamped National Charter Association. These were difficult years for the movement, which was reflected in declining sales of the *Northern Star*. During 1839 the average weekly sale of the journal had been 36,000 (making its proprietor an estimated £13,000 in profit); by 1843 it had fallen to 8,700; in 1844 it was a mere 7,400 and in 1845, 6,500.[19] In November 1844 O'Connor had moved the newspaper to London, establishing an office in the Strand, ostensibly to foster closer links with the trades and to promote the land scheme and, undoubtedly, in an attempt to arrest the decline in sales. However, the relationship between the putative land scheme and the movement proper remained ambiguous. As early as September 1843 O'Connor had unsuccessfully sought to convince a Chartist Conference in Birmingham to add the land to the Charter at the head of their agenda.[20] Similarly, a Conference in Manchester in April 1844 had rejected the scheme as impractical.[21] It was not until April 1845 that he persuaded a thinly attended conference in London to establish the Chartist Cooperative Land Society, although many details were still to be worked out and the plan continued to draw heavy criticism from friend and foe alike.[22]

In the aftermath of this limited success O'Connor redoubled his efforts at promoting the scheme. By the end of May he was promising a practical illustration in shrill tones: 'I have frequently told you that I never would recommend the people do a single act that I was not prepared to take part in myself'. When, he continued, 'you are either too indolent, too suspicious, or too unthrifty, to try it yourselves, I will endeavour to try it for you...' He would undertake to buy land and set up a colony with 30 or 35 cottages on it. 'It will be the proudest day of my life', he concluded, 'when I see the first batch of colonists entering their "own castles"'.[23]

In September O'Connor left England for an extensive study tour of Europe. He took his role seriously, heading his weekly reports in the *Northern Star* 'From "Our Own" Land "Commissioner"', a reference to the Devon Commission which had spent three years hearing testimony about land from eleven hundred witnesses in every county in Ireland and had recently presented its voluminous report to parliament. After a rough crossing from Dover, O'Connor arrived in the historic port of Ostend on the Flemish coast. Within hours he was visiting local farmers' markets and waxing lyrical, not only about the munificence on offer but also the healthy peasants who were selling it: 'O! What a sight!', he wrote, '... I wish the English workers could have seen the straight, majestic-looking peasants that I saw in this market...There was not a stunted one, nor an unhealthy one, nor an unhappy-looking one amongst them; *and not a single policeman to keep them in order.*' Belgium was, he enthused, a 'paradise of places'.[24] It was not all business. O'Connor visited the field of Waterloo and although he was more interested in the crops than the battlefield relics he related the scene before him with an eye to the famous conflict. He also devoted a considerable portion of his second epistle to a discussion of the virtues of Belgian manure and the efficiencies of the Belgian railways which he used to criss-cross the nation.[25]

From Belgium O'Connor moved on to tour Prussia, Germany, Nassau, Baden, France and Switzerland. After a delay at the border ('the Austrian Government is resolved that I shall not peep into its Italian territories', he wrote), he eventually went to Sardinia. His run in with the Austrian authorities had not dampened his appetite. At a hotel in Arona on the shores of Lake Maggiore, he told the readers of the *Star*, he had dined on 'cold veal and jelly; a splendid veal cutlet; a large piece of fat boiled beef; half a roasted fowl; a dish of French beans; bread, cheese; peaches; grapes; cakes of all sorts; and A BOTTLE OF WINE – the real juice of the grape, and all for ONE SHILLING AND EIGHT-PENCE...'[26]

Despite the occasional lapse into passages of travelogue O'Connor never lost sight of his broader message. 'You will be astonished to hear' he wrote after one week, 'If the land of Belgium were treated like the land of England, it would not produce anything; and if the land of England were cultivated as the land of Belgium is, it would feed half the world.'[27] Nothing he saw subsequently altered his opinions. On the contrary, from the foot of the Alps he suggested that he had seen enough in a month 'to convince me of the correctness of my views on the all important subject of THE LAND'.[28] Moreover, his European excursion had reinforced a sense of 'British' chauvinism even for an Irishman. 'As a country to live in', he wrote, 'I prefer England immeasurably to all others that I have seen'.[29] He was vaguely troubled from the moment he disembarked by the sight of so many 'officers in military uniforms with large moustachios and swords'. And, although he came to believe that, in Belgium at least, these officers were public servants duty bound to serve,[30] the contrast to Britain was still a stark one. '[W]e possess a power of reforming in England', he explained, 'which is not possessed by any other people: that is the power of meeting in public.' In Switzerland, Republic though it was, he was 'cautioned not to talk any politics' lest 'six or eight gendarmes will drag you off to a dungeon at once', he reported.[31] The *Northern Star* was prohibited in all the countries he toured except France and Belgium. Europeans, he continued, 'are governed wholly and entirely by the press of factions, and by military despotism'.[32] Travel had inspired a new enthusiasm for domestic reform: 'From all that I have seen, and heard, and learned, I am resolved never to relax my exertions, until I see every English, Irish and Scotch man, who wishes to live without "a master", enabled to do so'. He had returned, he insisted, 'more land mad than ever'.[33]

O'Connor had travelled to Europe at the same time as other Chartist leaders were seeking to align the movement more closely with the various causes of European freedom. Established in London in September 1845 the Fraternal Democrats believed that 'all men are brethren' and were committed to the doctrine that the 'earth with all its natural productions...[is]...the common property of all'.[34] The leading Chartist figure in the Democrats was George Julian Harney who had become editor of the *Northern Star* at the time of its relocation to London. With Harney in the editor's chair the *Star* office in Great Windmill Street became a hub for the various emigré movements in the metropolis and the paper devoted considerable space to the struggles abroad. O'Connor's letters from the continent, for example, were followed by a series on Germany by 'Your German Correspondent', Frederick Engels.[35] The contrast between O'Connor and the self-styled '*L'Ami du Peuple*' appeared stark. As Harney's biographer noted: 'Like his famous predecessor Cobbett in this, as in so many ways, Feargus was anti-socialist and anti-internationalist'.[36] A clash between the two men over the direction of the journal, and the movement at large, which became public in 1849 at the time of Harney's resignation, had been simmering since 1847. Early in 1848 O'Connor had written to Harney to insist 'what I have so often directed should be observed', that foreign news should be restricted to one column in the *Star*.[37] A couple of points need to be made. First, it is important to emphasise O'Connor's pragmatism. There had been 'much & very just complaint', he argued, 'of so much space being devoted to matters in which the *Star* readers and English people take not the slightest interest, to the exclusion of domestic matters'.[38] The comparison to Cobbett is apposite; O'Connor too had an acute sense of the popular mood. In this respect, as in so many others, O'Connor spoke for the Chartist majority, as Engels and Harney himself recognised. Engels had told Harney that he was 'the *only* Englishman who is really free of all prejudices that distinguish the Englishman from the Continental man' and urged him to take the lead in Chartist affairs. Harney accepted the compliment but not the suggestion. 'If I am "the only Englishman &c", it follows that I would be a chief without an army, a leader without followers.'[39] O'Connor's letters reveal him to be cosmopolitan in outlook but he was not an internationalist in a narrow political sense. In fact, the only international alliance that he consistently favoured involved England, Scotland, Wales and Ireland.[40]

The second point to emphasise is that the dispute with Harney underscored O'Connor's anti-socialism. O'Connor was a consistent critic of communist systems which he regarded as 'in practice...not less destructive of the rights of labour than the most grinding system that has been propounded by political economists': it 'must eventually end in the worst description of despotism – the despotism of self-surrender and non-reliance on self'.[41] He was particularly concerned to distinguish the land plan from any notions of collective ownership. The land plan 'has no more to do with Socialism than it has with the comet', he insisted, a reference to the 'great comet' sighted in June 1845.[42]

Having returned from the continent O'Connor brushed aside those critics who 'spitefully nibble at the details of the Land Plan'[43] and pressed ahead with the formal establishment of the Company at a national conference in Manchester in December 1845.[44] Despite persistent opposition and division O'Connor set up an office at 83 Dean St, Soho, formerly the residence of a notoriously foppish London artist, George Harlow (Marx lodged at 64 with Heinrich Bauer), and engaged lawyers to draw up the rules of the association. In March 1846 he purchased land for the first Chartist estate at Heronsgate near Rickmansworth in Hertfordshire for £1,860.[45] He, better than his opponents, knew the public mood and subscriptions began to steadily increase now that the realisation of the scheme seemed at hand.

By August 1846 the estate was ready to be unveiled in a ceremony described as a National Chartist Jubilee. On Monday 17 August a crowd estimated at between 12,000 and 20,000 Chartists from all over England, including a substantial convoy of vehicles which travelled up from London, converged on south-west Hertfordshire to celebrate the inauguration. On entering the gates of the estate a band played the 'Chartist land march' (words and music sold by a land company official, Thomas Martin Wheeler). 'The first object that met our view', reported the Star, 'was a huge tri-coloured banner floating high above an immense chestnut tree, bearing the inscription, "O'Connorville"'.[46] The show, however, was stolen by 'Rebecca the Chartist cow', resplendent in a silk 'vesture of tri-colour'. The festivities were enlivened by dancing, wandering minstrels, donkey racing, and 'nine-pin playing'. The reference to 'jubilee', a reminder of the promise in Leviticus 25:10 of the return of the land to the people, would not have been lost on any of those present.[47] O'Connor's speech was not surprisingly greeted with tremendous cheering. He devoted a large part of it to repudiating the criticism that had been directed at him (he was not a leveller, but an elevator, he quipped) by critics inside and outside the movement. By way of conclusion, he invited his listeners to imagine the scene, not at some indeterminate point in the future, but one year hence: 'if I live to…go from house to house, field to field, and from garden to garden, to see the industrious husband, the cheerful wife and prattling children all in their proper place and elements, and if they tell me that they are prosperous, contented and happy, I will bless God for making me the instrument of so much real bliss'.[48] What was once a glimmer in the mind's eye was now a reality as one London shoemaker enthusiastically wrote to the *Northern Star*: 'it is loose gravelly soil, and every foot we put on it we feel it is "our own", for once we feel independent'.[49] Independence was an idea close to many Chartist hearts, not merely O'Connor's. Ernest Jones summarised the seduction of O'Connorville in a poem published on the day of the 'jubilee':

From feverish couch by o'ertaxed labour pressed,
That yields man slumber, but denies him rest,
More weary still, when smoky morning breaks,
In crowded towns the pale mechanic wakes.
But why to-day, at twilight's earliest prime,
When morn's gray finger points to the march of time,
Why starts he upwards with a joyous strength
To face the long day slavery's cheerless length?
Has freedom whispered in his wistful ear,
'Courage, poor slave! deliverance is *near!*[50]

O'Connor's statement, which was published along with the report of the ceremony, was perhaps even more significant than his speech for the student of his biography. Signing himself as 'your faithful friend and bailiff', O'Connor concluded his letter by congratulating the 'working classes' on a glorious triumph, but the heart of the text was a paean of self-congratulation and vindication. 'The 17th of August is past', he commenced, 'and all England will testify that I have redeemed my pledge'. After a 'word about manure' he returned to the theme: 'I may now boastingly tell you of no small portion of the society's security – it consists in, my unimpaired constitution, undying zeal, and unconquerable pride…WHAT ENEMY CAN HOPE TO BEAT THAT'. The name chosen for the 'perfect paradise' was appropriate in every sense: 'O'Connorville'.

The inauguration augured well for the future; 1847 would prove to be the high point of O'Connor's English career. On the land front 600 branches of the Land Company were established; subscriptions flooded in; and sales of the *Northern Star* rose for the first time in a decade. A second Chartist estate at Lowbards near Gloucester had been purchased in October 1846 and, in February 1847, the *Star* published floor plans for the houses designed by O'Connor himself.[51] Was no task beyond him? In May, the first tenants moved into O'Connorville; O'Connor was in tears at the fulfilment of his dream, even though he regarded it as a 'meagre, unfinished sketch of that full-length portrait of freedom, happiness, and contentment which will eventually result from the novelty I have ventured to propound'.[52] A public meeting was held to celebrate the event and the reporter neatly summarised the delight of the large crowd at the 'magnificent' scene before them and, and at the same time, revealed what must have been a widespread understanding, even among O'Connor's supporters, of his tendency to view the world through rose-coloured glasses: 'even FEARGUS had not half described the place'.[53]

O'Connor shed no tears, however, at the news of the death of his nemesis, Daniel O'Connell, in the same month.[54] In June, another two estates were purchased: Snigs End near Lowbards and Minster Lovell in Oxfordshire (to be called Charterville). In August the Lowbards estate opened. The millennium was truly at hand. Nor had O'Connor entirely forsaken electoral politics. In July 1846 he had stood at a by-election in Nottingham. In accordance with the time-honoured practice the local MP, John Cam Hobhouse, had resigned and re-contested his seat when he accepted ministerial office. O'Connor seized the opportunity to attack the Whigs and won a substantial victory at the show of hands.[55] His success earned him, among other things, the thanks of the Brussels Communist Correspondence Committee (which included Marx and Engels, whom he had met the year before) and undoubtedly opened his mind to the possibility of future victory. From across the channel even the Brussels Communists looked forward to the day when O'Connor would capitalise on his support by going to the poll.[56] In June 1847, O'Connor's attention returned to possibility of election to the House of Commons and, not surprisingly, the site he chose for this political regeneration was Nottingham. 'Upon three occasions I have made your borough the skirmish ground for faction', he told the 'Independent Electors of Nottingham' in June, referring to his previous interventions largely in support of other candidates, 'when the next opportunity occurs, I shall make it the battlefield of principle'.[57]

O'Connor's election address provides a valuable index of his views at what was effectively the apex of his English career. The centrepiece was, understandably, the enactment of the People's Charter ('a full, free and fair representation of the people'), together with a familiar list of radical causes: disestablishment of the Church of England; direct taxation; repeal of the 1834 poor law; restrictions to working hours. He also declared that he was opposed to capital punishment; to war (except in the case of invasion); and, to the government secret service. There was little here for even moderate radicals to object to. Where he might have raised an eyebrow was in relation to the demand for the restoration of Frost, Williams and Jones, the Chartists transported to Van Diemen's Land, and the establishment of the Small Farm system as a government measure.[58] O'Connor also made it clear that he would not leave Ireland behind. 'Though the honour I seek is the representation of an English borough', he warned, 'I shall take part in all Irish questions'. Of course, he supported repeal of the union, interpreting it more stridently than in the past to mean the '*separation* of the two countries'; 'I shall at all times support the independence of my native country by endeavouring to rid her of a foreign *yoke*', he wrote. With Dan planted in the cold ground of Dublin's Glasnevin Cemetery, his former protégé undoubtedly had half an eye on his crown. O'Connor added a couple of procedural matters: he would not accept government office or inducement, and he would resign his seat at the conclusion of every session, effectively implementing one of the Chartist demands. Moreover, he would not test his support by any simple majority; only the support of 'three-fourths of the inhabitants' could convince him to resume his seat.[59]

Despite his victory at the show of hands the year before, the Nottingham press was not sanguine about O'Connor's chances. The radical middle-class newspaper, the *Nottingham Review*, for example, doubted he would receive 200 votes and urged him not to bother: 'we think him better employed at Lowband's, in nursing his money making land scheme, than in coming to Nottingham, where, he has not the shadow of a chance'.[60] The campaign was short and lacklustre (the local press commenting on the absence of the usual squibs, posters and flags); O'Connor had only arrived on the Monday prior to the nomination on Wednesday. Nevertheless, he was soon in action and at a large public meeting on Tuesday night he made much of his opponents failure to appear:[61]

> It appears that they who to-morrow and the day after will ask you for your sweet voices, are now in their hiding-places, afraid to face public opinion, lest they should receive public censure...

He reserved his sharpest criticism for his principal opponent, the Whig Cabinet Minister, Sir John Cam Hobhouse. Much to the amusement of the crowd O'Connor conjured up a vivid picture of Sir John and his committee huddled in a nearby public house 'counting over his notes' and trying to decide whether a bribe of £5 or £10 or £15 a head 'would be enough to carry the election', a reference to the parliamentary enquiry into serious allegations of bribery and intimidation against Hobhouse which had followed a local by-election in 1841.[62] 'To- morrow', O'Connor promised the crowd, 'we shall have a field day'.[63] He was not joking.

Even by his own high standards O'Connor's speech at the nomination was exceptional, not so much for his eloquence in articulating lofty sentiments but for the sheer force with which he forensically demolished his opponents. The Whigs candidates, Hobhouse and Thomas Gisborne (whom O'Connor had previously supported), spoke first. O'Connor took considerable pains to ensure that they were given a hearing – even threatening not to speak himself – but this probably had less to do with a sense of fair play than with giving his opponents enough rope with which to hang themselves. When it was his turn to address the crowd O'Connor turned his attention first to Hobhouse. 'I ask you', he said, 'if you ever heard so meagre, so unsatisfactory, so insignificant, so puerile, so childish an exhibition, as you have had to day from the minister of the Crown?' O'Connor then proceeded to mock Hobhouse's speech and his record in office with withering sarcasm. The reporter for the *Nottingham Review* struggled to find different ways to convey a scene that was repeated with stinging monotony: 'Great laughter', 'Laughter and cheers', 'Continued laughter', 'Great amusement in the crowd', 'Renewed laughter', 'Busts of merriment', 'Hooting and laughter', 'Loud laughter'.[64] O'Connor concluded his speech by cleverly linking his vision for a rural solution to Britain's malaise directly to Nottingham. 'Just consider this picture', he suggested, 'Look at Nottingham now, a barren waste all round it; picture Nottingham surrounded by thirty thousand acres of well-cultivated soil, with ten thousand peasants upon it'. It could happen: 'Yesterday', he told them, 'by agency, I purchased 500 acres more land. (Tremendous and long-continued cheering.)' He was a man of action: 'And when I say I will vote, I do not say it like my opponents; I do not say if any one brings it forward, I will support it; but I pledge myself to keep hammering at the ministers – (laughter) – till I make them do it. (Continued cheering.)' 'I devote twelve hours every day to the service of the poor', he continued, 'and I never travelled a mile, or eat [sic.] a meal, at their expense. (Hear, hear.) And yet I am supposed to be an individual not fit to be a representative in the House of Commons. Why?'[65]

It was a good question. The results, however, took everyone by surprise, perhaps even O'Connor himself. O'Connor was elected second behind the Tory, John Walter; Gisborne was third and Hobhouse last. The Whigs had given local electors plenty of cause to vote against them; the nonconformists had been offended by their support for state funding of schools run by religious organisations; Gisborne had voted against a measure designed to help the local framework knitters; Hobhouse had spoken but once in six years on an issue directly relevant to his constituency when he opposed Thomas Duncombe's measure to restrict the hours of child labour.[66] Nevertheless, the result was surprising. In searching for a reason the *Nottingham Review* (which had not given him a 'shadow's chance') focused on O'Connor's performance on the hustings:

But the speech of the day was Mr. O'Connor's, and it told with considerable power on all sections of the assembly. We are not going too far, when we assert that, though we saw reason to dissent here and there from the speaker's sentiments, and to question the entire justice of his reasoning and charges, his address was a masterly piece of oratory, teeming with sentiments the truest and noblest.[67]

The result reverberated around the nation. 'It is with feelings of inexpressible pleasure and exultation we have to announce the return of Mr. O'Connor as Member for Nottingham', boasted the *Star* with predictable ebullience, 'This a blow which will tell, not only in England, but in every part of Europe.' The *Manchester Examiner* thought, undoubtedly like many others, that Feargus had merely stood 'for the purpose of making a Chartist speech'; the *Nottingham Journal* thought the result 'altogether like a dream'.[68] O'Connor took the opportunity to pay tribute to his working-class supporters, most of whom had been denied the right to vote for him by the system that they were determined to change. 'Many had been astonished at his passing over from his own ranks to advocate the cause of the people', he told an impromptu crowd in the Nottingham Market Place, 'but he had always said that he had been promoted from the ranks of the aristocracy, to a commission in the democracy. He never would forget the fustian jackets, the blistered hands, and unshorn chins which had returned him.'[69] All over Britain Chartists began to hold meetings to rejoice at the victory; one celebration was even held across the Atlantic in Philadelphia.[70] As Gammage recalled, it appeared that all O'Connor touched would surely turn to gold: 'Everything appeared to go with him right joyously, and opposition seemed but the more to increase his power'.[71]

Victory had immediate implications for the rhythm of O'Connor's activities and it was soon announced that a manager of the Chartist Land Company had been appointed to allow him sufficient time to attend to his duties in Westminster.[72] Soon he was also musing over tactics in public: 'Twenty honest independent men', he told a meeting in Liverpool, 'were capable of breaking up any administration'.[73] The problem was that there were not twenty votes he could count on. Unlike his first period in the Commons when he was, ostensibly at least, part of the Irish party, he had few friends in Westminster in 1847. Although there were approximately sixty 'radical' MPs, few of them were of O'Connor's stripe.[74] His one likely close ally was Thomas Duncombe, who had joined the National Charter Association, and O'Connor immediately set about coming to terms with a characteristic admixture of brashness and obsequiousness. 'My terms are', he wrote to the longstanding London MP, 'that upon Irish questions I shall be free to act as I please; in all else I will *follow you*, but no other man. I will propose no national question of which you are the proper, the acknowledged, the loved leader...'[75] Duncombe's response is unknown.[76] Regardless, O'Connor was doomed to cut a lonely figure. As the editor of the *Nation* recorded in 1850, O'Connor, 'baited on all sides, exclaimed "the People's Charter and no surrender" – just as Barnaby Rudge's raven, perched on a tombstone, croaked "never say die"'.[77] Nevertheless, O'Connor took comfort from the fact that he had a special role to fill, indeed isolation appealed to his highly developed solipsistic sense of self. As he informed the audience at a grandiosely named 'O'Connor Festival' in Nottingham in November 1847: '[W]hen I speak in the House of Commons I do not speak, as Feargus O'Connor only; – I do not speak as the representative of Nottingham solely, but I speak as the mouth-piece of every industrious man in England, Ireland, Scotland and Wales'.[78] Moreover, he never lost sight of the value of a parliamentary speech in communicating to the nation at large; a speech, he opined, 'will be in the hands of thousands on Saturday; and if sound, it will be adopted'.[79]

O'Connor took his seat in November. Although the Palace of Westminster had re-opened in 1844, a decade after the fire which had substantially destroyed it, the new House of Commons chamber was not used until 1850. In 1847 the surroundings would have thus have been very familiar for the Member for Nottingham returning after a break of twelve years. Unlike many of the Irish MPs, who sat with the Whigs (an indication of how far they had lost touch with events in Ireland), O'Connor sat on the opposition benches, next to Duncombe, if he bothered to turn up, or between Disraeli and Peel 'like a constable between the Capulets and the Montagues of conservatism'.[80] What they thought of this arrangement is not known. O'Connor was, it appears, determined to accentuate his isolation by his flamboyant attire. According to one commentator, when Feargus was in the House it was 'difficult for any soberly-clad man to catch the Speaker's eye' which was 'infallibly' drawn to the Member for Nottingham's 'positive colours, and egotistical waistcoats, and watch chains'.[81] A contemporary engraving, albeit in black and white, offers a more restrained image (see plate 5).

O'Connor is recorded as making his first speech on 23 November during the Address in Reply. It neatly essayed two of his central passions: Ireland and the land. Describing himself as 'a soldier in the cause of Ireland' he promised that he 'would sit in that House, stand in that House, and sleep in that House' until the proposed coercion of Ireland was defeated. 'Instead of passing Coercion Bills', he pleaded, 'let them set the people to cultivate the land.' He had made the 'science of agriculture' a household topic in every cottage in England; a similar solution was available to Ireland: 'There was just one master grievance in Ireland; and if that were removed, it would do a thousand times more good than setting the people to knock down hills and dig holes', a reference to the government policy of making recipients of poor relief work for it. 'Give the tenantry perpetual tenures and corn-rents', he argued, 'and all would be right.'[82] The vexed issue of tenant rights would shape the relations between Irish nationalists and British governments until the Wyndham Act of 1903, but in 1847 O'Connor received no support in the Imperial Parliament.[83] In opposing coercion he promised that 'even if he should stand alone he would divide the House upon every single occasion on which he could do so'. Nor could he resist a swipe at O'Connell's feeble progeny and successors who appeared unable to see past the alliance that had sustained them during the 1830s: 'He was content to go into the lobby alone, and let the Irish Members go along with the Ministers if they pleased'.[84] Early in December O'Connor moved for the establishment of a Select Committee to enquire into the consequences of the Legislative Union with Ireland, ostensibly as a means of exposing the intentions of his fellow MPs. His motion attracted a derisory 23 votes.[85] Soon he resorted to the familiar charge of Whig hypocrisy. 'There was no better way of answering a Whig Government than from its own lips', he quipped. In fact he found hypocrisy superabundant among his colleagues: 'They sympathised with Poland; but while Poland was redolent only of the fresh blood of the martyrs who had fallen for their country, Ireland was stinking with the decomposed carcasses of her starving people...'[86]

It is ironic that as the Member for an English borough O'Connor spoke as often about Irish affairs as he had when he had represented Cork a decade earlier. Admittedly, in the midst of the famine Irish affairs were close to the top of the political agenda, but this is perhaps insufficient to explain the preponderance.[87] Even when speaking on general matters, which he frequently did, it was Irish examples which came most easily to his lips. Nottingham was rarely raised. Moreover, many of the examples he raised dated from the 1820s and 1830s. It was almost as if he was stuck in the past. What is perhaps more significant is that he did not mention the People's Charter in his first six months back in parliament. He did give a splendid speech calling for clemency for political prisoners (he evoked the powerful image of the government scouring prison hulks for pickpockets to release rather than recommend clemency for Frost, Williams and Jones languishing in Van Diemen's Land), but this was after he used an earlier opportunity to call for compensation for a captain of the Irish coast guard wronged in the late 1820s.[88]

Where his concerns did encompass both Britain and Ireland was in relation to a broader discourse about rights. The pretext for his intervention was the controversial Crown and Government Security Bill introduced by Lord John Russell's nervous administration as news of revolution spread through the capital cities of Europe. O'Connor spoke several times during the marathon debates. His argument was that the Bill effectively amounted suspension of Habeas Corpus and represented a serious erosion of the rights guaranteed by the venerable constitution. The government, he believed, was courting disaster:

He had always told the working classes that the constitution of this country was worth fighting for, and worth dying for, and that the right of freedom of speech always enabled the people to bring a moral force to bear upon the Government; but once gag the people, once put fetters upon the free expression of public opinion, and there would be an end to the boast of the British Constitution.[89]

'Let it become law', he threatened, 'and he would traverse the country, morning, noon, and night, and his constant cry would be, "Down with the base, bloody, and brutal Whigs!"' Popular constitutionalism was undoubtedly the 'master narrative' of nineteenth century politics,[90] but by 1848 baiting the Whigs had a hollow ring to it. Again, O'Connor seemed to be stuck in the past.

O'Connor felt that his isolation highlighted the lack of viable opposition within the parliament, which did not augur well for the nation.[91] Eventually he directly moved for the implementation of the People's Charter, but his speeches on those occasions lacked the passion of his other contributions in parliament. In 1849 his opening words were a recognition of the 'disadvantage under which he laboured' in the House. Although he insisted that before long the 'House must be the reflex of public opinion' and concluded on a defiant note of 'the Charter and no surrender', he obviously felt the isolation, admitting that he 'rose on the present occasion under unfortunate circumstances, not being backed, as in the previous year, by a monster petition'. He devoted most of his speech to the issue of annual parliaments, arguing that in an age of rapid progress this was the only way to 'legislate for the mind of the day'. When the resolution was put to the vote it attracted a paltry 13 votes.[92] In 1850 he rose to enunciate 'great truths' in what he called the 'annual farce' (given the state of the House) of moving for the implementation of the People's Charter but he had barely cleared his throat before another member drew attention to the state of the House and the debate was terminated for want of a quorum.[93] The 'discourtesy' and disinterest of his colleagues was surely reason enough, but O'Connor's apparent reluctance may well have also reflected the fact that his primary interest was now in Irish affairs and in the promulgation of the Chartist land plan. Ironically, it might have also been an indication that he shared the fears expressed by Daniel O'Connell in the early 1830s when Feargus had attempted to force him to introduce a motion for Repeal: that a vote in the House of Commons could reveal weakness as well as strength.

If 1847 had been a year of triumph for O'Connor, 1848 delivered a series of setbacks from which he never recovered. The year began well enough with the purchase in January of a site at Great Dodford for another Chartist estate.[94] From then on it was mostly all downhill. Parliament delivered the two most damaging blows. The first came as a result of the 1848 petition. Shortly after returning to the House of Commons O'Connor had been inundated with petitions from Chartists around the nation and by February 1848 the editor of the *Northern Star* was issuing advice on the strict rules that governed their presentation.[95] Early in 1848 the Chartists had resolved to again press their case in a National Petition and O'Connor expressed his desire to see it dwarf previous efforts. The 1842 petition had required sixteen men to carry it; this time let it be thirty, he argued, followed by a procession of 500,000. His target for signatures was equally ambitious: five million. His new mantra was: 'SIGN! SIGN!! SIGN!!!'[96] In a tragi-comic anticipation of what was to come he concluded one of his weekly epistles: 'Good night, my children. SIGN! SIGN!! SIGN!!! And do not allow us to be laughed at when we convey your will and pleasure to the door of the Senate House. Your affectionate father, FEARGUS O'CONNOR'.[97]

As 10 April, the date for the presentation of the petition approached, the political temperature in Britain increased dramatically. Every post brought news from the continent of 'a fresh revolution or dethronement';[98] the Queen left Buckingham Palace for the safety of Osborne; in anticipation of a rising of bloodthirsty Chartists, Irish rebels and vagabonds, every 'gentleman in London' enrolled as a Special Constable; Frederick Maurice, the Christian Socialist, was rejected; Louis Napoleon, the future emperor of the French, was assigned to patrol Hampstead Road with a greengrocer and Arthur Pell's brother; at the Foreign Office Lord Palmerston's clerks stood ready to 'mash' any insurgent Chartists or foreigners to 'jelly'.[99] On 6 April, Sir George Grey, the Home Secretary, had told the House that the proposed Chartist procession was illegal. O'Connor was on his feet immediately and with the indulgence of the House pointed to the precedents for such parades, including during the Reform Bill agitation when those in the Cabinet had encouraged them.[100] The public meeting at Kennington Common proceeded on 10 April but the procession was abandoned in compliance with the government ban. The Prime Minister reported to the Queen that O'Connor had been 'pale and frightened' when interviewed by the Chief Commissioner of London police, but there is no evidence to corroborate this.[101] On the contrary, it was only Feargus who crossed the heavily-fortified Thames. Even the four Chartist horses from O'Connorville trimmed in red, white and green, who had been enlisted to pull the petition cart, were not made to face Wellington's guns and barricades.

Later in the afternoon O'Connor tabled the petition claiming that it contained 5,706,000 signatures and anticipated a debate on its contents at the end of the week. The petition was given to the Standing Committee on Public Petitions for consideration which, as is well known, reported that it contained, in reality, 1,900,000 signatures. Among the rest the Committee identified a substantial number of false signatures some of which 'your Committee do not hazard offending the House or the dignity of their own proceedings by reporting'.[102]

Not even O'Connor's most strident opponents in the movement believed that he had been wrong to abandon the procession in the face of the government prohibition, or that he had wiled away the nights adding obviously bogus and indecent signatures to the document despite his determination to see it contain more than 5,000,000 names. And yet he has almost single-handedly been made to wear the 'enormous condescension of posterity' as a consequence. The tone for much of the subsequent historiography was set as early as 1850 by Charles Kingsley (who had served as a Special Constable) in *Alton Locke*, his fictionalised version of the events of two years earlier. Students of Chartism will remember the excruciating denouement to the chapter, 'the tenth of April', when O'Connor's 'courage failed him after all', the procession is abandoned, and the monster petition is 'dragged to the floor of the House of Commons amid roars of laughter – "inextinguishable laughter" – as of Tennyson's Epicurean Gods'.[103] If a historical actor was ever in need of rescuing it was Feargus O'Connor.[104]

O'Connor's response was a combination of tempestuous indignation and shrewd analysis. He regarded comments by members of the Committee as a slur upon his integrity and, having threatened one member with a duel, he was briefly arrested on the orders of the Speaker and compelled to apologise to the House. Amidst the rage, however, O'Connor actually did a very good job of defending himself. It was not possible, he told the House, for the petition to have been checked by the 13 clerks in 17 hours as was claimed.[105] As he subsequently wrote in the *Northern Star*, 'each clerk, besides the critical inspection of names, must have counted about 147,170 names, in round numbers, within the prescribed time' – this, he continued, worked out at 8,660 each hour, that is 150 every minute, or two and half every second for seventeen hours without interruption. O'Connor was correct: such an exercise was not possible. Simple arithmetic provided the 'most perfect circumstantial evidence', O'Connor concluded, that the Chartists and he were victims of an 'unjust, ungenerous and unjustifiable conspiracy'.[106] In fact, O'Connor's rhetoric was better than his arithmetic. The figures he published related to the lower, revised total and not the original which would have been all the more beyond the capacity of 13 clerks to count in 17 hours.[107] Taking up O'Connor's point, the Chartist Convention asked for the petition to be returned to them to check the veracity of the signatures and the total: it is perhaps not surprising that their request fell on deaf ears.[108]

Parliament's second blow came in relation to his beloved Land Company. Following O'Connor's election in 1847 a number of newspapers, including the *Nonconformist*, the *Dispatch*, *Lloyd's Newspaper* and the *Nottingham Journal*, had carried on an unremitting attack on the plan freely impugning

O'Connor's honesty into the bargain. Most vicious was a series of letters in the *Manchester Examiner*, a newspaper edited by a former League apparatchik, and penned by one of the League's most talented publicists, Alexander Somerville, under the signature 'One Who Has Whistled at the Plough'.[109] 'We regard him', boomed the editor, 'as by far the greatest quack that has appeared since CAGLIOSTRO.'[110] O'Connor met these attacks on his integrity with a mixture of indifference and indignation. As previously, it is clear that he believed that the barbs of his opponents only served to strengthen his bond with his followers, and he could always give as good as he got. Early in November 1847 O'Connor took the platform at the Manchester Hall of Science to meet his accusers. Such was the press of the crowd that Peter McDouall was left outside to address the estimated 5,000 or 6,000 people who could not gain entry; inside the Hall was packed by an estimated 3,000 women and men.[111] The galleries of the Hall had been festooned with cabbages grown on a Chartist estate as a 'nosegay for the Whistler' (Somerville later alleged that O'Connor had bought them at a London market).[112] To rapturous applause O'Connor ruthlessly excoriated his accusers and, at the same time, dismissed the attacks of the press as 'only fun for him'. When 'he lay down on his pillow', he told the crowd, 'he devoted half-an-hour to laughing at them – it was only like tickling him with sugar-sticks and he answered them occasionally with a tap of his bamboo'. The effect was incandescent, leaving the *Northern Star* struggling for adequate hyperbole: 'It was not enthusiasm, it was madness, a frenzy that cannot be described'.[113]

Despite the 'Glorious triumph of the "People's Bailiff"' soon the charges were being repeated in the House of Commons. In debate during February and March O'Connor indicated that he would seek to amend the Friendly Societies Act to encompass the scheme and save the subscribers the expense of full company registration under the current arrangements. Sir George Grey made it clear that the government was unlikely to support the amendment to include what he said was 'of the nature of a lottery'.[114] If O'Connor had assumed that the state would be willing to help him regularise the affairs of the company simply because it was in the public interest, or at least in the interests of the poor who had invested their meagre shillings and pence in the scheme, he was to be sadly mistaken. When this was made clear he defiantly told the House that, regardless, he 'was resolved to persevere. He would not be prevented from so doing by the difficulties or intricacies of the law. No power on earth should make him abandon the land plan which he had expended so much time and toil in maturing. He had created too many ardent hopes in the minds of those who had adopted his views to ever surrender them.'[115] 'No surrender' had become no surrender of the land plan.

O'Connor continued to face questions from his parliamentary colleagues about the affairs of the company and by May, the month that the Minster Lovell estate was partly occupied, the government agreed to establish a select committee to examine the scheme before the second reading of O'Connor's Bill in June. Oddly, O'Connor was both a member of the committee and its star witness. In the month that the Snigs End and Minster Lovell estates were opened the hearings commenced under the chairmanship of William Hayter, the Judge Advocate. O'Connor sought moral vindication if nothing else: 'I am ready to admit to this Committee that I have violated every law in my attempt to carry out this plan, but that I have violated no question of honour'.[116] The Committee's conclusions were published at the end of July. It found that the scheme was illegal; that O'Connor's proposed amendment would not help; and that the records and accounts of the company had been shoddily kept. O'Connor seized on the finding that he personally had not been guilty of fraud – on the contrary that he was out of pocket by £3,400 – and he remained defiant in the face of the political and legal reality: 'If the company is not legal', he wrote, 'it ought to be so'.[117] The findings, however, did not end the turmoil, they exacerbated it, condemning all parties to a protracted death. The people's bailiff was, in fact, the owner of large tracts of land purchased with the money of the members of an as yet unregistered company. Efforts to register the company continued while O'Connor promised to will the land to its current tenants and sought expressions of confidence in his conduct. Soon debts began to compound the morass of legal difficulties and confound the 'ardent hopes' that he had done so much to excite.

If the political class had gleefully taken two opportunities to damage O'Connor in 1848 he further added to his decline by his own hand. For years he retained the confidence of the 'fustian jackets' by promoting an independent working-class radicalism neatly summed up by the catch-cry 'no surrender'. As late as May 1848 O'Connor was still dismissing those he called the 'FOUR POINT HUMBUGS', including Richard Cobden, who preferred 'perfumed' Chartism; his Chartism would remain, he stated, 'unalloyed'.[118] During 1849, however, he began to resile from this stand and seriously consider the middle-class embrace; he even dallied with the ultimate heresy of a decade earlier: that 'the people could not carry all by themselves'.[119] It was the beginning of the end. His suitor (although he may not have intended it) was Sir Joshua Walmsley, MP for Bolton. In 1849 Walmsley founded the Metropolitan (later National) Parliamentary and Financial Reform Association on the twin objectives of extension of the franchise to all ratepayers and reform of the financial system (shifting from indirect to direct taxation and cutting government spending) which tapped a residue of support for the traditional radical critique of 'old corruption'.[120] Walmsley, a former Liverpool Mayor and wealthy and politically ambitious businessman, attracted the support of a cross section of parliamentary radicals and veterans of the Anti-Corn Law League, and he openly courted the Chartists of the metropolis.[121] His efforts quickly bore fruit, but the embrace of the Parliamentary and Financial Reform Association precipitated a schism in the National Charter Association. In April 1850 a group of prominent Chartists including Philip McGrath and Thomas Clark, both of them former Directors of the National Land Company and Members of the Executive of the National Charter Association, founded a rival organisation, the National Charter League, which adopted as 'one of its primary objectives' the creation of 'a friendly intercourse with all those, without reference to class distinction, who are labouring to bring about a change in our representative system'.[122]

O'Connor ran hot and cold on the question. According to Gammage, he 'became every day more in love with the financial and parliamentary reformers' during 1849 and he attended their meetings claiming that he 'had not come there to throw the apple of discord amongst them but to extend the olive branch of peace'. In April 1850, however, O'Connor invoked a familiar metaphor from the halcyon days of early Chartism when he indicated that he hoped to convince Walmsley and his associates to 'adopt the WHOLE HOG, BRISTLES AND ALL'. At the same time, Clark and McGrath were among O'Connor's oldest allies and he did not denounce them with the usual vehemence he reserved for 'seceders'.[123] In a further twist, at a National Conference in Manchester in January 1851 O'Connor backed away from the class alliance strategy thereby adding to the confusion and disunion in the ranks.[124] O'Connor followed up these tergiversations with a clumsy attack on the presence of European refugees in London that appeared to give succour to the xenophobia of *The Times* in the lead up to the Great Exhibition. Many Chartists were appalled. Under the headline 'Save Us From Our Friends', Harney lamented that O'Connor's 'vague denunciations and pitiful warnings can only serve the enemies of the people'.[125] He had a point. By the end of 1851 O'Connor had sold the *Northern Star* to its former editor and it was clear that he was now responding to the agendas of others in a way that would have been impossible a decade earlier. He looked increasingly like a man of the past. Time was now his enemy. As his career in English politics began to falter O'Connor sought salvation in Ireland.

Notes

1   Letter from Watkin to Cobden cited in N. McCord, *The Anti-Corn Law League*, London, 1958, pp. 102-3.
2   'Life and Adventures of Feargus O'Connor', *National Instructor*, 14 September 1850, p. 266.
3   *Manchester Times*, 12 March 1842; *Northern Star*, 19 March 1842.
4   See F. O'Connor, *The Trial of Feargus O'Connor and Fifty-eight Others on a Charge*

of Sedition, Conspiracy Tumult and Riot (1843), New York, 1970, pp. 106-9.

5   T. Cooper, *The Life of Thomas Cooper* (1872), Leicester, 1971, p. 211, suggests that when the printed placard was read to the delegates O'Connor had moved that it be issued in the name of the Executive rather than the Conference. The Placard itself, however, was headed 'The Executive Committee of the National Charter Association to the People'.

6   *Northern Star*, 26 March 1842.

7   *Northern Star*, 19 February 1842.

8   See A. Tyrrell, *Joseph Sturge and the Moral Radical Party in Early Victorian Britain*, London, 1982, pp. 129-30.

9   O'Connor, *The Trial of Feargus O'Connor*, p. 1.

10 Tyrrell records the 'moral repugnance' of the Sturge's sister, Sophia, at Joseph's dealings with O'Connor. See *Sturge*, p. 130.

11 O'Connor, *The Trial of Feargus O'Connor*, p. 9.

12 O'Connor, *The Trial of Feargus O'Connor*, p. 291.

13 O'Connor, *The Trial of Feargus O'Connor*, p. 291.

14 O'Connor, *The Trial of Feargus O'Connor*, p. 291.

15 O'Connor, *The Trial of Feargus O'Connor*, p. 289.

16 See my discussion of Griffin and Cartledge in 'Betrayal and Exile: A Forgotten Chartist Experience', M.T. Davis and P.A. Pickering (eds), *Unrespectable Radicals*, Aldershot, 2007, pp. 201-17.

17 O'Connor, *The Trial of Feargus O'Connor*, p. 390.

18 *Northern Star*, 1 November 1845. He was overlooking the government's subsequent attempt to prosecute Daniel O'Connell.

19 See *Northern Star*, 26 August 1848; A.R. Schoyen, *The Chartist Challenge: A Portrait of George Julian Harney*, London, 1958, p. 133n.

20 *Northern Star*, 16 September 1843.

21 *Northern Star*, 20 April 1844, 27 April 1844.

22 See R.G. Gammage, *History of the Chartist Movement 1837-1854* (1854), New York, 1969, pp. 268-70; A.M. Hadfield, *The Chartist Land Company*, Newton Abbot, 1970, pp. 17-18.

23 *Northern Star*, 31 May 1845.

24 *Northern Star*, 20 September 1845.

25 *Northern Star*, 20 September 1845; 27 September 1845; 4 October 1845.

26 *Northern Star*, 11 October 1845.

27 *Northern Star*, 20 September 1845.

28 *Northern Star*, 11 October 1845.

29 *Northern Star*, 4 October 1845.

30 *Northern Star*, 20 September 1845.

31 *Northern Star*, 4 October 1845. See also *Hansard* [House of Commons], 7 April 1848, col. 41.

32 *Northern Star*, 11 October 1845; 1 November 1845.

33 *Northern Star*, 4 October 1845; 1 November 1845.

34 *Northern Star*, 26 September 1846.

35 *Northern Star*, 1 November 1845; 8 November 1845.

36 Schoyen, *The Chartist Challenge*, p. 131.

37 See F. O'Connor to G.J. Harney, 2 January 1848, reprinted in F.G. and R.M. Black (eds), *The Harney Papers*, Assen, 1969, pp. 61-2.
38 O'Connor to Harney, 2 January 1848, *The Harney Papers*, pp. 61-2.
39 G.J. Harney to F. Engels, 30 March 1848, reprinted in *The Harney Papers*, pp. 241-2.
40 See *Northern Star*, 24 June 1843. In 1843 he told Thomas Allsop that 'he knew of no other circumstance that would induce me to take up a musket, but I certainly would do it to meet froggy on British or Irish ground'. See British Library of Political and Economic Science, *Allsop Collection*, Coll. Misc. 0525/2, letter 30.
41 *Labourer*, vol. 1, 1847, p. 149; vol. 3, 1848, pp. 54-5.
42 Cited in Hadfield, *Chartist Land Company*, p. 19. See also *Northern Star*, 27 January 1849.
43 *Northern Star*, 22 November 1845.
44 *Northern Star*, 22 November 1845; 13 December 1845; 20 December 1845.
45 See Hadfield, *Chartist Land Company*, p. 24. See also I. Foster, *Heronsgate: Freedom, Happiness and Contentment. The First 150 Years of the Estate*, Heronsgate, 1999. I am grateful to Owen Ashton for this reference.
46 *Northern Star*, 22 August 1846. See also M. Brook, 'A Chartist Flag', *Notes and Queries*, July 1957, p. 314.
47 *Bible*, Lev. 25:10: 'And ye shall hallow the fiftieth year, and proclaim liberty throughout all the land unto all the inhabitants thereof: it shall be a jubile unto you; and ye shall return every man unto his possession, and ye shall return every man to his family'. See M. Chase, 'From Millennium to Anniversary: The Concept of Jubilee in Late Eighteenth- and Nineteenth-Century England', *Past and Present*, no. 129, November 1990, pp. 132-147.
48 *Northern Star*, 22 August 1846.
49 *Northern Star*, 22 August 1846.
50 *Northern Star*, 22 August 1846.
51 *Northern Star*, 13 February 1847.
52 *Northern Star*, 8 May 1847.
53 *Northern Star*, 8 May 1847. See also *Northern Star*, 29 May 1847.
54 It appears that he passed no comment on O'Connell's death at all.
55 *Nottingham Review*, 10 July 1846.
56 *Northern Star*, 25 July 1846.
57 *Nottingham Review*, 11 June 1847.
58 *Nottingham Review*, 11 June 1847.
59 *Nottingham Review*, 11 June 1847.
60 *Nottingham Review*, 2 July 1847; 23 July 1847.
61 *Nottingham Review*, 30 July 1847.
62 See R.E. Zegger, *John Cam Hobhouse: A Political Life*, Columbia, 1973, chapter 10.
63 *Nottingham Review*, 30 July 1847.
64 *Nottingham Review*, 30 July 1847.
65 *Nottingham Review*, 30 July 1847.
66 *Nottingham Review*, 30 July 1847; Zegger, *John Cam Hobhouse*, p. 236.
67 *Nottingham Review*, 30 July 1847.
68 *Northern Star*, 7 August 1847; *Nottingham Review*, 6 August 1847 supplement.

69 *Nottingham Review*, 30 July 1847.

70 *Northern Star*, 7 August 1847; 14 August 1847; *Nottingham Review*, 13 August 1847. See also S. Roberts, 'Feargus O'Connor in the House of Commons 1847-1852', in O. Ashton, R. Fyson and S. Roberts (eds), *The Chartist Legacy*, London, 1999, pp. 104-6.

71 Gammage, *History of the Chartist Movement*, p. 285.

72 *Nottingham Review*, 10 September 1847.

73 *Nottingham Review*, 27 August 1847.

74 The estimation is Miles Taylor's. See M. Taylor, *The Decline of British Radicalism 1847-1860*, Oxford, 1995, p. 110.

75 T.H. Duncombe, *The Life and Correspondence of Thomas Slingsby Duncombe Late MP for Finsbury*, London, 1868, vol. 1, p. 373. Original emphasis.

76 As Stephen Roberts has pointed out, Duncombe rarely attended the House and effectively did not provide the lead to Feargus or anyone else. See Roberts, 'Feargus O'Connor in the House of Commons', p. 110.

77 *Nation*, 9 March 1850. O'Connor knew that this was his fate, often stating that he would go into the lobby alone if he had to be the lone vote against a measure. See, *inter alia*, *Hansard* [House of Commons], 7 April 1848, col. 42.

78 *Northern Star*, 20 November 1847.

79 *Nottingham Review*, 30 July 1847.

80 *Daily News* cited in I. and P. Kuczynski (eds), *A Young Revolutionary in Nineteenth-Century England: Selected Writings of Georg Weerth*, Berlin, 1971, p. 169.

81 *Blackwood's Edinburgh Magazine*, vol. 82, October 1857, p. 499. See also *Sentinel*, 10 February 1844.

82 *Hansard* [House of Commons], 24 November 1847, cols. 142-3. This issue would dominate the agenda of Anglo-Irish political relations for a generation.

83 See P.J. Bull, *Land, Nationalism, and Politics: A Study of the Irish Land Question*, Dublin, 1996.

84 *Hansard* [House of Commons], 29 November 1847, col. 320.

85 *Hansard* [House of Commons], 7 December 1847, cols. 797-8. Three O'Connells supported him.

86 *Hansard* [House of Commons], 9 December 1847, col. 890; 24 March 1848, col. 1012.

87 It attracted comment in the press. See *Northern Star*, 27 November 1847.

88 *Hansard* [House of Commons], 23 March 1848, cols. 9, 14-17; 6 April 1848, 1369-73. He had first raised the case in 1834.

89 *Hansard* [House of Commons], 18 April 1848, col. 454.

90 See J. Vernon, *Politics and the People: A Study of English Political Culture, c.1815-1867*, Cambridge, 1993, p. 296.

91 *Hansard* [House of Commons], 10 April 1848, col. 84-5.

92 *Hansard* [House of Commons], 3 July 1849, cols. 1268-1306.

93 *Hansard* [House of Commons], 12 July 1850, cols. 1282-4. An attempt had been made to count him out the previous year.

94 This estate was opened successfully in July 1849. See D. Poole, *The Last Chartist Land Settlement: Great Dodford 1849*, Dodford, 1999. I am grateful to Owen Ashton for this reference.

95   *Northern Star*, 12 February 1848. See also P.A. Pickering, 'And Your Petitioners &c: Chartist Petitioning in Popular Politics', *English Historical Review*, vol. CXVI, no. 466, 2001, pp. 368-388.

96   *Northern Star*, 4 March 1848.

97   *Northern Star*, 25 March 1848.

98   R. Cobden to Mrs Cobden, 27 March 1848, reprinted in J. Morley, *The Life of Richard Cobden*, London, 1903, p. 484.

99   See J.T. Ward, *Chartsim*, London, 1973, pp. 200-4 for a comprehensive survey of the alarm among the ruling classes.

100 *Hansard* [House of Commons], 6 April 1848, col. 1354.

101 See Ward, *Chartism*, p. 207.

102 *Hansard* [House of Commons], 13 April 1848, cols. 285-6.

103 C. Kingsley, *Alton Locke, Taylor and Poet: An Autobiography*, London, 1850, p. 292. Early twentieth century historians tended to follow suit. For Julius West, for example, the report of the Committee on Public Petitions was 'devastating'. Similarly, for the doyen of Chartist historians, Mark Hovell, the fact that the document featured so many names of unlikely Chartists such as Queen Victoria and the Duke of Wellington as well a host of fictitious names earned the Chartists 'ridicule'; it was a 'tragic fiasco' from which the movement 'never recovered'. See J. West, *A History of the Chartist Movement*, London, 1920, p. 250; M. Hovell, *The Chartist Movement*, Manchester, 1918, p. 292. Not much has changed. For John Ward, for example, writing in the 1970s, the petition turned Chartism into 'a joke' and, as recently as 1997, Miles Taylor described the 1848 petition as a debacle. J. Ward, *Chartism*, p. 209; Taylor, *The Decline of British Radicalism*, p. 105.

104 I am deliberately here invoking E.P. Thompson's well-known aspiration to rescue 'the poor stockinger, the Luddite cropper, the "obsolete" hand-loom weaver, the "utopian" artisan, and even the deluded follower of Joanna Southcott, from the enormous condescension of posterity'. See *The Making of the English Working Class*, Harmondsworth, 1980, p. 12.

105 *Hansard* [House of Commons], 13 April 1848, cols. 286, 299-301.

106 *Hansard* [House of Commons], 13 April 1848, cols. 285-6; *Northern Star*, 22 April 1848.

107 As I have explained elsewhere there is an alternative explanation of how the revised figure was arrived at by the Committee in the available time. To understand what happened it is important to appreciate that the method employed by the Petitions Committee for examining large petitions up to this point was simply to count the number of signatures on one yard of petition and then measure the total length to extrapolate the final total. What probably happened in the case of the Chartists in 1848 was that the usual simple procedure was employed but in reverse: after some suspect signatures were detected, part of the petition was counted and this was then extrapolated to provide a revised total. See Pickering, 'And Your Petitioners &c' pp. 368-388.

108 *Northern Star*, 22 April 1848.

109 *Manchester Examiner*, August-December 1847 *passim*. See also Gammage, *History of the Chartist Movement*, pp. 27-8.

110 *Manchester Examiner*, 19 October 1847. For Cagliostro see I.D. McCalman, *The*

seven ordeals of Count Cagliostro: the greatest enchanter of the eighteenth century, Pymble, 2003.

111 *Northern Star* 6 November 1847. One of those unable to gain entry was the young Philip Wentworth: 'I was only permitted to peril my life at the door where the crush was so great that I almost suffocated'. See 'Notes and Sketches by the Way', *Middleton Guardian,* 22 March 1890.

112 *Manchester Times,* 6 November 1847. For Somerville's account of the meeting see A. Somerville, *Conservative Science of Nations,* Toronto, 1860, pp. 226-7.

113 *Northern Star,* 6 November 1847.

114 *Hansard* [House of Commons], 17 March 1848, col. 698.

115 *Hansard* [House of Commons], 17 March 1848, col. 697.

116 *Labourer,* vol. IV, 1848, p. 54.

117 *Labourer,* vol. IV, 1848, p. 120.

118 *Northern Star,* 27 May 1848.

119 *Northern Star,* 6 October 1849.

120 *Northern Star,* 3 February 1849; F.E. Gillespie, *Labour and Politics in England 1850-1867,* New York, 1966, chapter 3; N.C. Edsall, 'A Failed National Movement: the Parliamentary and Financial Reform Association, 1848-54', *Bulletin of the Institute of Historical Research,* vol. XLIX, pp. 108-131.

121 Cooper, *The Life of Thomas Cooper*, p. 224; *Northern Star,* 17 November 1849. For Walmsley see M. Stenton, *Who's Who of British Members of Parliament 1832-1885,* London, 1976, vol.1, p. 396.

122 *Northern Star,* 6 April 1849.

123 *Northern Star,* 27 April 1849; 21 July 1849; 6 October 1849; 6 April 1850; 4 May 1850; 11 May 1850; Gammage, *History of the Chartist Movement,* pp. 348, 350.

124 *Northern Star,* 22 June 1850; 1 February 1851; Gammage, *History of the Chartist Movement,* pp. 357, 367-8; G.J. Harney to F. Engels, 25 January 1851, *The Harney Papers,* p. 26.

125 *Friend of the People,* 26 April 1851; *Northern Star,* 5 April 1851. See also M. Finn, *After Chartism: Class and nation in English radical politics, 1848-1874,* Cambridge, 1993, pp. 82-3. Finn argues that O'Connor's 'tergiversations...acted to expand the ideological horizons of working-class radicalism'. I have borrowed the term from her.

8: 'A PICTURESQUE AGITATOR'

O'Connor's Irish 'mission' – as it was later called[1] – involved separate trips to Dublin in 1849 and 1850. Returning to Ireland represented going back to his roots and the chance for a new beginning. During the first of his visits, in November 1849, O'Connor sought to dramatically regain the place among the leaders of Irish nationalism that he had foregone 15 years before. The pretext for the trip was to attend an 'aggregate meeting of nationalists' to be held in the Music Hall, Dublin on 21 November, which had been called by Charles Gavan Duffy. As a co-founder of the *Nation*, the journal of the Young Ireland movement, Duffy had helped to cause the split with O'Connell during the mid-1840s that culminated in the formation of an Irish Confederation in 1847 to rival his Repeal Association. Duffy's objective in calling the conference was twofold. First, he sought to launch a new organisation called the Irish Alliance which would effect a reconciliation among Irish nationalists. Second, he hoped to provide a national platform for an agitation on the issue of 'the land'. Foreshadowing the now famous Tenant Rights Conference in August 1850, Duffy called for the formation of 'tenant right associations from sea to sea'.[2] By calling an aggregate meeting of Irish nationalists, however, Duffy got more than he bargained for: he got Feargus O'Connor.

O'Connor had laid the foundation for his 'mission' by his stand on Irish questions in the House of Commons. While the remnants of O'Connell's 'tail' of Irish MPs sat mute (or voted in support of the government), O'Connor's strident opposition earned him praise from John Mitchel as Ireland's only determined representative.[3] Subsequently, Mitchel used the columns of his newspaper, the *United Irishman*, to broadcast the message that O'Connor, in the face of O'Connell's denunciations, had struggled for years to convey to the Irish people. 'Every Chartist is a *Repealer*,' Mitchel told his readers, 'In all there is nothing for which we should hate the Chartists. Hate them! why they are our brethren and allies: we are bound to help them to their ends, as they offer to help us to ours.'[4]

Unfortunately for O'Connor, by November 1849 many of his new Irish allies were in hiding, prison or Van Diemen's Land. Free of Mitchel's violent counsel and attempting to forge a new direction, the last thing Gavan Duffy wanted to do was embrace Arthur O'Connor's nephew. In response to O'Connor's announcement that he intended to attend the conference, Duffy's *Nation* condemned the 'threatened interruption': 'alliances and friendships must be spontaneous and voluntary; the affection or confidence of a people can not be carried by rape'.[5] Undeterred, O'Connor explained that the principal object of his mission was 'to announce the fact that at length it has been discovered that the cause of the working Celt and the working Saxon must be fought by the workers of both countries'.[6] During the conference O'Connor needed little encouragement from supporters among the crowd to hijack the proceedings and address the meeting. His speech was a classic statement of his belief that political action provided the means to achieve social objectives. '[T]he question is not simply the land', he told the delegates, 'the question is, how you are to get your land'. He had 'devoted much…time to social reform', he continued, including the Chartists' own Land Plan, 'but I tell you… you may look upon everything else that is proposed to you as mere moonshine, until your order is fully and fairly represented in the House of Commons'.[7] He pleaded for an understanding that the working people of England were 'as much oppressed and trampled on by the aristocracy as you are…' Despite a promise to say nothing divisive, O'Connor could not resist an attack on John O'Connell and the other 'lick-spittles' representing Ireland in the House of Commons, explaining that they must be replaced by the 'labouring man with the fustian jacket, the tanned trousers and the brawny hands'. In a country where nationalist – and religious – aspirations often cut across class lines, this was an explicit call for a class-based alliance with the English working class.[8] O'Connor concluded his speech by stating that it was the strategy of their 'enemies' to excite division between 'working Saxon and Celt' and he emphasised the support of the Chartist population for the cause of justice for Ireland. The press in both England and Ireland reported that the speech had been greeted with 'tremendous cheering' from the audience, and O'Connor claimed that he had taken part in bringing about a 'union of the working class of England and Ireland'.[9] Within weeks, however, it was clear that his appeal to the conference had failed to produce the desired response. Some who he had hoped to attract to the Chartist banner followed Gavan Duffy into the campaign for Tenants' Rights and the disappointment of the Independent Irish Party. Others could not see beyond the loyalties to religion and nation or the prejudices against O'Connor that had been carefully and systematically invoked by the O'Connellites.

Simultaneously, however, O'Connor had begun lending his support to a rival organisation, the Irish Democratic Association. Ostensibly the ground here looked better prepared. Accompanied by two of his closest Chartist allies, Thomas Clark and Philip McGrath, O'Connor undertook his second visit to Ireland in four months to attend the inaugural national conference of this organisation in Dublin early in March 1850. In preparation he also contributed a series of lengthy articles to a fledgling Dublin Chartist newspaper, the *Irishman*, which he described as a 'sterling representation of the Irish democratic mind'.[10] After an ephemeral appearance in mid-1848, the *Irishman* commenced publication under the control of Bernard Fullam in January 1849.[11] O'Connor's letters are among his last detailed political statements and, by way of conclusion, are worthy of consideration. The letters neatly fall into two groups – those seeking to explain the Charter and those relating to the land – and they contained four interconnected themes which provide a useful index of his ideas: Ireland, democracy, land and class.

Under the rubric 'United We Stand – Divided We Fall!', a phrase that invoked the American revolution, he argued that the 'first and chief object to be attained must be a thorough union of the Irish people', and in pursuit of this objective he would 'bury the past into oblivion' which might have come as a surprise to those Irish MPs he had attacked at Duffy's Conference weeks before.[12] By the time of the conference in March he was back to his old ways. In 1834 'they had disinherited him', he told the crowd, 'He was told that if he came to Ireland he should be ducked in the Liffey'. What is worse, they had 'cheered men and reviled principles'.[13] His crucial point about Irish affairs related to Repeal, the issue which had divided him from the O'Connellites in the first place. Whereas in the 1830s he was ahead of his colleagues, by the end of the 40s he felt that Repeal was not enough. Despite his longstanding record in support of Repeal he was now at pains to make the point that by itself it would be of little benefit: 'if you had a Repeal of the Union to-morrow, you would be helpless beggars'.[14] On the contrary, Repeal, 'under the present system, would make you greater slaves than ever by increasing your local taskmasters'.[15]

What then was the means for ensuring the 'regeneration' of Ireland? The answer was the People's Charter. In large part O'Connor's arguments would have been familiar to readers of the *Northern Star* (and of the parliamentary debates), although he did his best to give the tale an Irish twist. Readers would have been surprised to find him giving credit to his old adversary (and invoking his son). 'Daniel O'Connell with his own hand', he pointed out, 'drew up the document entitled the PEOPLE'S CHARTER', and, in the last session, John O'Connell had voted for it in the House of Commons. Moreover, O'Connor outlined an Irish version of the historical case that he had often employed in support of the case for reform. The English argument was a familiar one: 'every single point of the People's Charter, with the exception of Vote by Ballot, formerly constituted the basis of the English Constitution'.[16] Although he believed that Ireland had never had a legitimate parliament (while 'Catholics could vote, Catholics could not sit in Parliament, where they were obliged to support the tyrant's Church'), 'up to the reign of James the First you had equal electoral districts in Ireland'.[17] This provision, he insisted, was the most important point of the Charter: 'I would prefer it to Universal Suffrage with Septennial Parliaments'.[18] More importantly, he drew attention to the fact that his family, and the tradition of Irish politics that they represented, had advocated the principles of the Charter: 'he came forward to advocate their principles', he told the meeting in Dublin, 'because his family had suffered more in supporting them than any other family that ever was born'.[19] The quest to vindicate his persecuted father was with him still; he remained, in his own mind at least, in his father's shadow.

O'Connor's underlying instrumentalist view of politics applied equally on either side of the Irish Sea: politics provided the only mechanism to obtain social objectives. In an early letter he invoked the standard formula: the People's Charter was the means, and 'social happiness' was the end.[20] In a later letter he was more specific: 'it becomes your bounden duty to unite, as one man, for the means to the end – the PEOPLE'S CHARTER, as the means, and the LAND as the end'.[21] No reader of these letters could mistake the centrality of the land in his thinking. Under the headline, 'THE LAND ! THE LAND !! THE LAND !!!', he insisted that 'his whole life's study' had 'been devoted to the single consideration as to how the industrious labourer may be made independent of the grinding capitalist'. The answer was simple: 'I have come to the conclusion that this object cannot be achieved by any other means than the location of the people upon their own land, deriving a comfortable subsistence from its produce, furnished by their own labour'.[22] He had even been moved to verse to promote the case:

> Unite! Unite! ye Irish brave,
> Let the Land your watchword be;
> Scout, oh scout the servile slave
> That crouches when he may be free.
> Up like heroes, at the despots –
> Lick no more the tyrant's hand;
> Leave you pauper house mess-pots,
> And live like freeman on your Land.[23]

Many surely found the sentiments admirable if not the poetry.

O'Connor's certainty that what would work in England would work in Ireland and visa versa was sustained by the belief that the problems of both countries stemmed from the same source: class legislation. '[I]t is an indisputable fact that the English people are equally oppressed by class legislation with ourselves', he argued. 'Celt and Saxon have been placed in direct antagonism', he lamented, but 'their interests are one and indivisible' and, most importantly, 'their rights can only be achieved by their union and cooperation'.[24] This latter idea had fired the imagination of the United Irishmen and the United Englishmen when his progenitors had established their claim to a place in Irish and British history. But

Feargus O'Connor was not merely intoning the maxim of a previous generation; he gave the idea a particular emphasis on class. It is easy to forget how precocious this idea was in 1850, especially as this assertion that the working men of Ireland and England were 'all rowing in the same boat' had few proponents in subsequent generations.

Again, O'Connor's appeal failed. In part, he had also undermined his own claim. At the Conference he declared himself in favour not only of Repeal but also of separation, an indication of an emergent separatist nationalism in the late 1840s. As the cheering subsided following this declaration, O'Connor eschewed the use of 'violence, riot, or revolution' to achieve that objective. For many among his audience, however, democracy was not an alternative to armed rebellion. In Ireland the development of a separatist nationalism undermined the very premise of O'Connor's Irish mission. After O'Connor's speech, the secretary of the nascent organisation, Andrew English, called on his 'brother democrats' to 'cast aside forever...the debasing system of parliamentary agitation...even at the expense of losing the aid of their English friends'.[25] Like it or not Feargus was, in this sense, counted among the English friends. The message could not have been clearer. John Mitchel had welcomed the support of the Chartists on the basis that '[t]hey are as eager to get rid of us as we are to be free of them' and he abjured any attempts to articulate his cause within the British polity: 'we deny the right or power of the Imperial Parliament to legislate for us in any shape', he told readers of the *United Irishman*, 'even to give us the franchise'. In October 1850, Michael Doheny, a leading Confederate who had called himself an 'Irish Chartist' in 1848 before fleeing into self-imposed exile in the United States, argued that 'the objects of the English and Irish Democrats are not identical'. 'They are not even analogous, save to a limited extent', he wrote to the *Northern Star*, '[n]or would they be identical, in my estimate, if the "Repeal of the Union" were made the first point of the Charter.' The Charter could not deliver what was needed: 'total extinction of the English interest in Ireland'.[26] Many of those who cheered O'Connor at Dublin's Music Hall, both in November 1849 and in March 1850, believed, or would come to believe, that Ireland's salvation could only be achieved through force of arms. They were speaking a different language. His grand nephew, Arthur O'Connor, seemed to understand the distinction when he tried to shoot Queen Victoria with a rusty pistol in 1872.[27] O'Connor's appeal to the 'fustian jackets' of Ireland was thus both too late and too early. Nevertheless, it owes him a place in Irish political history that he has been denied.

In England he suffered the same fate. Indeed, by the time that he first appeared in the *Dictionary of National Biography* in 1894, in an article by Graham Wallas, O'Connor was dismissed as a man without 'a single consistent political idea'.[28] This is unfair. On the one hand, it is hard to imagine any political figure remaining entirely consistent during a career that spanned decades, countries and economic systems. It would be odd, surely, if O'Connor's views did not develop. Although many of O'Connor's views were, in fact, the same in 1850 as they had been in 1820 (and were expressed using the same rhetoric), O'Connor's mature thinking was eclectic, heterogeneous, even fractured. It is important to recognise that this was not unusual. Borrowing the idea of 'bricolage' from anthropology, as Jon Mee has done in his study of William Blake, is helpful here. Mee employs the notion to understand Blake's syncretic combination of romantic millenarianism and enlightenment rationalism, ideas that, to modern readers, might seem mutually exclusive. Like Blake and many other early nineteenth century radicals, O'Connor was a 'bricoleur'.[29] Irish Repeal, democracy, nostalgic agrarianism, class and independence were an irreducible cluster of discrete ideas, or at least they drew upon separate, and somewhat incompatible, discourses. The fact that O'Connor knitted them together anyway should not be cause for concern; rather it is a reminder that individuals are always complex and surprising.

Nor were O'Connor's ideas original, but they were important. His problem, again, was his timing. O'Connor's passion for the land was shared by many of his supporters but it was increasingly anachronistic in a rapidly changing world. His instrumental view of politics was also being challenged by new ways of understanding society and his plea for an independent working-class politics contained within it a challenge to his right to lead. By 1850, many of those individuals Feargus had encouraged and sustained were now advocating solutions involving trade unions, self-help, co-operation, socialism or a change in the ownership of the means of production. O'Connor regarded some of these solutions as anathema. On many occasions he claimed that he longed for the day when men like himself would no longer be needed, and not long after his re-election he told the House of Commons that he looked forward to what we would nowadays call generational change when 'sluggish humdrum minds' were replaced by the 'active spirits of the present day'.[30] He lived to see his wish fulfilled. It is only with the benefit of hindsight that we can see Feargus O'Connor as a transitional figure but it is, nevertheless, a compelling conclusion. He was essentially a man with eighteenth century political beliefs who actually adapted better to the reality of nineteenth century class politics than many others. This flexibility, expressed ultimately in suit of fustian that he wore with pride in 1841, produced inconsistency and incongruity, but it allowed him to survive in the interstices of a changing political landscape. O'Connor lived on the edge of the future and rode it successfully like one of the wild horses of his youth for more than a decade. In the end it overtook him.

Wallas was correct to the extent that it is not by ideas alone that we can understand the nature of O'Connor's leadership. Part of the explanation arises from his status; for James Epstein and John Belchem, for example, he was a 'bridging', if somewhat liminal figure, a 'gentleman' leader of the type which characterised nineteenth century popular politics.[31] O'Connor was a 'friend of the people' in that sense, with Hunt and Cartwright on one side and Jones and Bright on the other, but a couple of caveats are called for. Much was made (both then and now) of his pretensions to Royal Irish ancestry, denoting himself 'Feargus Rex', and pompously addressing letters to Queen Victoria as 'My Dear Cousin',[32] without due recognition of their, at least in part, self-deprecating and mocking tone. O'Connor was no republican but he was not above a joke at the Queen's expense or his own. He would have undoubtedly been aware that, as the truculent Tom Cooper put it bluntly, not 'half a dozen Chartists cared a fig about his boasted descent from "Roderick O'Connor, the King of Connaught, and last king of all Ireland"'.[33] Cooper did suggest that O'Connor's upper-class status 'lent him influence' and it is also true that his oft-repeated claim to financial disinterestedness, sacrifice and incorruptibility was an important political asset despite the emergence of a vigorous class consciousness among the Chartist rank and file. 'He had', he frequently boasted, 'never travelled a mile, eaten a meal, or slept a night at the people's expense.' By 1850 he claimed that he had spent £130,000 on the cause.[34] That he did so is not surprising. As Philip Wentworth recalled in relation to the success of *Northern Star*, 'When a boy I used to hear the enemies of Fergus O'Connor charge him with drawing a princely revenue from this brilliant luminary, but I know now ridiculously mendacious the charge was'.[35] Nevertheless, for all that O'Connor's boast did not change the circumstances in which he offered it did. During the 1830s his claim implied wealth and the gentlemanly attribute of philanthropy; from the mid-1840s it was no longer an indication of wealth but an explanation for his growing penury. O'Connor's became a story of downward social mobility that reached, as we shall see, its nadir after his death. Moreover, any claim to lead on the basis of his status was forever changed when he appeared dressed as a working man in 1841. In many ways there was no going back to a complacent sense of leadership by virtue of birth; although he never wore the suit of fustian again he could never really take it off. 'In their O'Connor', commented the young German socialist, Georg Weerth, 'the English people see themselves.'[36]

O'Connor's leadership owed less to status than to his style and to his charismatic personality. 'A popular chief', Harney told Engels, 'should be possessed of a magnificent bodily appearance, an iron frame, eloquence, or at least a ready of fluency of tongue...O'C has them all – at least in degree.'[37] T.W. Wheeler agreed; O'Connor was:

Of commanding stature, blessed with a constitution so rare that what was fatigue to other men was only natural exercise to him, rich in natural eloquence, full of genuine Irish humour, teeming with anecdote, facile, ready-witted, varying from the deepest pathos to the loudest indignation...[38]

O'Connor himself often claimed that he had attended more public meetings than any man alive.[39] This was, as we have seen, no idle boast. His indefatigable peripatetic approach must have made him seem ubiquitous and was particularly well suited to the needs of the developing national movement. No reader of the *Northern Star* can be in any doubt that Chartism was an agglomeration of community-based local cells, each proud of their contribution to the greater collective (class and nation). O'Connor helped to bind them together, not only with ink and paper, but also, by his physical presence, with flesh and blood. Moreover, his intensely personal, almost visceral, sense of politics was particularly appropriate for, and effective in, an age of increasing alienation. After all, this was the period when the young Frederick Engels found the doors of working-class homes barred against the social atomisation of the industrial city.[40] Although working-class community was more resilient than Engels allowed, O'Connor did speak to a genuine longing for intimacy. His capacity to make each member of an audience of 20 or 20,000 feel as though he was speaking to them personally was at the core of his political genius and one of the keys to understanding his popularity. He was both famous and familiar; the Lion of Freedom and Feargus.

O'Connor's style drew heavily on a romantic theatricality that spanned both the court room and the stage which, as Gillian Russell has shown, had a crucial role in political communication in Georgian Britain. Crucially, Russell tells us, this form of theatricality was not seen as inauthentic or meretricious. On the contrary, theatricality provided its exponent with a means to express sympathy, defined primarily at the time as a '(real or supposed) affinity between certain things, by virtue of which they are similarly or correspondingly affected by the same influence, affect or influence one another...or attract or tend towards each other'.[41] In other words, 'Theatricality *was* sympathy', a potent communicative force for lawyers, actors and politicians. Russell develops her argument in relation to Thomas Erskine, the electrifying court room lawyer of the 1790s, but it seductively beckons O'Connor whose autopoiesis embraced the law, the theatre and politics. By the time O'Connor was a household name, Thomas Carlyle had coined the neologism 'theatricality' and given it the pejorative connotation that it has subsequently carried.[42] Nevertheless, it is clear that many working men and women who heard and saw O'Connor perform accepted it as a genuine and heartfelt expression of sympathy. It is also possible to understand this aspect of O'Connor's performance in terms of the rise of sentimentality during the long eighteenth century. In fact, at a time when sentiment was seen as directly related to class – the 'skin, pores, muscles, and nerves of a day-labourer are different from those of a man of quality: So are his sentiments, actions and manners. The different stations of life influence the whole fabric, external and internal', noted David Hume in 1739[43] – O'Connor exemplifies the democratisation of affect. The question we should ask of his audiences is not what did he encourage them to think, but how did he make them feel? 'When he addressed in the rich brogue of his native country "the blistered hands and unshorn chins of the working classes,"' recalled W.E. Adams, 'he appeared to touch a chord which vibrated from one end of the kingdom to the other.'[44] If O'Connor had a personal motivation it was surely vindication of his father, but beyond this he was inspired by a deep sense of outrage against inequality and poverty, by a genuine sympathy for the plight of the poor in the Irish countryside or the British city.

O'Connor had returned from Ireland with nowhere to go in political terms. Long before he sold the *Northern Star* at the end of 1851 the agenda of the Chartist movement was being set by others. Moreover, he still faced a raft of ongoing legal problems and successive inquiries in relation to the land plan. It is at this time that regular reports of eccentric behaviour began to appear. Feargus appeared to many to be a broken man, his flaming red hair quickly turning white; a fondness for brandy over indulged.[45] According to Ernest Jones it was the parliamentary enquiry into the affairs of the land company that had been the turning point: 'It was evident', he told readers of his *People's Paper*, 'the great mind was beginning to totter on its throne, and balancing itself to and fro before plunging in its fall'.[46] At an inquiry into the company's finances before the Master of the Chancery in February 1852 O'Connor's behaviour had lurched from the ridiculous to the sublime. On the one hand, he had bemused the court by offering the Master a pinch of snuff and the opposing counsel a mutton chop, but he also showed a flash of incisive political analysis: 'If Prince Albert had built these cottages and located these lands', he suggested:[47]

> there would have been offices to promote them in every street in London for the benefit of these poor people, under the patronage of the philanthropic prince; but now if my Lord or Lady Nincompoop happens to be driving through these estates and the daughter of the carriage happens to say "Lor' mama, look at those beautiful cottages!", the anxious parent pulls down the blind, exclaiming, "My dear, it is that ruffian Feargus O'Connor built them. (Loud cheering)".

Later the same day O'Connor had scandalised an audience by interrupting a play at London's Lyceum theatre and he regularly irritated his parliamentary colleagues with what were considered to be excessive displays of effusive affection or intimidation.[48] Justin McCarthy remembered that O'Connor's eyes still gleamed but 'with the peculiar, quick, shallow, ever-changing glitter of madness'.[49]

Contemporary and historical medical opinion suggests that by this time
O'Connor was in the grips of *dementia paralytica* and Bayle's disease, a physical and mental condition caused by syphilis contracted many years earlier. The
consumption of an estimated fifteen glasses of brandy a day was undoubtedly
contributing to his neurasthenic excesses.[50] The drinking was not a recent habit;
signing a letter penned in 1843 'a drunken barbarian', he told his friend Thomas Allsop that he had been drunk for seven weeks.[51] The fact that he almost
certainly had contracted syphilis in the early 1830s is the one clear indicator we
have in relation to his sexual activity. A fellow Chartist, W.E. Adams, recalled
that Feargus's speaking tours often mirrored those taken by the well-known ac-
tress Louisa Nisbett. Adams suggested that their relationship was of long standing (from the mid-1830s) and with understandable exaggeration he claimed
that it caused as much gossip in radical circles as Charles Stewart Parnell and
Mrs O'Shea.[52] The rumours, however, have not convinced Louisa's most recent biographers, who do not mention O'Connor at all. On the contrary they
show that she was married twice, in 1831 and 1844, and lived the balance of her
years at St Leonards in Sussex.[53] There were also persistent rumours that some
of the Chartist children named Feargus O'Connor owed more to 'the Lion of
Freedom' than their name. Born in March 1844 to a painter's wife the most
prominent of these pretenders was Edward O'Connor Terry who went on to
be a celebrated musical comedy actor.[54] Many of O'Connor's opponents would
have found this to be convincing evidence of his pedigree. Having said that, it
is clear that O'Connor never had a stable family life, and spent the majority of
his life in the company of men. Illness and intemperance were compounded by
impecuniousness. As he wrote to T.M. Wheeler as early as January 1850, he was
'actually penniless'.[55]

Soon O'Connor's eccentric public behaviour got him into trouble with the
law. When he volubly interrupted the play at the Lyceum in February 1852 he
had assaulted a police officer and was sentenced to seven days in prison, which
he served as a common felon in Coldbath Fields prison.[56] O'Connor had no
friends in the mainstream press, which delighted in presenting his discomfiture
in the worst possible light. Nevertheless, it is clear that O'Connor's behaviour
was increasingly bizarre. At about this time Wheeler started following his old
friend and mentor through the streets of London in an attempt to ensure 'that
no harm befel [sic.] him, or that he did not interfere with others'.[57] After his incarceration O'Connor took a brief trip to the United States, apparently 'without
the knowledge of his friends', arriving in New York on 21 May and installing
himself in the fashionable Irving House Hotel on Broadway. His stay in the first
city of the great republic was noteworthy for eccentric antics: obstreperously or-

dering meals not on the bill-of-fare, addressing other guests as 'Your Majesty', reciting poetry and parliamentary speeches in the restaurant, 'telling anecdotes of the Queen, her husband, O'Connell, Peel and Little Johnny Russell', and suggesting to 'ladies' at Stewart's Marble Palace they should 'wear beards on their chins'. On the basis that 'European lunatics are not only secure from molestation, but feted, and made much of' in New York, the *New York Herald* felt sure that O'Connor was going to involve himself in the 'Presidential movements' then under way. By the end of the month, however, O'Connor had returned to England, arriving in Liverpool on 31 May.[58]

O'Connor's next public outburst was to systematically interrupt the proceedings of the Westminster Law Courts.[59] It was his behaviour inside parliament, however, that led to decisive action to remove what had effectively become an intolerable irritant. He was, commented *The Times*, 'the terror of the House'.[60] Having 'assaulted' several members and slapped Palmerston on the back before a speech, O'Connor was taken into custody by the Sergeant-at-Arms in June 1852 and a medical examination concluded, not surprisingly, that he might be a danger to himself and to others. A hastily convened Select Committee subsequently ordered that he be confined to Old Manor House Asylum in Chiswick. From his desk Ernest Jones fumed at the 'derisive and inhuman laughter that echoed in the House of Commons' at the news of O'Connor's situation,[61] a legacy no doubt of a lingering hatred for the man who had tormented them inside and outside the House. One MP spoke up for O'Connor, not 'as the friend of the hon. Member, but simply because he understood that he had no friends'.[62] Their victory was now complete: O'Connor was for a second time deprived of his seat by a vote from his colleagues – men who loathed him – rather than by the decision of an electorate.

At a time when the treatment of the 'insane' was described as akin to the treatment vermin[63] O'Connor might have had grim prospects, but he was fortunate to be confined to a 'rich' asylum run by the comparatively forward thinking Dr Harrington Tuke (no relation to the Tukes who ran the well-known asylum based on 'moral treatment' in York) in a handsome house in a fashionable quarter of Chiswick.[64] Like his better known namesakes Harrington Tuke believed in the treatment of mental illness without restraint and O'Connor's regime was limited to bitter tonic, mineral acids, occasional aperients and a small quantity of wine.[65] When Ernest Jones first visited his former mentor he found him 'playing *with the Doctor's little child*'; on his next visit O'Connor was playing billiards ('winning a game with considerable skill').[66]

At the same time, Jones painted a picture of decline which he attributed to the failure of the land company. When the plan was under development, Jones recalled, 'I always found him in the most joyous state of excitement at its success'. With the benefit of hindsight Jones stated 'I feared that, should anything frustrate the success of his plan, the effect on him would be terrible, as his whole soul seemed bound up in the undertaking'.[67] Now, not only was a 'general paralysis' afflicting him but also:

> his mind is a perfect wreck, and the extinction of his once mighty intellect may be seen in the mild dimness of his clouded eyes. There is no wildness or fierceness in their expression – but a manifest dying out of the light of mind.[68]

Despite the medical view that he was hopelessly insane without a lucid moment, O'Connor was not completely oblivious to his fate, believing himself to be a state prisoner like his father. Upon recognizing Jones and Dougal McGowan, the former printer of the *Northern Star*, on one visit, O'Connor broke into a rousing chorus ('in a voice of thunder form') of the Lion of Freedom.[69] There surely could not have been a more poignant and pathetic *mise-en-scène* had Jones chosen to use his considerable skill with a pen to concoct it.

Subsequently O'Connor's sister, Harriet, and his nephew, Roger, bickered publicly about his care and about the control of his meagre assets – estimated by a court to be £1,167-7 in June 1853.[70] By August 1855 Harriet had succeeded in having Feargus released into her care. He died in agony ten days later at her home in Notting Hill.[71] O'Connor's death had briefly returned the democratic movement to the centre of national political stage. The 'magnificent' funeral procession through the streets of London drew a crowd of mourners and onlookers estimated at not less than 50,000. 'Perhaps no ceremonial of this description', speculated G.W.M Reynolds, 'saving the burial of Nelson, Queen Caroline and the Duke of Wellington – has attracted during the present century such vast crowds to witness it'.[72] O'Connor's coffin was conveyed from Harriet's residence in Notting Hill to Kensal Green Cemetery followed by an ever-increasing *cortège*. An 'injudicous' decision to close the cemetery gates 'against the vast mass of people' provoked a democratic and defiant response that would have brought a smile to the face of the deceased: 'the crowd, who were greatly irritated, unceremoniously broke them open'. O'Connor's body was taken to the cemetery Chapel where an Anglican priest performed a service. What he said was not recorded. At the graveside, where the vast crowd had converged, one of the second lieutenants of Chartism, William Jones from Liverpool, offered a eulogy. Jones dwelt on O'Connor's 'self-sacrifice', 'devotion' and 'incorruptible honesty', and insisted that 'he was a man more sinned against than sinning':

Poverty, neglect, and misrepresentation were but too often the reward of those who faithfully fought the battle of the people; and when the proud and too sensitive spirit, though worn and exhausted by the struggle, still refused to leave the path of honour, the generous heart broke, the strong brain lost its powers of reason, and the champion of the people and of liberty sank into the grave.[73]

Whether the Liverpudlian eulogist had been influenced by the fracas at the gates is unclear but he stressed, by way of conclusion, the real nature of O'Connor's service to the people: the gift of self confidence. Although 'it could not be said', mused Jones, that Feargus

had overturned thrones, or even that the work to which he had devoted his life had been fully accomplished, yet they would point on his behalf to the mental emancipation he had achieved for the people of this country, for he had removed much of the political ignorance which had disgraced their minds and confirmed their slavery. (cheers.)[74]

Jones, a 'working man', a watchmaker by trade, from the industrial heartlands of England where O'Connor had his most loyal supporters, was living proof.[75]

The unseemly squabble over O'Connor's dying carcass proved to be a dress rehearsal for the dispute over his commemoration. At a time when Britain was in the grip of what *The Times* called 'monument mania' it is not surprising that there soon were calls for O'Connor to be honoured by the erection of a monument. On this point Reynolds undoubtedly caught the public mood: 'if ever there was a man who deserved a monument at public expense', he editorialised, 'Mr Feargus O'Connor is that man'.[76] Ignoring the prevailing trend the Tory London *Standard* was thankful that 'the national taste does not run' to 'statues and memorials to individuals…or we should, no doubt, before this have had a statue or monument raised to Mr Feargus O'Connor'.[77] By 1860 two monuments had been erected: one at the grave site in London and the other in the Nottingham Arboretum.[78]

The London monument to O'Connor was nearly a casualty of the wider malaise that aflicted metropolitan Chartism in the 1850s. By the time of O'Connor's death the sharpest rivalry in the movement, both in the capital and in the nation at large, was between Ernest Jones and G.W.M. Reynolds. A barrister by training, Ernest Jones was an artist by inclination. In 1855 he was busily engaged attempting to re-establish a national democratic organisation, and in promoting his last important newspaper venture, the *People's Paper*.[79] George Reynolds had cut his teeth as a political agitator in the 1840s before embarking on a successful career as a writer of popular fiction. His novels made him a 'household name' in the 1840s, long before he returned to journalism.[80] Towards the end of the decade Reynolds sought to establish a career as a radical leader, throwing his considerable energy into reviving the flagging fortunes of London Chartism and, early in the 1850s, commencing a radical journal, *Reynolds's Newspaper*, which attracted an ever increasing audience.[81]

Almost inevitably O'Connor's death and its commemoration became a pawn in the leadership struggle between Jones and Reynolds. Controversy was touched off when the *Morning Advertiser*, a moderate liberal journal, reported that O'Connor had been interred in a 'mean, unbricked grave, in one of the obscurest corners of the cemetery'.[82] Despite the undoubtedly malicious intent, the article highlighted the fact that 'the great leader of the working classes was without a coffin or any preparation'. The problem, it emerged, was that at the time of his death O'Connor 'did not possess a shilling'.[83] The undertaker reported that he had received financial assurances from Reynolds, a 'blank cheque' that was later withdrawn.[84]

This revelation gave Jones an irresistible opportunity to smite his political rival, even if it meant infuriatingly arguing in favour of both sides of the question. On the one hand, Jones was harshly critical of Reynolds's apparent *volteface* as evidence of insincerity and parsimony, and, with a note of indignant pomposity, he personally took charge of the debt.[85] On the other hand, he took a principled stand against patronage that was clearly designed to touch a deep chord among the rank and file: 'We can only say that the dignity of the Chartist body and the working classes should spurn charity for burying their champion', he contended, 'Let the people bury the people's leader.'[86] For his part Reynolds had stumbled into an invidious position. When he learned that a working men's committee had been formed he had hastily withdrawn the 'blank cheque' – making a donation of £5 instead – in deference to the very principle that Jones was now using to attack him. In this way, Jones and Reynolds ensured that any monument would again raise the question that had dogged O'Connor's leadership: how was a gentleman by birth to lead a predominantly working-class movement?[87]

By the end of 1855 the situation appeared to have reached its nadir when Jones began to have a change of heart and called for unity. 'Let me now ask you this question', he wrote, 'shall O'Connor have a monument worthy of his name? If so, then unite, subscribe, organise!…let him not slumber unmarked and unrecorded among the proud tombs of aristocrats and usurers, without a monument!'[88] In the wake of Jones's call for unity the situation improved quickly. By mid-February 1856 a total of £66-15-6d in debts for the funeral and associated activities had been cleared, and the two warring committees had been merged into a central body.[89] Within months, firm plans for a monument at Kensal Green were announced; a design had been submitted that was 'highly approved of' by the Central Committee and Jones concurred, declaring it to be 'most appropriate, chaste and elegant'.[90]

The committee estimated that the proposed monument, comprising approximately 14 tons (14.2 tonnes) of 'good Sicilian marble', together with the extra land and associated work, would cost about £200. Consequently, a new program of fundraising was commenced.[91] At the eleventh hour, however, dissension returned. Many readers of the *People's Paper* of Saturday 11 April 1857 would have been bemused to learn that the O'Connor Monument had been erected on Kensal Green 'in a private surreptitious sort of way, the Monument Committee not even knowing anything about it...' Jones did not try to hide his outrage: 'By this secret proceeding a public ovation to Feargus O'Connor has been scandalously burked'.[92] Contrary to Jones's claim, however, at least some members of the Central Committee were certainly aware of what had occurred, but they offered no explanation of their conduct.[93] Clearly some Committee members deemed the implied internal victory of a surreptitious act of proprietorship to be more important than a symbolic public display of Chartist power. The monument had fulfilled its worst potential, standing as a symbol of disunity.

Moreover, the indecorous squabble over the clandestine erection of the monument encouraged further recrimination. According to some correspondents, the completed monument was unworthy of O'Connor. A mason from Paddington, for example, suggested that 'the design is completely spoilt by the execution of the Portland stone...It is a disgrace to the position it stands in, and to those who executed it'.[94] The monument was both smaller and less expensive than had been envisaged, but at over twenty feet in height and weighing more than seven tons (7.1 tonnes) it was an imposing structure (see plate 6). Built from Yorkshire and Portland stone with a marble front panel (costing in total £140) the monument comprises a hexagonal spire in the 'pointed gothic' style that had become *de rigueur* in mid-Victorian funerary architecture, surmounted by a 'gilded star', and standing on a hexagonal base.[95]

On the base was carved the O'Connor family coat of arms together with their motto, 'Fair and easy goes far'. On the front panel was a lengthy inscription:

TO THE MEMORY OF
FEARGUS O'CONNOR,
ELECTED M.P. FOR THE COUNTY OF CORK IN
1833, ALSO FOR THE BOROUGH OF
NOTTINGHAM IN 1847.

BORN, JULY 18TH, 1794
DIED, AUGUST 30TH, 1855.
AGED 61,
WHOSE PUBLIC FUNERAL WAS DEFRAYED,
AND THIS MONUMENT ERECTED, BY
A SUBSCRIPTION CHIEFLY FROM
THE WORKING CLASSES.

—

READER, PAUSE!
THOU TREADEST ON THE GRAVE OF A
PATRIOT. WHILE PHILANTHROPY IS A
VIRTUE, AND PATRIOTISM NOT
A CRIME, WILL THE
NAME OF
O'CONNOR
BE ADMIRED, AND THIS MONUMENT RESPECTED.[96]

The inscription highlights the ambiguity at the heart of O'Connor's Chartist career. The juxtaposition of O'Connor's aristocratic background – the family crest and motto – and the celebration of his philanthropy, a traditional attribute of a 'gentleman leader', with the pointed reference to the independence of those working people who 'chiefly' paid for his funeral and his monument was uneasy at best. The Chartist press reported that the monument was also inscribed with the words '*Meen Secker Reague*' (which have long since eroded away). This was almost certainly a phonetic rendition of '*Cier-Rige*', the title adopted by O'Connor's father denoting himself as leader or chief of the people of Eri. It seems likely that O'Connor's Chartist friends understood his desire to vindicate his father and perhaps even they appreciated his need to emerge from his father's shadow. They offered him salvation in stone.[97]

If the London monument summed up the contradiction at the heart of O'Connor's leadership, the Nottingham monument highlighted his legacy in an unequivocally positive way. This statue stood as assertion of the rights of citizenship and a demonstration of democratic accountability. It pointed firmly to the future. The Nottingham Monument Committee was formed in September 1855 and a pattern of meeting every Sunday evening was established to raise funds that would be sustained over the next four years.[98] It was remarkably successful. By 1858 the committee had engaged J.B. Robinson of Derby to execute a life size statue of O'Connor to stand on a pedestal of approximately eight foot. The monument, as it stands today, is thus about 14 foot high and depicts Feargus, his dress formal, including a full-length flowing cape, in the act of giving a speech. O'Connor's right foot is forward, his left hand on his breast inserted Napoleon-like in his jacket, and his right hand clutching a roll of papers – the People's Charter. This was O'Connor as he appeared for most of his public life: the gentleman leader (see plates 7 and 8). The inscription is uncontroversial:

FEARGUS O'CONNOR ESQ MP
THIS STATUE WAS ERECTED BY HIS ADMIRERS
1859

Later the Committee estimated, with understandable exaggeration, that their campaign had benefited from the support of 'thousands of subscribers' over the years.[99] One member went further: the subscriptions had come from 'the working classes who could only give their pence'.[100] The message was clear: O'Connor's 'admirers' were working people.

The real struggle in Nottingham related to the site. The story of how the radicals forced the local authorities to grant them a site in the Arboretum, the 'people's park', was the real legacy of Feargus O'Connor.[101] There is no detailed record of the debate in the local council, but one particularly vitriolic critic was in no doubt about what had taken place: both 'liberals and conservatives' had become caught up in what he called a simple contest for 'mob popularity'.[102] Historians have estimated that in 1865 as much as 39 per cent of the Nottingham electorate was 'working class' in social composition (much higher than Birmingham, Leeds, Manchester or Newcastle).[103] Thus it is likely that the spectre of democratic accountability – combined with the lingering memory of O'Connor's victory in 1847 – had had a persuasive impact on the Council. The Chartists had put forward a good case based on their putative political power; as one later wrote: 'the Arboretum is the property of the people... the admirers of O'Connor are largely in the majority, therefore they have a right to erect a monument in their own grounds...'[104] By the end of the decade not only had the gates of Nottingham's 'people's park' been thrown open, but the right of equal access to public space was now watched over by the statue of the man who had helped to set 'the people' on the road to democracy. The statue remains in its beautiful setting, but it is denied a place even in the register of local cultural heritage. In London, O'Connor's careworn monument teeters precariously on subsiding ground. No one will hear it fall. The contrast to the restored monument to reformers nearby is stark.

Anyone who had heard O'Connor speak at the inauguration of Hunt's monument in Manchester in 1842 would have known the value that he placed on these tributes, but his own monuments did not guarantee either his place in history or in popular affection. The fierce loyalty of a generation of Chartist women and men was deeply held. William Henry Chadwick, the self-proclaimed 'last of the Manchester Chartists', who wore his treasured O'Connor medal (see plates 2 and 3) with pride until the day he died in 1908, was one; William Farish, who 'never ceased to entertain a sort of lingering love for the burly Hibernian' was another; Thomas Martin Wheeler who 'never for one moment ceased to venerate' Feargus was another; so too was Allan Pinkerton, who insisted that as long as he (Pinkerton) lived O'Connor would 'have at least one Friend'. Pinkerton had taken his loyalty to Dundee, Illinois; Charles Jardine Don carried his to Melbourne, Victoria. Don had not long taken his seat as the first working man in the colonial assembly when another member offered a snide aspersion against O'Connor. He 'would not sit in his place', boomed Don, 'and hear Feargus O'Connor abused'.[105] The devotion of the O'Connor loyalists died with them. No one took their place. Even before he died O'Connor's ideas had lost their central place in popular thinking. His solutions for Ireland and for Britain were both premature and too late. Time was his enemy. O'Connor was, as one commentator perceptively put it, 'a picturesque agitator'.[106] After his death there was nothing to see.

Notes

1   *Northern Star*, 16 March 1850. See also *Northern Star*, 6 April 1850.

2   *Cork Examiner*, 23 November 1849; *Freeman's Journal*, 21 November 1849.

3   *Hansard* [House of Commons], 6 December 1847, col. 729; *Northern Star*, 18 December 1847. On the Second Reading half a dozen Repealers, including M.J. O'Connell, voted for the Bill, while John O'Connell and William Smith O'Brien, a leader of the moderate wing of the Confederate Council, voted with O'Connor in the minority.

4   *United Irishman*, 24 February 1848. See also R. Davis, *The Young Ireland Movement*, Dublin, 1987, p. 191.

5   *Nation*, 17 November 1849; *Cork Examiner*, 19 November 1849.

6   *Northern Star*, 24 November 1849.

7   *Cork Examiner*, 23 November 1849.

8   *Cork Examiner*, 23 November 1849. For the significance of fustian see P.A. Pickering, 'Class Without Words: Symbolic Communication in the Chartist Movement', *Past and Present*, no. 112, August 1986, pp. 144-162.

9   See *Cork Examiner*, 23 November 1849; *Freeman's Journal*, 21 November 1849; *Irishman*, 24 November 1849; *Clonmel Chronicle*, 24 November 1849; *Kilkenny Journal*, 24 November 1849; *Northern Star*, 24 November 1849.

10 *Northern Star*, 1 December 1849.

11 Although often consumed with recrimination and mutual mistrust, the emerging generation of Chartist leaders could at least agree about the value of the *Irishman*. According to G.M.W. Reynolds it was the 'only true organ of the democratic party of the Emerald Isle' and George Julian Harney, 'England's Marat', used the columns of his *Red Republican* to 'heartily recommend' it to 'British and Irish Republicans' as

'a master-piece of democratic eloquence'. With his knack of getting to the heart of the matter, Feargus O'Connor commented that while Duffy's revived *Nation* sought to represent 'the pockets of the shopocracy', the *Irishman* championed 'the interests of the toiling millions'. *Reynolds Political Instructor*, 3 April 1850; *Red Republican*, 27 July 1850; 17 August 1850; *Northern Star*, 18 May 1850. See also Harney's *Democratic Review*, May 1850.

12 *Irishman*, 1 December 1849.

13 *Northern Star*, 9 March 1850.

14 *Northern Star*, 15 December 1849.

15 *Northern Star*, 8 January 1850. At the Conference O'Connor also used the word 'separation' as he had in the House of Commons.

16 *Northern Star*, 15 December 1849.

17 *Northern Star*, 29 December 1849.

18 *Northern Star*, 15 December 1849.

19 *Northern Star*, 9 March 1850.

20 *Northern Star*, 15 December 1849.

21 *Irishman*, 19 January 1850.

22 *Irishman*, 19 January 1850.

23 *Irishman*, 19 January 1850.

24 *Irishman*, 1 December 1850. See also *Northern Star*, 9 February 1850.

25 *Northern Star*, 3 August 1850; *Nation*, 9 March 1850; 22 June 1850. O'Connor had used the term separation as early as 1846. See *Northern Star*, 7 November 1846.

26 *United Irishman*, 26 February 1848; 4 March 1848; *Northern Star*, 12 October 1850. See also D.G. Boyce, *Nationalism in Ireland*, London, 1995, pp. 154-191.

27 See L.M. Geary, 'O'Connorite Bedlam: Feargus and his grand-nephew, Arthur', *Medical History*, vol. 34, no. 2, 1990, pp. 136f.

28 *Dictionary of National Biography*, vol. XIV, pp. 839-840. G.D.H. Cole agreed. For Cole O'Connor's 'ideas were a jumble'. See *Chartist Portraits*, London, 1941, p. 301.

29 See J. Mee, *Dangerous Enthusiasm: William Blake and the Culture of Radicalism in the 1790s*, Oxford, 1992. See also I. McCalman, *Radical Underworld: Prophets, revolutionaries and pornographers in London, 1795-1840*, Cambridge, 1988. The notion of bricolage comes from Claude Levi-Strauss. I am grateful to Iain McCalman for bringing this to my attention.

30 *Hansard* [House of Commons], 28 February 1848, col. 1445.

31 J. Epstein, *In Practice: Studies in the Language and Culture of Popular Politics in Modern Britain*, Stanford, 2003, p. 130.

32 See, for example, Sir Robert Peel's sarcastic remarks at O'Connor's expense, *Hansard* [House of Commons], 25 April 1834, col. 91. See also *Sentinel*, 10 February 1844; W.E. Adams, *Memoirs of a Social Atom* (1903), New York, 1968, pp. 204-5; J.T. Ward, *Chartism*, London, 1973, p. 199.

33 T. Cooper, *The Life of Thomas Cooper* (1872), Leicester, 1971, p. 180.

34 See Adams, *Memoirs of a Social Atom*, pp. 204-5.

35 P. Wentworth, 'Notes and sketches by the way', *Middleton Guardian*, 15 March 1890. See also P.A. Pickering, 'Chartism and the Trade of Agitation in Early Victorian Britain', *History*, vol. 76, no. 247, June 1991, pp. 221-237; J. Epstein,

'National Chartist Leadership: Some Perspectives', in O. Ashton, S. Roberts and R. Fyson (eds), *The Duty of Discontent*, London, 1995, pp. 42-5.

36   I. and P. Kuczynski (eds), *A Young Revolutionary in Nineteenth-Century England: Selected Writings of Georg Weerth*, Berlin, 1971, pp. 106-7.

37   G.J. Harney to F. Engels, 30 March 1846, reprinted in F.G. and R.M. Black (eds), *The Harney Papers*, Assen, 1969, p. 241.

38   W. Stephens, *A Memoir of Thomas Martin Wheeler, Founder of the Friend-in-need Life and Sick Assurance Society, Domestic, Political and Industrial*, London, 1862, p. 66.

39   *Northern Star*, 25 March 1848; F. O'Connor, *The Trial of Feargus O'Connor and Fifty-eight Others on a Charge of Sedition, Conspiracy Tumult and Riot* (1843), New York, 1970, p. 290.

40   F. Engels, *The Condition of the Working Class in England* (1845), London, 1979, pp. 58, 86, and 301-2. See also P.A. Pickering, *Chartism and the Chartists in Manchester and Salford*, Basingstoke, 1995, chapter 1.

41   G. Russell, 'The Theatre of Crim. Con.: Thomas Erskine, Adultery and Radical Politics in the 1790s', in M.T. Davis and P.A. Pickering (eds), *Unrespectable Radicals? Popular Politics in the Age of Reform*, Aldershot, 2007, pp. 57-70. See also T. C. Davis, 'Theatricality and civil society', in T.C. Davis and T. Postlewait (eds), *Theatricality*, Cambridge, 2003, pp. 127-155.

42   Russell, 'The Theatre of Crim. Con.' p. 65.

43   D. Hume, *A Treatise of Human Nature* (1739-40), edited by D.F. and M.J. Norton, Oxford, 2000, p. 259. I am grateful to John Brewer for this reference.

44   Adams, *Memoirs of a Social Atom*, p. 157. Cole recognized this quality in O'Connor. See *Chartist Portraits*, p. 301: 'His feeling for such sufferings was strong and genuine; and this it was that was that made the wretched and the oppressed all over England look to him as their friend, and go on forgiving and loving him whatever he did amiss'.

45   See A.M. Hadfield, *The Chartist Land Company*, Newton Abbot, 1971, p. 69.

46   *People's Paper*, 16 April 1853.

47   Cited in the excellent article by Laurence Geary, 'O'Connorite Bedlam', p. 129.

48   *Hansard* [House of Commons], 8 June 1852, cols. 273-4; 9 June 1852, cols. 367-73; *People's Paper*, 16 April 1853.

49   J. McCarthy, *Reminiscences*, London, 1899, vol. 2, pp. 259-61; D. Read and E. Glasgow, *Feargus O'Connor: Irishman and Chartist*, London, 1961, p. 140.

50   Geary, 'O'Connorite Bedlam', p. 131; see also T. Frost, *Forty Years' Recollections Literary and Political*, London, 1880, p. 182.

51   British Library of Political and Economic Science, *Allsop Collection*, Coll. Misc. 0525/2, letter 7.

52   Adams, *Memoirs of a Social Atom*, pp. 208-9.

53   *Oxford Dictionary of National Biography*, 2004, vol. 40, pp. 924-5. A reference to the affair with O'Connor was in the original *DNB* article but has inexplicably been removed from the revised article. See *Dictionary of National Biography*, vol. XIV, pp. 517-19.

54   Read and Glasgow, *Feargus O'Connor*, p. 142.

55   Stephens, *A Memoir of Thomas Martin Wheeler*, p. 53.

56 *Notes to the People*, vol. 2, p. 859.

57 Stephens, *A Memoir of Thomas Martin Wheeler*, p. 62.

58 *New York Times*, 22 June 1852; *New York Evening Post* reprinted in *The Times*, 26 May 1852; *New York Herald* reprinted in *The Times*, 28 May 1852; *The Times*, 31 May 1852; *People's Paper*, 22 May 1852; 29 May 1852; 5 June 1852.

59 Geary, 'O'Connorite Bedlam', pp. 129-31.

60 *The Times*, 9 June 1852.

61 *Notes to the People*, vol. 2, no. 44, p. 859. Laurence Geary has pointed to the 'extraordinary lack of charity' displayed by the political class in general. See Geary, 'O'Connorite Bedlam', p. 131n.

62 *Hansard* [House of Commons], 10 June 1852, col. 417. The MP was Jacob Bell, Member for St Albans.

63 Cited in Andrew Scull, 'Museums of Madness Revisited', *Society for the Study of the Social History of Medicine*, 1993, p. 3.

64 E. Walford, *Old and New London: A Narrative of Its History, Its People, and Its Places*, London, n.d. [1878], vol. 6, pp. 556, 559; 'Chiswick: Manors', *A History of the County of Middlesex*, vol. 7 London, 1982, pp. 71-4. URL: http://www.british-history.ac.uk/report.asp?compid=22561.

65 Geary, 'O'Connorite Bedlam', p. 132.

66 *People's Paper*, 12 March 1853; 19 March 1853. According to J.B. Leno, Tuke 'looked on the Chartist leader as a friend rather than a patient. We knew also that he had received little by way of payment for the great care and attention he had bestowed on him'. See *The Aftermath: with an Autobiography of the Author*, London, 1892, p. 57.

67 *People's Paper*, 16 April 1853.

68 *People's Paper*, 12 March 1853. See also *Notes to the People*, vol. 2, p. 733. Jones described O'Connor as a 'worn out warrior'.

69 *People's Paper*, 16 April 1853.

70 Geary, 'O'Connorite Bedlam', p. 134.

71 W.J. O'Neill Daunt, *A Life Spent for Ireland*, London, 1896, p. 127.

72 *Reynolds's Newspaper*, 16 September 1855. See also W. Tinsley, *Random Recollections of An Old Publisher*, London, 1900, vol. 1, p. 45; Daunt, *A Life Spent for Ireland*, p. 127.

73 *Reynolds's Newspaper*, 16 September 1855; *Annual Register*, appendix to chronicle, 1855, p. 303.

74 *Reynolds's Newspaper*, 16 September 1855.

75 According to J.B. Leno, Jones was known as the 'eloquent boy' in Chartist ranks. See *The Aftermath*, p. 57.

76 *Reynolds's Newspaper*, 9 September 1855. For 'monument mania' see *The Times*, 12 August 1850. I am grateful to Alex Tyrrell for this reference.

77 *Standard*, 1 September 1855.

78 For a fuller discussion see P.A. Pickering, 'The Chartist Rites of Passage: Commemorating Feargus O'Connor', in P.A. Pickering and A. Tyrrell, *Contested Sites: Commemoration, Memorial and Popular Politics in Nineteenth-Century Britain*, Aldershot, 2004, pp. 101-126.

79 See M. Taylor, *Ernest Jones, Chartism, and the Romance of Politics*, Oxford, 2003.

80 See R. McWilliam, 'The Mysteries of G.W.M. Reynolds: radicalism and melodrama in Victorian Britain', in M. Chase and I. Dyck (eds), *Living and Learning: Essay in Honour of J.F.C. Harrison*, Aldershot 1996, pp. 182-198; L. James and J. Saville, 'Reynolds. G.W.M.', *Dictionary of Labour Biography*, London, 1976, vol. 3, pp. 146-151.

81 When Jones boasted of the circulation of the *People's Paper* in comparison with its rivals, he did not include *Reynolds's News* in the list. By 1855 Reynolds was selling approximately 150,000 copies of his newspaper a week. By 1872 the weekly circulation had grown to over 350,000 copies. See V. Berridge, 'Popular Sunday papers and mid-Victorian society', in G. Boyce, J. Curran, and P. Wingate, *Newspaper History: from the 17th century to the present day*, London, 1978, p. 263.

82 *Morning Advertiser*, 11 September 1855.

83 *People's Paper*, 15 September 1855.

84 *People's Paper*, 15 September 1855. The letter implied that Reynolds had leaked the details of the burial to the *Advertiser*. See *Reynolds's Newspaper*, 23 September 1855.

85 *People's Paper*, 22 September 1855.

86 *People's Paper*, 15 September 1885.

87 For a fuller discussion see P.A. Pickering, 'Class without Words', pp. 144-162.

88 *People's Paper*, 22 December 1855.

89 *People's Paper*, 23 February 1856; 1 March 1856; *Reynolds's Newspaper*, 24 February 1856.

90 *People's Paper*, 22 March 1856.

91 *People's Paper*, 6 September 1856. By this time the campaign had sufficient momentum for Jones to feel confident enough to hand over the money that had been sent to him creating, for the first time, a single fund.

92 *People's Paper*, 11 April 1857.

93 The directors of the cemetery may have interceded to prevent a public unveiling, but the very fact that such an intervention was not reported in the radical press makes it unlikely. Earlier the press had reported that the Company had 'approved' the inscription. See *Reynolds's Newspaper*, 10 August 1856.

94 *People's Paper*, 30 May 1857.

95 *People's Paper*, 16 May 1857; 30 May 1857; J.S. Curl, *The Victorian Celebration of Death*, Newton Abbot, 1972, pp. 22-6. The Chartists offered no explanation of why they chose this style in particular.

96 *People's Paper*, 16 May 1857. The inscription was purportedly drafted by T.M. Wheeler. See Stephens, *A Memoir of Thomas Martin Wheeler*, p. 63.

97 It is also possible that the words were actually the Gaelic '*Meas Sether Riogh*' meaning respected good/strong leader. See W. Shaw, *Gaelic and English Dictionary Containing all the words in the Scotch and Irish dialects of the Celtic that could be collected from the Voice, and Old Books and Mss*, London, 1780; R. O'Connor, *Chronicles of Eri; Being the History of Gael Sciot Iber: or, the Irish People*, London, 1822, vol. 1, frontispiece. The words are not, as implied in the report in the *People's Paper*, a translation of the family motto 'fair and easy goes far'.

98 *People's Paper*, 29 September 1855; 17 November 1855.

99 *Nottingham Telegraph*, 12 February 1859.

100 *Nottingham Telegraph*, 17 September 1859.

101 See Pickering, 'The Chartist Rites of Passage', pp. 114-118.

102 *Nottingham Telegraph*, 12 February 1859.

103 D. Fraser, *Urban Politics in Victorian England: The Structure of Politics in Victorian Cities*, London, 1979, p. 223.

104 *Nottingham Telegraph*, 26 February 1859. As Jones demonstrated in three successive elections, the Chartists believed that they could repeat Feargus's triumph. See A.C. Wood, 'Nottingham 1835-1865', *Transactions of the Thoroton Society of Nottinghamshire*, vol. LIX, 1955, p. 81.

105 T.P. Newbould, *Pages from a Life of Strife: Being Some Recollections of William Henry Chadwick, the Last of the Manchester Chartists*, London, [1910], pp. ix-x, facing p. 33; *The Autobiography of William Farish: The Struggles of a Handloom Weaver with some of his writings*, n.p. 1889, pp. 76-7; Stephens, *A Memoir of Thomas Martin Wheeler*, p. 63; A. Pinkerton to G.J. Harney, 11 May 1850, reprinted in *The Harney Papers*, p. 67; *Hansard* [Legislative Assembly, Victoria], 15 December 1859, col. 249.

106 Daniel Madden cited in Sir B. Burke, *Vicissitudes of Families*, Second Series, London, 1861, p. 42.

BIBLIOGRAPHICAL NOTE

A full statement of the sources used in this book will be found in the notes at the end of each chapter. Detailed lists of the sources for the study of Chartism can be found in two book length bibliographies: J. Harrison and D. Thompson (eds), *Bibliography of the Chartist Movement 1837-1976*, Sussex, 1978; O.R. Ashton, R. Fyson and S. Roberts (eds), *The Chartist Movement 1839-1994*, London, 1995. The first attempt to describe O'Connor's life was in a 'Political Sketch' in the Cork *Southern Reporter* in January 1833. Since then there have been several, including his own fragmentary account, 'Life and Adventures of Feargus O'Connor, Esq., MP with a sketch of the persecutions of his family', which was serialised in the *National Instructor* between May 1850 and March 1851. Among the most important studies of his life are the two book length accounts by Donald Read and Eric Glasgow (*Feargus O'Connor: Irishman and Chartist*, London, 1961) and Jim Epstein (*The Lion of Freedom: Feargus O'Connor and the Chartist Movement, 1837-1842*, London, 1982), as well as shorter essays by Margaret Cole (*Makers of the Labour Movement*, London, 1948, pp. 86-105) and G.D.H. Cole (*Chartist Portraits*, London, 1941, pp. 300-336); dictionary entries by Graham Wallas (*Dictionary of National Biography*, London, 1894, vol. XIV, pp. 845-847) and Jim Epstein (*Oxford Dictionary of National Biography*, Oxford, 2004, vol. 41, pp. 461-464); and Glenn Airey's unpublished study: 'Feargus O'Connor 1842-1855: A Study in Chartist Leadership', PhD thesis, Staffordshire University, 2003. It is notable that O'Connor was not included in the first eleven volumes of the *Dictionary of Labour Biography*.

Index